Anonymous

Foods and food adulterants

Anonymous

Foods and food adulterants

ISBN/EAN: 9783337201111

Printed in Europe, USA, Canada, Australia, Japan

Cover: Foto ©Andreas Hilbeck / pixelio.de

More available books at **www.hansebooks.com**

U. S. DEPARTMENT OF AGRICULTURE.

DIVISION OF CHEMISTRY.

BULLETIN   No. 13.

FOODS

AND

FOOD ADULTERANTS.

BY DIRECTION OF

THE COMMISSIONER OF AGRICULTURE.

PART FIRST:

DAIRY PRODUCTS.

WASHINGTON:
GOVERNMENT PRINTING OFFICE.
1887.

19330—No. 13

LETTER OF SUBMITTAL.

Sir: I have the honor to submit herewith for your inspection and approval Bulletin No. 13, devoted chiefly to a discussion of the best methods of detecting the adulteration of foods.

The first part, which is now placed in your hands, treats of dairy products. Much interest has lately been manifested among those engaged in agriculture in respect of the adulteration of butter, and this part of the subject has been treated with greater detail than any other.

It has been my object in this work to determine the best methods of analysis of the various products in question, and all the recent improvements in analytical methods have been thoroughly tried, and those which have given good results have been adopted in the analytical work which has been done.

Within the last year my division has been supplied with apparatus for photo-micrography, and the illustrations in the following pages are entirely the work of the division unless otherwise stated.

Great benefit has been derived from this method of fixing photographic appearances, as the illustration of the crystalline characters of butters and butter substitutes sufficiently show. The examination of condiments, &c., the report of which will soon follow, was made almost entirely with the microscope, and the illustrations will show how satisfactory this kind of work proves to be. In the matter of photographic illustration no attempt has been made to confine the exhibition to phenomenally fine specimens, but the ordinary appearance of the field of vision has been reproduced. This, I think, is of greater advantage to the general investigation than would be the publication only of the strikingly good negatives. It is believed that by following the methods of analysis recommended in the report it will be possible to detect without fail any adulteration of butter that could possibly prove a commercial success. All other forms of adulteration will be suppressed by the laws of trade. In addition to the report herewith submitted the following parts of the bulletin are almost ready for the press, viz, condiments, sugar, sirup and honey, drinks and canned goods, flour and meal, tea and coffee, and baking powders. Other parts will follow as soon as time is afforded to submit all the process involved to a thorough examination in the laboratory.

Respectfully,

H. W. WILEY,
Chemist.

Hon. NORMAN J. COLMAN,
Commissioner of Agriculture.

3

CONTENTS.

4

BUTTER AND ITS ADULTERATIONS.

The adulteration of butter with other fats has of late years attracted the attention not only of the analyst but also of the political economist and health officer.

This matter has been deemed of sufficient importance to demand regulation by law of Congress. This law provides for the inspection and analysis of commercial butters and their substitutes.

Following is the text of the act:

AN ACT defining butter, also imposing a tax upon and regulating the manufacture, sale, importation, and exportation of oleomargarine.

Be it enacted by the Senate and House of Representatives of the United States of America in Congress assembled, That for the purposes of this act the word "butter" shall be understood to mean the food product usually known as butter, and which is made exclusively from milk or cream, or both, with or without common salt, and with or without additional coloring matter.

SEC. 2. That for the purposes of this act certain manufactured substances, certain extracts, and certain mixtures and compounds, including such mixtures and compounds with butter, shall be known and designated as "oleomargarine," namely: All substances heretofore known as oleomargarine, oleo, oleomargarine-oil, butterine, lardine, suine, and neutral; all mixtures and compounds of oleomargarine, oleo, oleomargarine-oil, butterine, lardine, suine, and neutral; all lard extracts and tallow extracts; and all mixtures and compounds of tallow, beef-fat, suet, lard, lard-oil, vegetable-oil, annotto, and other coloring matter, intestinal fat, and offal fat made in imitation or semblance of butter, or when so made, calculated, or intended to be sold as butter or for butter.

SEC. 3. That special taxes are imposed as follows:

Manufacturers of oleomargarine shall pay six hundred dollars. Every person who manufactures oleomargarine for sale shall be deemed a manufacturer of oleomargarine.

Wholesale dealers in oleomargarine shall pay four hundred and eighty dollars. Every person who sells or offers for sale oleomargarine in the original manufacturer's packages shall be deemed a wholesale dealer in oleomargarine. But any manufacturer of oleomargarine who has given the required bond and paid the required special tax, and who sells only oleomargarine of his own production, at the place of manufacture, in the original packages to which the tax-paid stamps are affixed, shall not be required to pay the special tax of a wholesale dealer in oleomargarine on account of such sales.

Retail dealers in oleomargarine shall pay forty-eight dollars. Every person who sells oleomargarine in less quantities than ten pounds at one time shall be regarded as a retail dealer in oleomargarine; and sections thirty-two hundred and thirty-two, thirty-two hundred and thirty-three, thirty-two hundred and thirty-four, thirty-two hundred and thirty-five, thirty-two hundred and thirty-six, thirty-two hundred and thirty-seven, thirty-two hundred and thirty-eight, thirty-two hundred and thirty-nine, thirty-two hundred and forty, thirty-two hundred and forty-one, and thirty-two hundred and forty-three of the Revised Statutes of the United States are, so far as applicable, made to extend to and include and apply to the special taxes imposed by this section, and to the persons upon whom they are imposed: *Provided*, That in case any manufacturer of oleomargarine commences business subsequent to the thirtieth day of June in any year, the special tax shall be reckoned from the first day of July in that year, and shall be five hundred dollars.

SEC. 4. That every person who carries on the business of a manufacturer of oleomargarine without having paid the special tax therefor, as required by law, shall, besides being liable to the payment of the tax, be fined not less than one thousand and not more than five thousand dollars; and every person who carries on the business of a wholesale dealer in oleomargarine without having paid the special tax therefor, as required by law, shall, besides being liable to the payment of the tax, be fined not less than five hundred nor more than two thousand dollars; and every person who carries on the business of a retail dealer in oleomargarine without having paid the special tax therefor, as required by law, shall, besides being liable to the payment of the tax, be fined not less than fifty nor more than five hundred dollars for each and every offense.

SEC. 5. That every manufacturer of oleomargarine shall file with the collector of internal revenue of the district in which his manufactory is located such notices, inventories, and bonds, shall keep such books and render such returns of material and products, shall put up such signs and affix such number to his factory, and conduct his business under such surveillance of officers and agents as the Commissioner of Internal Revenue, with the approval of the Secretary of the Treasury, may, by regulation, require. But the bond required of such manufacturer shall be with sureties satisfactory to the collector of internal revenue, and in a penal sum of not less than five thousand dollars; and the sum of said bond may be increased from time to time, and additional sureties required at the discretion of the collector, or under instructions of the Commissioner of Internal Revenue.

SEC. 6. That all oleomargarine shall be packed by the manufacturer thereof in firkins, tubs, or other wooden packages not before used for that purpose, each containing not less than ten pounds, and marked, stamped, and branded as the Commissioner of Internal Revenue, with the approval of the Secretary of the Treasury, shall prescribe; and all sales made by the manufacturers of oleomargarine, and wholesale dealers in oleomargarine, shall be in original stamped packages. Retail dealers in oleomargarine must sell only from original stamped packages, in quantities not exceeding ten pounds, and shall pack the oleomargarine sold by them in suitable wooden or paper packages, which shall be marked and branded as the Commissioner of Internal Revenue, with the approval of the Secretary of the Treasury, shall prescribe. Every person who knowingly sells or offers for sale, or delivers or offers to deliver, any oleomargarine in any other form than in new wooden or paper packages as above described, or who packs in any package any oleomargarine in any manner contrary to law, or who falsely brands any package or affixes a stamp on any package denoting a less amount of tax than that required by law, shall be fined for each offense not more than one thousand dollars, and be imprisoned not more than two years.

SEC. 7. That every manufacturer of oleomargarine shall securely affix, by pasting, on each package containing oleomargarine manufactured by him, a label on which shall be printed, besides the number of the manufactory and the district and State in which it is situated, these words: "Notice—The manufacturer of the oleomargarine herein contained has complied with all the requirements of law. Every person is cautioned not to use either this package or the stamp thereon again, nor to remove the contents of this package without destroying said stamp, under the penalty provided by law in such cases." Every manufacturer of oleomargarine who neglects to affix such label to any package containing oleomargarine made by him, or sold or offered for sale by or for him, and every person who removes any such label so affixed from any such package, shall be fined fifty dollars for each package in respect to which such offense is committed.

SEC. 8. That upon oleomargarine which shall be manufactured and sold, or removed for consumption or use, there shall be assessed and collected a tax of two cents per pound, to be paid by the manufacturer thereof; and any fractional part of a pound in a package shall be taxed as a pound. The tax levied by this section shall be represented by coupon stamps; and the provisions of existing laws governing the engraving, issue, sale, accountability, effacement, and destruction of stamps relating to tobacco and snuff, as far as applicable, are hereby made to apply to stamps provided for by this section.

SEC. 9. That whenever any manufacturer of oleomargarine sells, or removes for sale or consumption, any oleomargarine upon which the tax is required to be paid by stamps, without the use of the proper stamps, it shall be the duty of the Commissioner of Internal Revenue, within a period of not more than two years after such sale or removal, upon satisfactory proof, to estimate the amount of tax which has been omitted to be paid, and to make an assessment therefor and certify the same to the collector. The tax so assessed shall be in addition to the penalties imposed by law for such sale or removal.

SEC. 10. That all oleomargarine imported from foreign countries shall, in addition to any import duty imposed on the same, pay an internal-revenue tax of fifteen cents per pound, such tax to be represented by coupon stamps as in the case of oleomargarine manufactured in the United States. The stamps shall be affixed and canceled by the owner or importer of the oleomargarine while it is in the custody of the proper custom-house officers; and the oleomargarine shall not pass out of the custody of said officers until the stamps have been so affixed and canceled, but shall be put up in wooden packages, each containing not less than ten pounds, as prescribed in this act for oleomargarine manufactured in the United States, before the stamps are affixed; and the owner or importer of such oleomargarine shall be liable to all the penal provisions of this act prescribed for manufacturers of oleomargarine manufactured in the United States. Whenever it is necessary to take any oleomargarine so imported to any place other than the public stores of the United States for the purpose of affixing and canceling such stamps, the collector of customs of the port where such oleomargarine is entered shall designate a bonded warehouse to which it shall be taken, under the control of such customs officer as such collector may direct; and every officer of customs who permits any such oleomargarine to pass out of his custody or control without compliance by the owner or importer thereof with the provisions of this section relating thereto, shall be guilty of a misdemeanor, and shall be fined not less than one thousand dollars nor more than five thousand dollars, and imprisoned not less than six months nor more than three years. Every person who sells or offers for sale any imported oleomargarine, or oleomargarine purporting or claimed to have been imported, not put up in packages and stamped as provided by this act, shall be fined not less than five hundred dollars nor more than five thousand dollars, and be imprisoned not less than six months nor more than two years.

SEC. 11. That every person who knowingly purchases or receives for sale any oleomargarine which has not been branded or stamped according to law shall be liable to a penalty of fifty dollars for each such offense.

SEC. 12. That every person who knowingly purchases or receives for sale any oleomargarine from any manufacturer who has not paid the special tax shall be liable for each offense to a penalty of one hundred dollars, and to a forfeiture of all articles so purchased or received, or of the full value thereof.

SEC. 13. That whenever any stamped package containing oleomargarine is emptied, it shall be the duty of the person in whose hands the same is to destroy utterly the stamps thereon; and any person who willfully neglects or refuses so to do shall for each such offense be fined not exceeding fifty dollars, and imprisoned not less than ten days nor more than six months. And any person who fraudulently gives away or accepts

8   FOODS AND FOOD ADULTERANTS.

from another, or who sells, buys, or uses for packing oleomargarine, any such stamped package, shall for each such offense be fined not exceeding one hundred dollars, and be imprisoned not more than one year. Any revenue officer may destroy any emptied oleomargarine package upon which the tax-paid stamp is found.

SEC. 14. That there shall be in the office of the Commissioner of Internal Revenue an analytical chemist and a microscopist, who shall each be appointed by the Secretary of the Treasury, and shall each receive a salary of two thousand five hundred dollars per annum; and the Commissioner of Internal Revenue may, whenever in his judgment the necessities of the service so require, employ chemists and microscopists, to be paid such compensation as he may deem proper, not exceeding in the aggregate any appropriation made for that purpose. And such Commissioner is authorized to decide what substances, extracts, mixtures, or compounds which may be submitted for his inspection in contested cases are to be taxed under this act; and his decision in matters of taxation under this act shall be final. The Commissioner may also decide whether any substance made in imitation or semblance of butter, and intended for human consumption, contains ingredients deleterious to the public health; but in case of doubt or contest his decisions in this class of cases may be appealed from to a board hereby constituted for the purpose, and composed of the Surgeon-General of the Army, the Surgeon-General of the Navy, and the Commissioner of Agriculture; and the decisions of this board shall be final in the premises.

SEC. 15. That all packages of oleomargarine subject to tax under this act that shall be found without stamps or marks as herein provided, and all oleomargarine intended for human consumption which contains ingredients adjudged, as hereinbefore provided, to be deleterious to the public health, shall be forfeited to the United States. Any person who shall willfully remove or deface the stamps, marks, or brands on package containing oleomargarine taxed as provided herein shall be guilty of a misdemeanor, and shall be punished by a fine of not less than one hundred dollars nor more than two thousand dollars, and by imprisonment for not less than thirty days nor more than six months.

SEC. 16. That oleomargarine may be removed from the place of manufacture for export to a foreign country without payment of tax or affixing stamps thereto, under such regulations and the filing of such bonds and other security as the Commissioner of Internal Revenue, with the approval of the Secretary of the Treasury, may prescribe. Every person who shall export oleomargarine shall brand upon every tub, firkin, or other package containing such article the word "oleomargarine," in plain Roman letters not less than one half inch square.

SEC. 17. That whenever any person engaged in carrying on the business of manufacturing oleomargarine defrauds, or attempts to defraud, the United States of the tax on the oleomargarine produced by him, or any part thereof, he shall forfeit the factory and manufacturing apparatus used by him, and all oleomargarine and all raw material for the production of oleomargarine found in the factory and on the factory premises, and shall be fined not less than five hundred dollars nor more than five thousand dollars, and be imprisoned not less than six months nor more than three years.

SEC. 18. That if any manufacturer of oleomargarine, any dealer therein or any importer or exporter thereof shall knowingly or willfully omit, neglect, or refuse to do, or cause to be done, any of the things required by law in the carrying on or conducting of his business, or shall do anything by this act prohibited, if there be no specific penalty or punishment imposed by any other section of this act for the neglecting, omitting, or refusing to do, or for the doing or causing to be done, the thing required or prohibited, he shall pay a penalty of one thousand dollars; and if the person so offending be the manufacturer of or a wholesale dealer in oleomargarine, all the oleomargarine owned by him, or in which he has any interest as owner, shall be forfeited to the United States.

SEC. 19. That all fines, penalties, and forfeitures imposed by this act may be recovered in any court of competent jurisdiction.

SEC. 20. That the Commissioner of Internal Revenue, with the approval of the Secretary of the Treasury, may make all needful regulations for the carrying into effect of this act.

SEC. 21. That this act shall go into effect on the ninetieth day after its passage; and all wooden packages containing ten or more pounds of oleomargarine found on the premises of any dealer on or after the ninetieth day succeeding the date of the passage of this act shall be deemed to be taxable under section eight of this act, and shall be taxed, and shall have affixed thereto the stamps, marks, and brands required by this act or by regulations made pursuant to this act; and for the purposes of securing the affixing of the stamps, marks, and brands required by this act, the oleomargarine shall be regarded as having been manufactured and sold, or removed from the manufactory for consumption or use, on or after the day this act takes effect; and such stock on hand at the time of the taking effect of this act may be stamped, marked, and branded under special regulations of the Commissioner of Internal Revenue, approved by the Secretary of the Treasury; and the Commissioner of Internal Revenue may authorize the holder of such packages to mark and brand the same and to affix thereto the proper tax-paid stamps.

Approved, August 2, 1886.

ARTIFICIAL BUTTER.

The French chemist, Mége-Mouries, in 1870 first described a method of making artificial butter on a large scale.

Mége, who was employed on the Imperial farm at Vincennes, was led to undertake this study through a desire to furnish to the poorer classes and to sailors an article which should be cheaper and more stable in its composition than ordinary butter.

He endeavored to imitate the physiological process which he supposed took place when cows were insufficiently fed, and when, therefore, the butter which they furnished was derived from their own fat. From beef he obtained a fat " which melted at almost the exact temperature of butter, possessed a sweet and agreeable taste, and which for most purposes could replace ordinary butter, not, of course, the finest kinds, but which was superior to it in possessing the advantageous peculiarity of keeping for a long time without becoming rancid."

Before the breaking out of the Franco-Prussian war Mége had established a factory at Poissy. The war suspended the operations of this factory, but at the cessation of hostilities they were again commenced.

Following is the method employed in the year 1873, in the manufacture of artificial butters:

The fat of best quality from recently killed bullocks is finely cut in a kind of sausage grinder in order to break up the membranes. The fragments fall into a tank heated with steam, which for every 1,000 parts of fat contains 300 parts of water and 1 part of carbonate of potash and 2 stomachs of sheep or pigs.

The temperature of the mixture is raised to 45° C. After two hours, under the influence of the pepsin in the stomachs, the membranes are dissolved and the fat melted and risen to the top of the mixture.

The fat is next drawn off into a second tank, kept at a somewhat higher temperature, and 2 per cent. of common salt added. After two hours more the fat becomes clear and takes on a yellow color and acquires somewhat the taste and odor of fresh butter. The fat is now drawn off into vessels and allowed to cool. It is then cut into pieces, wrapped in linen, and put in a hydraulic press and kept at a temperature of about 25° C. By pressure the fat is separated into two portions, viz: stearine 40 to 50 per cent., and fluid oleo 50 to 60 per cent. The stearine remaining in the presses is used in candle-making. Mége's patent, possessing as it does historical interest, is given in full.

A full citation of the various patents taken out in foreign countries is found in "Sell's Kunstbutter."[1]

The patents taken out in this country for the manufacture of artificial butter are given below:

LIST OF PATENTS GRANTED IN THE UNITED STATES FOR THE MANUFACTURE OF BUTTER SUBSTITUTES.

Hippolyte Mége, No. 146012, dated December 30, 1873.

To all whom it may concern:

Be it known that I, Hippolyte Mége, of Paris, France, have discovered a new and improved process of transforming animal fats into butter, of which the following is a full, clear, and exact description:

The butter which is obtained from milk is produced by the cow elaborating her own fat through her cellular mammary tissues at the low rate of temperature of the body.

The animal fat from which the butter-cells in milk are produced is composed chiefly of oleine, margarine, and stearine, and small quantities of other substances.

The natural process performed by the cow consists, mainly, first, in separating the oleomargarine from the stearine without developing disagreeable odors or flavors in the oleomargarine; and, secondly, in producing a slight change in the oleomargarine, by which it assumes the character of butter.

My invention, hereinafter described, is based upon a discovery made by me, that when the fat is rendered at a low temperature, considerably below that heretofore employed in the ordinary rendering of fat, it has the taste of molten butter, and does not acquire that peculiarly disagreeable flavor heretofore supposed to be necessarily attached to melted fat or tallow, and which is designated as "tallowy flavor."

I have succeeded in obtaining excellent results by rendering the crude fat at a temperature of 103 Fahrenheit, which is below the temperature at which the tallowy flavor is created. The temperature may be raised above this point in order to facilitate the operation, provided care be taken to avoid attaining the temperature at which the tallowy flavor is created.

The precise limit to which it is safe to increase the rendering-temperature can be ascertained by trial under various circumstances with the different kinds of fat. The temperature must, however, be far below that heretofore ordinarily used in rendering fats when no such object as I propose—to wit, the making of a butter-like product—was had in view. I do not think it would be safe to vary many degrees above that specifically indicated.

I have also discovered that, in order to neutralize any fermentation of the fat before or during its treatment, the raw fat should, as soon as possible after the death of the animal, be plunged in a solution of fifteen (15) per cent. of common salt and one per cent. of sulphate of soda, the effect of which would be to prevent such fermentation.

[1] Arbeiten a. d. Kaiserlichen Gesundheitsamte, pp. 484-493.

In carrying out my process I first crush, grind, or disintegrate the fat by any suitable machinery, such as rollers or millstones, in order to break up the cellular tissues in which the fat is contained in the animal, and thus cause it to be more easily melted or rendered by the application of low temperatures. This fat thus disintegrated is to be slowly raised to a temperature of 103° Fahrenheit in a vessel in which the temperature can be raised at will until the rendering shall be complete. The temperature, as before stated, must be so regulated that the rendered fat will have the taste of molten butter, and care should be taken not to heat it so as to induce the change which produces the usual disagreeable taste of melted fat or tallow, instead of the taste of molten butter, which temperature is considerably below that heretofore ordinarily used in rendering fat, and will be found to vary not many degrees above the point already stated.

I also add to the fat while being rendered, for the purpose of aiding in this process, two liters of gastric juice to a hundred (100) kilograms of fat. This gastric juice is made by macerating, for three hours, half of the stomach of a pig or sheep, well washed, and three litres of water containing thirty grams of bi-phosphate of lime. After maceration this macerated substance is passed through a sieve, and then added to the fat under treatment in the proportion of two litres to one hundred (100) kilograms.

The separation of the organized tissues from the fat is aided by the introduction of salt during the rendering; and as soon as there are no lumps of fat visible in the kettle I add about one per cent. of common salt. I stir it for some time. The rendered fat is then allowed to stand until it attains perfect limpidity, when it can be drawn off. By this means the separation is well made, and the organized tissues which do deposit are not altered. I then allow the melted fat to stand in a vessel, maintained at a temperature of about 86° to 98°, until the stearine is crystallized. The mixture of stearine and oleomargarine may then be put in a centrifugal machine; and by the operation of this machine the oleomargarine will pass through the cloth and the stearine remain within; or the mixture may be subjected to pressure in a press. The effect produced in either case is that the oleomargarine practically separates from the stearine and flows out. The oleomargarine thus separated from the stearine, when cooled, constitutes a fatty matter of very good taste, which may replace the butter used in the kitchen. If it is desired, however, to transform it into more perfect butter, I employ the following means: I mix the oleomargarine, as it comes from the press or centrifugal machine, with milk and cream, equal to ten per cent. of the weight of the oleomargarine, the temperature of the milk and cream being about seventy-one (71) degrees, and thoroughly agitate them together. I then let the mixture become completely cold and solid, and then cause it to be worked between rollers, which give it the homogeneousness and the consistency which are the qualities of the natural butter.

The above process of agitating the oleomargarine with milk is intended to be adopted when the butter is to be immediately used. If the butter is intended to be preserved, it will be better to mix the oleomargarine at animal heat with ten per cent. of its weight of water instead of milk or cream, and then agitate the two together, as above described.

I have also found it expedient to mix with the cream or milk, in the first case above described, before agitating, or with the water in the other case above described, before agitating, a fiftieth part of mammary tissue, which is the udder of the cow, minced fine, a one-hundredth part of bicarbonate of soda, and some coloring matter.

It may be desirable to add ordinary butter, and this I do by mixing the oleomargarine and the ordinary butter together at a temperature of about 70° Fahrenheit.

What I claim as my invention, and desire to secure by Letters Patent, is—

(1) The rendering of animal fat at a low temperature, substantially as above set forth, for the production of a fatty matter devoid of disagreeable taste.

(2) As a new product of manufacture, fat rendered at the low temperature, substantially as above described, devoid of disagreeable taste.

(3) The combined process of rendering animal fat at a low temperature and then separating the oleomargarine for the purpose of producing a material adapted to be used as ordinary butter for culinary purposes, or to be further treated for making more perfect butter, substantially as above described.

(4) As a new product of manufacture, oleomargarine obtained from fat rendered at a low temperature and separated from the stearine, substantially as above described.

(5) The agitating of oleomargarine with water or milk for the purpose of making a more perfect imitation of butter, substantially as above described.

(6) The butter-like product produced by the agitation of oleomargarine with water or milk, substantially as above described.

(7) The treatment with artificial gastric juice for facilitating the process of rendering the fat at a low temperature, substantially as above described.

(8) The treatment of the oleomargarine with the mammary tissue of the cow, or mammary pepsin, substantially as above described.

(9) The addition of ordinary butter to oleomargarine, substantially as above described.

H. MÉGE.

Witnesses:
ROBT. M. HOOPER,
M. D. DESHLER.

William E. Andrew, No. 153,999, dated August 11, 1874.

The process, herein described, for rendering fats, consisting in the application of dry heat or dry hot air to liquefy, and pressure to separate, the oily portion from the membrane, and removing the liquid portions from contact with the membranous portions as fast as separated.

William E. Andrew, No. 166,955, dated August 24, 1875.

Complete process of manufacturing artificial butter, herein described, consisting first in rupturing and destroying the globular condition of animal oil by agitation and then refrigerating the same, then combining the product thus obtained with butter, cream, or milk and churning until a thorough amalgamation takes place.

William E. Andrew, No. 172,942, dated February 1, 1876.

The process of clarifying liquid tallow or oil by injecting into the oil, under force, in the form of mist or fine spray, water prepared with chloride of sodium or nitrate of potash, and heated to a higher degree of temperature than the oil.

Garret Cosine, No. 173,591, dated February 15, 1876.

The process of making artificial butter by mixing together oleine and margarine from animal fats, and from fruit and vegetable nuts, and lactic acid and loppered cream or milk.

William E. Andrew, No. 179,883, dated July 18, 1876.

(Mechanical.)

Alfred Springer, No. 187,327, dated February 13, 1877.

The process of producing edible fat or tallow by heating the crude fat at a temperature of 140° to 145° Fahrenheit, in contact with common salt, saltpeter, borax, and boracic and salicylic acids, withdrawing the separated fat and incorporating therewith a second and smaller charge of the above chemicals, with the addition of benzoic acid.

Amor Smith, No. 188,428, *dated March* 13, 1877.

Method of separating oleomargarine from the fat of kine, that is to say, by separating it directly from the stearine and membrane at a low heat, without having first heated the mass to a higher point, for the purpose of removing the membrane from the stearine and oleine.

Royal W. Barnard, No. 198,334, *dated December* 18, 1877.

Method of reclaiming sour "tubby," or rancid butter, which consists in treating the same with a solution of brine containing an alkaline carbonate mixed with a solution of tartaric acid, or its equivalent.

Thomas F. Wilkins, No. 226,467, *dated April* 13, 1880.

Butter containing metaphosphoric acid intimately incorporated therewith, whereby the butter is preserved.

Otto Roysen, No. 236,483, *dated January* 11, 1881.

Process of making a substitute for butter, consisting in adding to oleomargarine an alkaline solution, and agitating the mixture until partial saponification ensues, and then adding a minute quantity of butyric acid.

Thomas F. Wilkins, No. 9,892, *reissued, dated October* 11, 1881.

The method herein described of preserving fats and other organic matter by mechanically mingling phosphoric acid therewith.

Samuel H. Cochran, No. 258,992, *dated June* 6, 1882.

The combination of beef-suet oil, cotton-seed oil and its equivalents, purified and flavored as described, with beef-stearine and slippery-elm bark.

Hippolyte Mège, No. 10,137, *reissued, dated June* 13, 1882.

Treating animal fats so as to remove the tissues and other portions named, with or without the addition of substances to change the flavor.

Samuel H. Cochran, No. 10,171, *reissued, dated August* 1, 1882.

A combination of beef-suet oil, cotton-seed oil and its equivalents, with beef-stearine.

Samuel H. Cochran, No. 262,207, *dated August* 8, 1882.

Compound composed of the oil obtained from swine fat, cotton-seed oil and its equivalents, deodorized and purified by slippery-elm bark and beef-stearine.

John Hobbs, No. 263,042, *dated August* 22, 1882.

The vegetable stearine to be used can be obtained from any pure vegetable, seed, or nut oils by pressing them at a temperature as above set forth, or it may be obtained in the market at times as vegetable stearine.

Mixing "vegetable stearine" or "margarine" obtained substantially as described, with what is called "animal oleomargarine" and emulsionizing the said mixture with milk, cream or other watery fluid.

Nathan I. Nathan, No. 263,199, *dated August* 22, 1882.

Process of manufacturing artificial butter by uniting oleomargarine with leaf lard, the latter having been previously cleaned, fused, strained, and subjected to a washing action in a solution of water, borax, and nitric acid, then rewashed and the united mass heated and subjected to the ordinary churning operation.

George S. Marshall, No. 264,545, *dated September* 19, 1882.

Process of deodorizing, purifying and flavoring stearine obtained from animal ' fats, or vegetable oils, by boiling the same with water and mixing therewith powdered orris-root.

William Cooley, No. 264,516, *dated September* 19, 1882.

An artificial cream composed of an oleaginous substance mechanically blended, or otherwise incorporated with milk, buttermilk, or cream, the oleaginous material being in a state of minute and even division, and each particle encased in a coating of caseine.

Henry Lauferty, No. 265,833, dated October 10, 1882.

Improvement in the manufacture of artificial butter, or oleomargarine, which consists in treating in the manner described both the milk and the oleomargarine oil separately with sal-soda, prepared and taken in the proportions as specified, then mixing or churning the creamy substance produced from the treated milk with the prepared oleomargarine oil, and coloring, salting, and working the mixture.

Hugo Berthold, No. 266,417, dated October 24, 1882.

A coloring compound for admixture with oleomargarine oil after the usual churning operation, consisting of saccharine matter, glycerine, annotto, and oil of ben, mixed togther.

George H. Webster, No. 266,568, dated October 24, 1882.

Process of making artificial butter, which consists in minutely dividing leaf-lard, rendering and straining it, mixing a butter-coloring matter with it, immersing it for thirty-six hours in cold brine, transferring it from the brine to dry tables or shelves and keeping it there covered with salt for thirty-six hours ; then heating it to about 130° Fahrenheit and mixing it with lukewarm buttermilk, a small quantity of clarified tallow, and a minute quantity of pepsin, and allowing the mixture to settle ; then transferring the liquid lard and tallow to a vessel containing comminuted butter of about half the weight of the lard, thoroughly mixing the contents of the vessel by stirring, pouring the mixture into cold water, and thoroughly working it in the usual manner.

William H. Burnett, No. 266,580, dated October 24, 1882.

The butter-like product described, consisting of the ingredients specified, to wit, lard, beef-suet, butter, glycerine, salt water, and coloring material.

Oscar H. Coumbe, No. 266,778, dated October 31, 1882.

A new article of manufacture, oleard, consisting of vegetable oil, in combination with cooked farinaceous flour.

Oscar H. Coumbe, No. 266,777, dated October 31, 1882.

An improved article of commerce known as butteroid, and consisting of cottonseed or other vegetable oil treated with a solution of caustic soda, in combination with farinaceous flour first thoroughly cooked in salt water.

Henry R. Wright, No. 267,637, dated November 14, 1882.

Process of making artificial butter or creamine, which consists in mixing together the oils derived from animal fat at low temperatures with sweet cream, the oil of butter, vegetable oil, and coloring matter ; then allowing these ingredients to become sour while together ; then removing the whey, and finally churning the mass.

Joseph H. McDonald, No. 270,451, dated January 9, 1883.
    (Mechanical.)

John Hobbs, No. 271,239, dated January 30, 1883.
    (Mechanical.)

John Hobbs, No. 271,240, dated January 30, 1883.
    (Mechanical.)

John Hobbs, No. 271,244, dated January 30, 1883.
    (Mechanical.)

John Hobbs, No. 271,241, dated January 30, 1883.
    (Mechanical.)

John Hobbs, No. 271,243, dated January 30, 1883.
    (Mechanical.)

John Hobbs, No. 271,242, dated January 30, 1883.
    (Mechanical.)

John Hobbs, No. 280,822, dated July 10, 1883.

Process of refining fats, which consists in first finely grinding the fat of the leaf of the hog, mixing it thoroughly with salt, placing it in tanks of cold water for two or three days, when it is worked over, as described, then rendering it at a low temperature, and as quickly as possible, with or without adding the solution mentioned, then drawing it off from the tissue, clarifying it and again drawing it off and cooling it.

Samuel H. Cochran, No. 285,878, dated October 2, 1883.

The mode above described of giving a butter-flavor to animal fats or oils, which consists in mixing therewith in the manner above described a quantity of dairy or creamery butter in its normal or hard condition.

Samuel H. Cochran, No. 285,973, dated October 2, 1883.

(Mechanical.)

Samuel H. Cochran, No. 285,974, dated October 2, 1883.

(Mechanical.)

Andrew J. Chase, No. 286,778, dated October 16, 1883.

The method herein described of manufacturing butter from animal oils, said method consisting in subjecting the oils to a low temperature, and at the same time agitating them, both during the process of solidifying and afterwards.

John Hobbs, No. 289,100, dated November 27, 1883.

The manufacture of deodorized fats or oxyline, the use or employment of the substance herein mentioned—vegetable stearine—in combination with the other ingredients named--oleomargarine-stearine and oleomargarine-stock.

George Lawrence, No. 295,180, dated March 18, 1884.

Process of treating milk with fatty and other matters by passing it and them, mingled with gases, through one or more steam-ejectors, for separating and mixing the particles.

Samuel Schwarzschild, No. 299,685, dated June 3, 1884.

(Mechanical.)

Emma J. Woodruff, No. 327,636, dated October 6, 1885.

Adding to the milk white-wine rennet, sugar, salt, bicarbonate of soda, bicarbonate potassium, alum, and butter.

Lyman Guinnip, No. 334,430, dated January 19, 1886.

Consisting in mingling two bodies of cream of different age, then churning the same, then removing a portion thereof from the churn and mingling with the removed part a quantity of butter, then churning the residue until butter begins to separate, then adding butter thereto, as specified, and churning the mixture, and finally adding thereto the portion first abstracted, and churning the whole until the butter is made.

William A. Murray, No. 335,084, dated January 26, 1886.

Mixing 1 gallon of sweet milk with 1 ounce of liquid rennet, 25 grains (Troy) of nitrate of potash, 1 ounce granulated sugar, half-teaspoonful of butter-coloring, and 8 pounds of butter, churned together and worked.

Carl August Johansson, No. 336,324, dated February 16, 1886.

(Mechanical.)

George Wm. Sample, No. 336,438, dated February 16, 1886.

(Mechanical.)

Charles Marchand, No. 338,538, dated March 23, 1886.

(Mechanical.)

Edward J. Oatman, No. 346,062, dated July 20, 1886.

Producing an emulsion from milk or its derivates and a suitable oleaginous material, which consists in thoroughly dividing and commingling the ingredients by injecting a steam jet into the mixture.

The common method of manufacture employed in this country is set forth by Armsby:[1]

Although numerous patents have been taken out for the manufacture of imitation butter, and a great variety of materials have been named in the specifications, the process as now conducted is comparatively simple. The raw materials are beef-tallow, leaf-lard, and the best quality of butter, together with small amounts of milk or cream and of butter-color.

From the beef-tallow is prepared the oleomargarine oil of Mége. The caul fat of freshly killed beeves is, after thorough washing first in tepid and then in iced water, allowed to stand in a cold room until thoroughly cold. It is then rendered at a temperature between 130° and 175° F. The resulting oil is allowed to cool slowly until a considerable portion of the stearine and palmitin have crystallized out, and the pasty mass is then subjected to hydraulic pressure. The still fluid (about two-thirds of the whole) flows out into a tank of cold water, where it solidifies into a granular mass which is known in the trade as "oleo" oil or simply "oleo". The name "oil" is somewhat misleading, as the product is a granular solid of a slightly yellow color. Fresh leaf-lard treated in substantially the same way as the beef-tallow, yields the "neutral lard" or "neutral" of the trade, also a granular solid of a white color.

The objects of this treatment are twofold: first, to produce fats as free as possible from taste or odor; second, to remove some of the difficultly fusible stearine and palmitin, in order that the finished product may melt readily in the mouth.

Having thus secured the fats in proper condition, the manufacturer proceeds to mix the "oleo" and "neutral", the proportions varying according to the destination of product; a warm climate calling for more "oleo," a cold one for more "neutral," and to flavor the mixture with butter. This flavoring is conducted in large, steam-jacketed vessels provided with revolving paddles, by which their contents can be thoroughly agitated. Here the "oleo" and "neutral" are melted and thoroughly agitated with a certain proportion of milk, or sometimes of cream, and a proper amount of butter-color. Forty-eight gallons of milk per 2,000 pounds of product are stated to be a common proportion. After sufficient agitation, the melted mass is run into cold water, and as it cools is broken up by paddles so as to granulate the mass. After thorough washing, it is salted and worked exactly like butter. The product is known as oleomargarine. Although it contains hardly more than a trace of butter fat, the latter flavors the whole mass so strongly that, when well salted, as it usually is, it might readily pass with an inexpert or careless consumer for a rather flavorless butter. Oleomargarine is the cheapest product made. By adding to the material in the agitator or "churn" more or less pure butter, what is known as butterine is produced, two grades of which are commonly sold, viz, "creamery butterine" containing more, and "dairy butterine" containing less butter.

The method of manufacture used by the firm of Armour & Co., of Chicago, is thus described by Mr. Philip D. Armour:[2]

The fat is taken from the cattle in the process of slaughtering, and after thorough washing is placed in a bath of clean, cold water, and surrounded with ice, where it is allowed to remain until all animal heat has been removed. It is then cut into small pieces by machinery and cooked at a temperature of about 150° until the fat, in liquid form, has separated from the fibrine or tissue, then settled until it is perfectly clear. Then it is drawn into graining vats and allowed to stand a day, when it is ready for the presses. The pressing extracts the stearine, leaving the remaining product, which is commercially known as oleo oil, which, when churned with cream or milk or both and with usually a proportion of creamery butter, the whole being properly salted, gives the new food-product, oleomargarine.

[1] Science, vol. 7, pp. 471-472.
[2] Senate Mis. Doc. No. 131, Forty-ninth Congress, first session, p. 224.

In making butterine we use neutral lard, which is made from selected leaf lard in a very similar manner to oleo oil, excepting that no stearine is extracted. This neutral lard is cured in salt brine for forty-eight to seventy hours at an ice-water temperature. It is then taken, and, with the desired proportion of oleo oil and fine butter, is churned with cream and milk, producing an article which, when properly salted and packed, is ready for market.

In both cases coloring matter is used, which is the same as that used by dairymen to color their butter. At certain seasons of the year, viz, in cold weather, a small quantity of salad oil made from cotton seed is used to soften the texture of the product, but this is not generally used by us.

Gustavus F. Swift, of the firm of Swift & Co., of the town of Lake (near Chicago), describes as follows the method in use in the manufacture of artificial butter by his company:[1]

The fat is taken from the cattle in the process of slaughtering, and after thorough washing is placed in a bath of clean, cold water and surrounded with ice, where it is allowed to remain until all animal heat has been removed. It is then cut into small pieces by machinery and cooked at a temperature of about 150° until the fat in liquid form has separated from the fibrine or tissue; then settled until it is perfectly clear. Then it is drawn into draining vats and allowed to stand a day, when it is ready for the presses. The pressing extracts the stearine, leaving the remaining product, which is commercially known as oleo oil, which, when churned with cream or milk, or both, and with usually a proportion of creamery butter, the whole being properly salted, gives the new food product, oleomargarine.

In making butterine we use neutral lard, which is made from selected leaf-lard in a very similar manner to oleo oil, excepting that no stearine is extracted. This neutral lard is cured in salt brine for forty-eight to seventy hours at an ice-water temperature. It is then taken, and with the desired proportion of oleo oil and fine butter, is churned with cream and milk, producing an article which, when properly salted and packed, is ready for market.

In both cases coloring matter is used, which is the same as that used by dairymen to color their butter. At certain seasons of the year, viz, in cold weather, a small quantity of sesame oil, or salad oil made from cotton seed, is used to soften the texture of the product.

WHOLESOMENESS OF ARTIFICIAL BUTTER.

On this subject there is a wide difference of opinion. It is undoubtedly true that a great deal of artificial butter has been thrown upon the market that has been carelessly made, and therefore harmful to the health. On the other hand a butter substitute, made carefully out of the fat of a perfectly healthy bullock or swine, is not prejudicial to health.

Prof. Henry Morton, of the Stevens Institute, Hoboken, N. J., made the following statements before the Senate Committee on Agriculture, pending the consideration of the "Oleomargarine" bill:[2]

The subject is one which has been of great interest to all scientific men from the time of the original discovery by Mége, which was made, as you are aware, during the siege of Paris. Many persons have been interested in it and have followed it up. I have been frequently called upon to examine processes and superintend operations where modifications in the manufacture have been suggested, and so on, and specimens have been brought to me as a chemist, to examine from time to time microscopic-

---

[1] *Op. cit.*, p. 225.   [2] *Op. cit.*, p. 47.

ally and chemically. When the substance was first introduced, the question was raised as to whether it could be distinguished from butter by any test, and I was led in that way to investigate the subject, and to examine as to all the properties which it exhibited, as well as to compare different samples of it, and I have in my experiments in this line examined great numbers of specimens of oleomargarine prepared as butter and of oleomargarine oil for the preparation of butter, from all parts of the country, and also have visited factories very frequently and spent long periods there. I have remained as long as a week in one of these factories continuously—sometimes spending the night as well as the day there, in order to watch the process completely and see the operation from beginning to end, to see what was put in and what was not, and to observe what was done and what was not done.

In the course of these examinations I have reached the conclusion, founded on these observations, that the material is of necessity, a pure one, and cannot possibly be unwholesome, and is, in fact, in that sense a thoroughly desirable and safe article of food. I will express as briefly as I can my reasons for this opinion, and state the facts on which they are founded.

In the first place I have found, as a matter of observation, that fat which is to be used in the manufacture of oleomargarine, if it is in the slightest degree tainted before the manufacture begins, if it is not strictly fresh, if it is not taken almost directly from the slaughtered animal, if it is allowed to stand in a barrel for a few hours in ordinary weather or in cold weather, if put in a barrel with any animal heat in it for a few hours, then an incipient change begins which, in the succeeding process, is exaggerated so that an utterly offensive material is produced, which could not be used for any such purpose.

Prof. C. F. Chandler says:[1]

In all of these reports I have taken the ground that this is a new process for making an old article, and that article is butter. This is a new process for making butter. It is made of materials which are in every respect wholesome and proper articles of food, whether it be made solely from the oleomargarine extracted from beef fat, or whether it has added to it more or less leaf lard properly prepared, or more or less sesame oil or cotton-seed oil, and whether it be or not colored with annatto or the other coloring matters used. I take the ground that there is nothing in any one of these materials in any sense unwholesome, and nothing in any one of them which makes it inferior as an article of food to dairy butter. I regard the discovery of Mége-Mouries, of a process by which beef fat and hog fat can be extracted from adipose tissue and converted into a wholesome article of food free from any disagreeable taste or odor, as one of the most important discoveries made in this century, a discovery by which it is possible to make a perfectly pure and satisfactory, as well as wholesome, article of food at a reasonable price. I have visited various factories where this article is manufactured, from the time the industry began down to date. I am perfectly familiar with the materials employed and the different processes, and know there is nothing whatever used either in material or process which is unwholesome or in any way deleterious to the public health.

Professor Chandler further has reported as follows to the Board of Health of New York City:[2]

NEW YORK, *May 2*, 1881.

To the Board of Health of the Health Department:

Having been directed by this board to investigate the subject of oleomargarine, in response to the resolutions of the Board of Aldermen, I would beg leave to submit the following report:

The resolutions directing the inquiry are as follows:

Whereas there is existing at the present time in the minds of the public great alarm and distrust in relation to the adulteration of food products; and

[1] *Op. cit.*, p. 67.   [2] *Op. cit.*, p. 70.

Whereas the committee on public health of the assembly of this State has been for some time investigating the adulteration of food products, and especially oleomargarine ; and

Whereas this committee have conducted such investigation by calling as witnesses principally dealers in butter and have not examined as witnesses medical or chemical experts to determine the value of oleomargarine as food ; therefore

Resolved, That the board of health of this city be, and they are hereby requested and directed to take immediate measures to investigate in the most thorough manner, by medical and chemical aid, the purity, healthfulness, and value of said product as an article of food, and to report to this body the results of their investigation, with such recommendations, if any be necessary, as may relate to the manufacture and distribution of the same as an article of food.

This subject has been before the board on former occasions, and I have little to add to what has been previously stated.

Oleomargarine, invented by the distinguished French chemist, Mége-Mouries, is manufactured in New York City in a few large establishments. The material is fresh beef suet, brought directly from the slaughter-houses. It is thoroughly washed, rendered very carefully, strained to remove a portion of the hard stearine, and then churned with milk to convert it into artificial butter, which contains the same constituents as dairy butter. The process is extremely ingenious and simple and executed by machinery. Nothing objectionable exists in the original material, nor is anything objectionable added during the process, and the operations are conducted with the utmost cleanliness. The product is palatable and wholesome, can be made of uniform quality the year round, is in every respect superior as an article of food to a large proportion of dairy butter sold in this city, and can be manufactured at a much lower price. I regard it as a most valuable article of food and consider it entirely unexceptional in every respect. In this opinion I am supported by the best scientific authorities in the country. The following distinguished chemists, after carefully studying the manufacture, have made the most decided statements in favor of this new article of food :

Prof. George F. Barker, University of Pennsylvania.
Dr. Henry A. Mott, jr., New York.
Prof. G. C. Caldwell, Cornell University, Ithaca, N. Y.
Prof. S. W. Johnson, Yale College, New Haven, Conn.
Prof. C. A. Goessmann, Massachusetts Agricultural College, Amherst, Mass.
Prof. Henry Morton, Stevens Institute, Hoboken, N. J.
Prof. Charles P. Williams, Philadelphia, Pa.
Prof. W. O. Atwater, Wesleyan University, Middletown, Conn.
Prof. J. W. S. Arnold, University of New York.

I would further say that this question is one on which there is no difference of opinion among scientific investigators familiar with the chemistry of dairy products and fats. I have never seen a statement emanating from any person having any standing among scientific men in which a contrary opinion is advanced. There has recently been a very strong confirmation of my opinion published in England. A bill came before the House of Commons in England, directed against this kind of butter from America, and, after considerable discussion, was defeated by a vote of 75 to 59. In the discussion the strongest opponent to legislation against it was Dr. Lyon Playfair, one of the most distinguished chemists and sanitary authorities in England. A pupil of Graham and Leibig, he has filled the chairs of chemistry in the Royal Institution of Manchester and at the University of Edinburgh, was appointed chemist to the Museum of Practical Geology by Sir Robert Peel, represented the universities of Edinburgh and Aberdeen in Parliament, was postmaster-general in the first Gladstone cabinet, has been member of several sanitary commissions, and is now a leading member of Parliament. In his remarks he stated that " bad butter was a fraud upon the poor, and oleomargarine would sooner or later drive it out of the market;" he "thought that good oleomargarine at one shilling a pound was a great deal better and cheaper than bad butter at one shilling four pence a pound," and he said that "as a general rule the former (oleomargarine) did not become so readily rancid as the latter (butter)."

I would further state that, as there is nothing unwholesome in oleomargarine, no legislation in regard to this article is necessary to protect the public health.

C. F. CHANDLER,
President.

Prof. G. F. Barker says:[1]

UNIVERSITY OF PENNSYLVANIA,
Philadelphia, March 22, 1880.

To the United States Dairy Company:

GENTLEMEN: In reply to your inquiry, I would say that I have been acquainted for several years with the discovery of Mége-Mouries for producing butterine from oleomargarine fat. In theory the process should yield a product resembling butter in all essential respects, having identically the same fatty constituents. The butterine prepared under the inventor's patents is, therefore, in my opinion, quite as valuable a nutritive agent as butter itself. In practice the process of manufacture, as I have witnessed it, is conducted with care and great cleanliness. The butterine produced is pure and of excellent quality, is perfectly wholesome, and is desirable as an article of food. I can see no reason why butterine should not be an entirely satisfactory equivalent for ordinary butter, whether considered from the physiological or commercial standpoint.

Prof. G. C. Caldwell, of Cornell University, gives the following testimony:[2]

CHEMICAL LABRATORY, CORNELL UNIVERSITY,
Ithaca, N. Y., March 20, 1880.

I have witnessed, in all its stages, the manufacture of "oleomargarine" and of oleomargarine butter or "butterine."

The process for oleomargarine, when properly conducted, as in the works of the Commercial Manufacturing Company, is cleanly throughout, and includes every reasonable precaution necessary to secure a product entirely free from animal tissue, or any other impurity, and which shall consist of pure fat made up of the fats commonly known as oleine and margarine. It is, when thus prepared, a tasteless and inodorous substance, possessing no qualities whatever that can make it in the least degree unwholesome when used in reasonable quantities as an article of food.

In the manufacture of butterine, since nothing but milk, annotto, and salt, together with, perhaps, a little water from clean ice, are added to this oleomargarine, to be intimately mixed with it by churning and other operations, I have no hesitation in affirming that this also, when properly made according to the Mége patent, and other patents held by the United States Dairy Company, and when used in reasonable quantities, is a perfectly wholesome article of food ; and that, while not equal to fine butter in respect to flavor, it nevertheless contains all the essential ingredients of butter, and since it contains a smaller proportion of volatile fats than is found in genuine butter it is, in my opinion, less liable to become rancid.

It cannot enter into competition with fine butter; but in so far as it may serve to drive poor butter out of the market, its manufacture will be a public benefit.

Prof. S. W. Johnson, of Yale College, makes the following statement:[3]

SHEFFIELD SCIENTIFIC SCHOOL OF YALE COLLEGE,
New Haven, Conn., March 20, 1880.

The United States Dairy Company:

GENTLEMEN: I am acquainted with the process discovered by M. Mége for producing the article known in commerce as oleomargarine or butterine.

[1] *Op. cit.*, p. 73.   [2] *Op. cit.*, p. 73.   [3] *Op. cit.*, p. 74.

I have witnessed the manufacture in all its stages, as carried out on the large scale, and I can assert that when it is conducted according to the specifications of M. Mége it cannot fail to yield a product that is entirely attractive and wholesome as food, and one that is for all ordinary culinary and nutritive purposes the full equivalent of good butter made from cream.

Oleomargarine butter has the closest resemblance to butter made from cream in the external qualities—color, flavor, and texture. It has the same appearance under the microscope, and in chemical composition differs not in the nature, but only in the proportions of its components. It is, therefore, fair to pronounce them essentially identical.

While oleomargarine contains less of those flavoring principles which characterize the choicest butter, it is, perhaps for that very reason, comparatively free from the tendency to change and taint, which speedily renders a large proportion of butter unfit for human food.

I regard the manufacture of oleomargarine or butterine as a legitimate and beneficent industry.

S. W. JOHNSON,
Professor of Theoretical and Agricultural Chemistry,
Director of the Connecticut Agricultural Experiment Station.

Dr. C. A. Goessmann, of Amherst, indorses in general the above statements:[1]

AMHERST, MASS., *March* 20, 1880.

United States Dairy Company, New York:

GENTLEMEN: I have visited on the 17th and 18th of the present month your factory, on West Forty-eighth street, for the purpose of studying your mode of applying Mége's discovery for the manufacture of oleomargarine butter or butterine. A careful examination into the character of the material turned to account, as well as into the details of the entire management of the manufacturing operation, has convinced me that your product is made with care, and furnishes thus a wholesome article of food. Your oleomargarine butter or butterine compares in general appearance and in taste very favorably with the average quality of the better kinds of the dairy butter in our markets. In its composition it resembles that of the ordinary dairy butter; and in its keeping quality, under corresponding circumstances, I believe it will surpass the former, for it contains a smaller percentage of those constituents (glycerides of volatile acids) which, in the main, cause the well-known rancid taste and odor of a stored butter.

I am, very respectfully, yours,

C. A. GOESSMANN, PH. D.,
Professor of Chemistry.

To these I may add the names of Prof. Charles P. Williams, of the State University of Missouri, Dr. Henry Mott, jr., Prof. W. O. Atwater, and Prof. J. W. S. Arnold.[2]

Armsby[3] says in respect of the healthfulness of oleomargarine:

Very exaggerated and absurd statements have been made regarding the unhealthfulness of butterine and oleomargarine. The charges have in general been that the fat used is practically uncooked, and that raw animal fat is unwholesome; that filthy fat and fat from diseased animals are used, and that the product contains, or is liable to contain, the germs of disease; and that in cleansing these diseased and filthy fats dangerous chemicals are used, which are not subsequently completely removed.

That the fats used are of themselves unwholesome there is no proof whatever. They contain nothing that butter-fat does not also contain, and differ from it only by the absence of about 6 per cent. of the glyceride of certain soluble fatty acids, viz, caprinic,

[1] *Op. cit.*, p. 74. [2] *Op. cit.*, pp. 73, 74, 75. [3] Science, vol. 7, No. 172.

caprylic, capronic, and butyric acids. The only experiments upon the digestibility of imitation butter are two, by A. A. Mayer, upon oleomargarine. These showed a difference of only about 2 per cent. in favor of butter. That the higher flavor of butter acting upon the nervous system would give it a greater nutritive value than the flavorless "neutral" or "oleo" may be conceded; but that an article which even experts fail to distinguish from genuine butter is at any serious disadvantage in this respect may well be doubted.

The manufacturers claim that imitation butter can only be made from the best quality of fat from freshly-killed animals, and I know of no evidence which disproves their assertions. The sensational article recently published in a prominent agricultural paper in the Northwest, accompanied by cuts of the num crous organisms found in butterine, is of no significance in this connection, both because the species described are all harmless, and because no comparative examinations of genuine butter were made. It is highly probable that many samples of the latter would show as miscellaneous an assortment of formidable looking, harmless organisms as did the butterine.

On the other hand, however, there is at present no guaranty, except the statement of the manufacturers, that diseased fat is not or cannot be used, the manufacture being conducted entirely without any official inspection, and visitors being in most (not all) cases excluded. I believe that the chances of disease being conveyed in this way are small, but they are not yet proved to be non-existent.

As regards filthy processes of manufacture, it may safely be asserted that butterine could not successfully imitate butter were it not as clean as most things are which pass for clean in this dirty world.

The charge that dangerous chemicals are used in the manufacture may be disposed of in a few words. If a dangerous amount of any chemical which is claimed to be used were left in the finished product the latter would be inedible. Should trace of these chemicals be found their significance would not lie in themselves, but in the indication they would furnish that the original fats were impure and required chemical treatment.

Sell[1] has made an examination of the evidence for and against the unwholesomeness of artificial butter and has reached the following conclusions:

The artificial butter prepared from the fat of healthy animals, apart from possibly a somewhat less digestibility, in comparison with milk-butter furnishes in general no reason for the supposition that it can affect injuriously human health.

There is ground for the suspicion that a part of the artificial butter occurring in commerce is manufactured out of such material or by such processes as do not with certainty exclude the danger of conveying to man disease whether produced by vegetable spores or animal parasites.

There is ground for suspicion that a part of the artificial butter is made from nauseating substances.

The possibility of injury to health from a carelessly-prepared artificial butter must not be neglected.

Dr. Thomas Taylor presented this aspect of the case to the Senate Committee.[2]

It has already been mentioned that in the earlier processes employed in the manufacture of artificial butter the stomachs of sheep and pigs were digested with the fats employed.

[1] Arbeiten a. d. Kaiserlichen Gesundheitsamte, pp. 494, 500.
[2] Op. cit. pp. 42-46 and 273-4.

Tidy and Wigner [1] have investigated the action of mammary tissue on fats used as butter substitutes.

By digesting a pure animal fat with the chopped-up tissues of the udders of cows the authors found a marked chemical change produced. Oleomargarine or tallow when treated in this way give rise to both soluble and volatile fatty acids. Since both milk and butter contain a certain amount of mammary tissue, in the form of casts from the mammary glands, it is believed that they also would exert an influence on animal fats. Butter appears to act more vigorously than milk in this way, probably because it contains a larger percentage of mammary tissue.

NUTRITIVE VALUES OF BUTTER AND OLEOMARGARINES.

On this subject Atwater [2] has collected valuable information, he says:

The value of butter, as of any other food material for nourishment, depends upon the amounts of its nutritive ingredients, their digestibility, and their uses in the nutrition of the body.

CHEMICAL COMPOSITION.

The food values of real and imitation butter, as compared with each other and with other food materials, can be best shown by first comparing their composition.

It appears that the nutrients of the leaner kinds of meat and fish consist mostly of protein, that the fatter meats and fish contain considerable fat with the protein, that the vegetable foods have for the most part very little fat, and abound especially in carbohydrates, while the nutriments of butter and oleomargarine consist almost exclusively of fats. Indeed, the protein and carbohydrates in both must be regarded as impurities. The quantities of fat are shown by analysis to be very nearly the same in both.

DIGESTIBILITY.

Regarding the relative digestibility of butter and oleomargarine the experimental facts at hand are meager. They imply, as would be expected from the composition, that there is very little difference between the two. The study of the question is rendered difficult by the fact that what is ordinarily called the digestibility of a food includes several different things, the ease with which it is digested, the time required for digesting it, and the proportions of its several constituents that are digested.

As to the comparative ease and time of digestion of butter and oleomargarine nothing is definitely known, though there is little ground for assuming that, in the alimentary canal of a healthy person, at any rate, one would be digested and taken into the circulation much more readily than the other. The actual amounts digested are capable of more nearly accurate experimental estimate. During the past few years very many experiments have been made, in Germany especially, to test the quantities of the more important constituents of different foods digested by domestic animals, and a considerable number have been carried out with men and children.

The only comparative experiments on the digestibility of butter and oleomargarine that have been reported are two series conducted by Professor Mayer, a German chemist. One series was with a full-grown man and the other with a boy of nine years of age, both strong, healthy persons. The outcome was that both the man and the boy digested from 97.7 to 98.4 per cent. of the fat of the butter, and from 96.1 to 96.3 per cent. of the fat of the oleomargarine. The average difference was about 1.6 per cent. in favor of the butter. There are, however, certain unavoidable sources of

[1] Analyst, 1883, pp. 113 et seq.   [2] Bradstreet's, Saturday, June 19, 1886.

error in such experiments, and it is very probable that the proportions actually digested were somewhat larger than these figures imply. Very likely each of the two persons may have digested practically all of the fat of the butter, and all but 1 or 2 per cent. or even less of that of the oleomargarine. In these experiments the butter and oleomargarine were eaten with bread, cheese, white of eggs, potatoes, peas, and sugar.

The digestibility of butter has been tested in two or three other series of experiments. Thus Dr. Rubner, in Munich, found that a healthy man, on a diet of butter, bread, and meat, digested 97.3 per cent. of the total fat of the food, of which the bulk came from the butter. In some experiments by myself, in which a man received a diet of fish (haddock) and butter, 91 per cent. of the total fat, nearly all of which came from the butter, was found to be digested.

The experiments of Rubner and myself were conducted in the same manner as those of Mayer, and exposed to the same slight sources of error. The results of all of them are just what would naturally be expected, namely, that very nearly all of the fat of butter and of oleomargarine is digested in a healthy organism.

It might seem that the relative digestibility of the two materials could be tested by experiments in artificial digestion; that is to say, by treating both substances with digestive fluids, or with materials similar to them, and observing the results. Such experiments are not accurate tests of the actual digestibility of the substances in the body, since the conditions which obtain in the alimentary canal cannot be exactly imitated by any artificial means which physiological chemistry has yet suggested. Professor Mayer, taking into account that the fats are more or less split up in the process of natural digestion, has made some experiments to test the comparative readiness with which butter and oleomargarine are split up, and finds a very slight difference in favor of butter. As the result of all his experiments he concludes that, while the butter appears to be a little more digestible than oleomargarine, the difference is too small to be of practical consequence for healthy persons. At the same time there may be cases, especially those of invalids and children just past the nursing period, when butter would be preferable; but, considering simply the nutritive values for ordinary use, Professor Mayer considers the choice between the two to be essentially one of comparative cost, an opinion from which there is, so far as I am aware, scarcely any dissent among those who have devoted the most study to this class of subjects.

It is a common and perhaps correct theory, though it lacks experimental confirmation, that the flavor of the fats peculiar to butter may in some way increase its value for nutriment. But, granting this to be true, it would be hardly reasonable to assume that a difference in flavor which even experts may fail to detect could make any considerable difference in the nutritive effect of two substances otherwise so similar as real and imitation butter.

To recapitulate briefly, butter and oleomargarine have very nearly the same chemical composition; in digestibility there may be a slight balance in favor of butter, though for the nourishment of healthy persons this difference can hardly be of any considerable consequence; for supplying the body with heat and muscular energy, which is their chief use in nutrition, they are of practically equal value, excelling in this respect all other common food materials. Such, at any rate, is the practically unanimous testimony of the latest and best experimental research.

While it is true that chemical analysis and certain digestive experiments have not hitherto shown that pure butter possesses any marked superiority over butter surrogates as a food, yet it must not be forgotten that butter has a much more complex composition than lard or tallow or cotton-seed oil; that it is a natural food, and doubtless possesses many digestive advantages which science has not yet been able to demonstrate.

THE MANUFACTURE OF ARTIFICIAL BUTTER IN THE UNITED STATES.

The following information has been kindly furnished by the Hon. Joseph S. Miller, Commissioner of Internal Revenue:

TREASURY DEPARTMENT, OFFICE OF INTERNAL REVENUE,
Washington, March 4, 1887.

SIR: In reply to your letter of 1st instant, I have the honor to state that there are thirty-seven factories engaged in the manufacture of artificial butter now in operation in the United States, located as follows:

Location.	No. of factories.	Location.	No. of factories.
Denver, Col.	2	Buffalo, N. Y.	1
Chicago, Ill.	11	Columbus, Ohio	1
Kokomo, Ind.	1	Cleveland, Ohio	3
Kansas City, Kans.	1	Philadelphia, Pa.	3
Armourdale, Kans.	1	Pittsburgh, Pa.	1
Cambridge, Mass.	1	Allegheny, Pa.	1
Brooklyn, N. Y.	2	Providence, R. I.	3
New York, N. Y.	3	Pawtucket, R. I.	2

There are two hundred and fifty-nine wholesale dealers in the United States, located as follows:

Location.	No. of wholesale dealers.	Location.	No. of who'esa'e dealers.
Birmingham, Ala.	2	Salt Lake, Utah	1
Fort Smith, Ark.	1	Hoboken, N. J.	1
Hot Springs, Ark.	1	Jersey City, N. J	1
Little Rock, Ark.	2	Deming, N. Mex.	1
Pine Bluff, Ark.	1	Fairbanks, Ariz.	1
Denver, Col.	4	Saratoga Springs, N. Y.	1
Jacksonville, Fla.	1	Rochester, N. Y.	1
Atlanta, Ga.	1	Youngstown, Ohio	2
Englewood, Ill.	1	Philadelphia, Pa.	12
Springfield, Ill.	1	Allegheny City, Pa	1
Cairo, Ill.	2	Woonsocket, R. I.	1
Council Bluffs, Iowa.	1	Memphis, Tenn.	8
Elwood, Kans.	1	El Paso, Tex.	2
Louisville, Ky.	3	Dallas, Tex.	1
New Orleans, La.	5	Dennison, Tex.	1
Boston, Mass.	30	Milwaukee, Wis.	3
Fall River, Mass.	1	Ashland, Wis.	1
Lowell, Mass.	3	Eau Claire, Wis.	1
Aspen, Col.	1	Worcester, Mass.	3
Pueblo, Col.	1	Houghton, Mich.	1
Durango, Col.	1	Detroit, Mich.	6
Buena Vista, Col.	1	Grayling, Mich.	1
Hartford, Conn.	2	Saginaw, Mich.	1
New Haven, Conn.	4	Luddington, Mich.	1
Leadville, Col.	4	Saint Paul, Minn.	2
Chicago, Ill.	21	Helena, Mont.	2
Peoria, Ill.	1	Jefferson City, Mont.	1
Danville, Ill.	1	South Butte, Mont.	1
Indianapolis, Ind.	1	Ogden, Utah.	1
Kansas City, Kans.	2	Dover, N. H.	1
Topeka, Kans.	1	Newark, N. J.	1
Covington, Ky.	1	Sante Fé, N. Mex.	1
Baltimore, Md.	2	Albuquerque, N. Mex.	1
Salem, Mass.	1	New York, N. Y.	15
New Bedford, Mass.	2	Buffalo, N. Y.	2
Gloucester, Mass.	2	Cincinnati, Ohio.	6
Lawrence, Mass.	2	Cleveland, Ohio.	8
Springfield, Mass.	1	Pittsburgh, Pa.	14
Ironwood Mich.	1	Providence, R. I.	16
Bay City, Mich.	3	Pawtucket, R. I.	1
East Saginaw, Mich.	1	Nashville, Tenn.	1
Muskegon, Mich.	1	San Antonio, Tex.	1
Grand Rapids, Mich.	4	Fort Worth, Tex.	2
East Saint Louis, Ill.	1	Richmond, Va.	1
Butte, Mont.	2	Oshkosh, Wis.	1
Missoula, Mont.	1	Hurley, Wis.	2
Omaha, Nebr.	3	Chippewa Falls, Wis.	1

The quantity manufactured and removed for consumption or sale at 2 cents per pound during the months of November and December, 1886, and January, 1887, is as follows:

	Pounds.
November	4,742,569
December	2,786,278
January	2,501,114
Total	10,029,961

The quantity exported from the United States during the period above, all exportations being from the port of New York, is as follows:

	Pounds.
November	3,247
December	58,689
January	52,761
Total	114,697

Respectfully,

JOS. S. MILLER,
Commissioner.

Hon. N. J. COLMAN,
Commissioner of Agriculture, Washington, D. C.

COLORING MATTERS IN BUTTER.

The pure animal fats, prepared in the manner described, are almost colorless. The tint of genuine butter is imparted to these bodies by various coloring matters. The principal artificial colors which have been employed are:

Annotto (*Bixa orellana*).
Turmeric (*Curcuma longa* and *viridiflora*).
Saffron (dried stigmas *Crocus sativus*).
Marigold leaves (*Calendula officinalis*).
Yellow wood (*Morus tinctoria*).
Carrot juice (*Daucus carota*).
Chrome yellow ($PbCrO_4$)
Dinitrocressol—kalium.

ANNOTTO.

This substance is used more than any other in imparting to artificial butter a yellow tint. Indeed it is used to color genuine butter, which often in winter is almost white in its natural state.

The coloring substance called *annotto, arnatta,* or *roucou* is the reddish pulp surrounding the seeds in the fruit of *Bixa orellana*, a middling-sized tree growing in Guiana and other parts of South America. The pulp is separated by bruising the fruit, mixing it with water, then straining through a sieve, and allowing the liquid to stand till the undissolved portion subsides. The water is then poured off and the mass which remains, having been sufficiently dried, is formed into flat cakes or cylindrical rolls and sent into the market. Another mode is to bruise the seeds, mix them with water, and allow the mixture to ferment. The coloring matter is deposited during the fermentation, after which it is removed and dried. In commerce there are two kinds of annotto the Spanish or Brazilian and French, the former coming in baskets from Brazil, the latter in casks from French Guiana. The French, which is also called *flag annotto*, has a disagreeable smell, probably from having been prepared by the fermenting process, but is superior as a dye-stuff to the Spanish, which is without any disagreeable odor. Annotto is of a brownish red color, usually rather soft but hard and brittle when dry, of a dull fracture, of a sweetish peculiar odor, and a rough, saline, bitterish taste. It is inflammable, but does not melt with heat. It softens in water, to which it imparts a yellow color, but does not dissolve. Alcohol, ether, the oils, and alkaline solutions dissolve the greater part of it. It contains a peculiar crystallizable coloring principle, to which M. Preisser, its discoverer, gave the name of *bixin*. It is frequently adulterated with red ocher, powdered bricks, colcothar, farinaceous substances, chalk, sulphate of calcium, turmeric, &c. The mineral substances, if present, will be left behind when the annotto is burned.[1]

SAFFRON.

Saffron has a peculiar, sweetish, aromatic odor, a warm, pungent, bitter taste, and a rich deep orange color, which it imparts to the saliva when chewed. The stigmas of which it consists are an inch or more in length, expanded and notched at the upper extremity, and narrowing towards the lower, where they terminate in a slender, capillary, yellowish portion, forming a part of the style. When chewed it tinges the saliva deep orange-yellow. Saffron should not be mixed with the yellow styles. When pressed between filtering paper it should not leave an oily stain. When soaked in water it colors the liquid orange-yellow, and should not deposit any pulverulent mineral matter nor show the presence of organic substances differing in shape from that described.[2]

Adulteration of saffron.—Saffron is often adulterated with cheaper yellow vegetable coloring matter, turmeric, annotto, the flowers of the marigold (*Calendula officinalis*), Carthamus flowers, the flowers of *Arnica montana, Scolymus hispanicus, Pulicaria dysenterica, Punica granatum, Pæonia, Crocus vernus*, &c.[3]

Of these the marigold flowers are perhaps the most commonly used. They have a natural yellow color, and when they are saturated with carmine or aniline red, and dried, they possess a striking similarity to the genuine saffron. If they are put for a few minutes in water, however, they assume their original form, and are then easily distinguished from the stigmas of the saffron flower.

If a mixture of saffron stigmas and the substitutes just mentioned be put into a vessel of water where the individual pieces are widely separated, the saffron stigmas soon become surrounded with a yellow extract, while the others suffer no change or impart only a weak carmine tint to the water.

The use of mineral coloring matters like the chromate of lead is highly reprehensible from a sanitary point of view.

Annotto and saffron in butter may be detected by the following method, proposed by Cornwall:[4]

About 5 grams of the warm filtered fat are dissolved in about 50cc. of ordinary ether, in a wide tube, and the solution is vigorously shaken for ten to fifteen seconds with 12 to 15cc. of a very dilute solution of caustic potash or soda in water, only alkaline enough to give a distinct reaction with turmeric paper, and to remain alkaline after separating from the ethereal fat solution. The corked tube is set aside and in a few

---

[1] U. S. Dispensatory, p. 1572.

[2] U. S. Dispensatory, p. 501.

[3] Schimpfer, Anleit. z. Mikroskopischen Untersuchung d. Nahrungs- und Genussmittel, p. 101.

[4] Chem. News, vol. 55, p. 49.

hours, at most, the greater part of the aqueous solution, now colored more or less yellow by the annotto, can be drawn from beneath the ether with a pipette or by a stopcock below, in a sufficiently clear state to be evaporated to dryness and tested in the usual way with a drop of concentrated sulphuric acid.

Sometimes it is well to further purify the aqueous solution by shaking it with some fresh ether before evaporating it, and any fat globules that may float on its surface during evaporation should be removed by touching them with a slip of filter-paper; but the solution should not be filtered, because the filter-paper may retain much of the coloring matter.

The dry-yellow or slightly orange residue turns blue or violet blue with sulphuric acid, then quickly green, and finally brownish or somewhat violet (this final change being variable, according to the purity of the extract).

Saffron can be extracted in the same way; it differs from annotto very decidedly, the most important difference being in the absence of the green coloration.

Genuine butter, free from foreign coloring matter, imparts at most a very pale yellow color to the alkaline solution; but it is important to note that a mere green coloration of the dry residue on addition of sulphuric acid is not a certain indication of annotto (as some books state) because the writer has thus obtained from genuine butter, free from foreign coloring matter, a dirty green coloration, but not preceded by any blue or violet blue tint.

Blank tests should be made with the ether; it is easy to obtain ether that leaves nothing to be desired as to purity.

Turmeric is easily identified by the brownish to reddish stratum that forms between the ethereal fat solution and the alkaline solution before they are intimately mixed. It may be even better recognized by carefully bringing a feebly alkaline solution of ammonia in alcohol beneath the ethereal fat solution with a pipette, and gently agitating the two, so as to mix them partially.

Martin[1] gives a method of separating and determining artificial coloring matters in butter. To 5 grams of fat, dry, are added 25cc. CS_2 and the mixture well shaken with water made slightly alkaline with NaOH or KOH and the mixture gently shaken. The alkaline water will dissolve all the coloring matter. This is now determined qualitatively by the spectroscope or quantitatively by making up a comparative mixture with the coloring matter found. Butters act better when treated as above than oleomargarine.

The relative amount of color in butters is thus estimated by Babcock:[2]

The relative amount of color in butters may be determined with accuracy as follows: One gram of the fresh butter is digested with 15cc. of refined kerosene till the fats are completely dissolved and the solutions filtered. The filtrate will be colored in proportion to the coloring matter of the butter, and may be compared to that from another butter or preferably to a standard solution by means of a Dubosque colorimeter. A standard color for comparison may be prepared by adding a small quantity of any of the commercial butter colors to kerosene oil. This standard will keep for a long time without changing, if kept from the light.

The scale of the colorimeter on the side which the butter solution occupies is always set at the same degree, while the scale for the other standard is made variable. The reading of this side will, therefore, vary with the amount of color in the sample.

If some of the kerosene oil in which the butters are dissolved be substituted for the solution of butter, a small reading will be obtained which should be deducted

[1] Analyst, 1885, p. 163.
[2] Fifth An. Rep't B'd Control, N. Y. Exp. Sta., p. 335–336.

from that for each of the butters. The numbers remaining are directly proportional to the colors of the butters. In the butters thus far examined a fair colored Jersey butter was taken for a standard and called 100. The others were calculated to this standard from the scale reading.

The use of a small amount of vegetable coloring matters mentioned above does not seem to be prejudicial to health.

EXAMINATION OF BUTTERS.

The examination of butters to detect adulterations may be divided into two parts: (1) Determination of physical properties; (2) determination of chemical properties.

Physical properties.—The physical properties of fats which are useful in butter analysis are their crystalline state, specific gravity, and melting point.

Pure fresh butter prepared in the ordinary manner is not crystalline. The microscope shows the absence of all forms of crystalline structure, and thin films of the butter fat have no influence whatever on polarized light.

On the contrary, old butters, or butters which have been melted and allowed to crystallize, and oils and fats which have been once in a fluid state, show, as solids, quite a distinct crystalline structure readily revealed by the microscope and affecting, in a marked manner, the polarized ray.

Recently much attention has been excited by a discussion of the application of polarized light to the qualitative examination of suspected butters, and since many analysts have not the time to fully investigate this matter I have thought it useful to enter upon the discussion of it in considerable detail.

Polarization is a term applied to a phenomenon of light, in which the vibrations of the ether are supposed to be restricted to a particular form of an ellipse whose axes remain fixed in direction. If the ellipse becomes a straight line it is called " plane polarization." This well-known phenomenon is most easily produced by a Nicol prism, consisting of a crystal of carbonate of calcium (Iceland spar). This rhombohedral crystal, the natural ends of which form angles of 71° and 109°, respectively, with the opposite edges of its principal section, is prepared as follows:

The ends of the crystal are ground until the angles just mentioned become 68° and 112°. The crystal is then divided diagonally at right angles with the planes of the ends and with the principal section, and after the new surfaces are polished they are joined again by Canada balsam. The principal section of this prism passes through the shorter diagonal of the two rhombic ends. If now a ray of light fall on one of the ends of this prism, parallel with the edge of its longer side, it suffers double refraction, and each ray is plane polarized, the one at right angles with the other. That part of the entering ray of light

which is most refracted is called the ordinary and the other the extraordinary ray. The refractive index of the film of balsam being inter-
mediate between those of the rays, permits the total reflection of the
ordinary ray, which, passing to the blackened sides of the prism, is absorbed. The extraordinary ray passes the film of balsam without de-
viation and emerges from the prism in a direction parallel with the
incident ray, having, however, only half of its luminous intensity.

Two such prisms, properly mounted, furnish the essential parts of a
polarizing apparatus. They are called the "polarizer" and the "analyzer," respectively.

If now the plane of vibration in each prism be regarded as coincident
with its principal section, the following phenomena are observed: If
the prisms are so placed that the principal sections lie in the prolonga-
tion of the same plane, then the extraordinary polarized ray from the
polarizer passes into the analyzer, which practically may be regarded
in this position as a continuation of the same prism. It happens, therefore, that the extraordinary polarized ray passes through the analyzer
exactly as it did through the polarizer, and is not reflected by the film
of balsam, but emerges from the analyzer in seemingly the same condition as from the polarizer. If now the analyzer be rotated 180°,
bringing the principal section again in the same plane, the same phenomenon is observed. But if the rotation be in either direction only 90°,
then the polarized ray from the first prism, incident on the second, de-
ports itself exactly as the ordinary ray, and on meeting the film of balsam is totally reflected. The field of vision, therefore, is perfectly dark.

In all other inclinations of the planes of the principal sections of the
two prisms the ray incident in the analyzer is separated into two, an ordinary and extraordinary, varying in luminous intensity in proportion to
the square of the cosine of the angle of the two planes.

Thus by gradually turning the analyzer, the field of vision passes
slowly from maximum luminosity to complete obscurity.

The expression "crossed Nicols" refers to the latter condition of the
field of vision.

Selenite plate.—In the practical application of polarized light to the examination of facts, an important use is made of a selenite plate (crystallized sulphate of calcium). A disk of selenite, interposed between the
polarizer and analyzer imparts a coloration to the field of vision which
varies with the relative position of the principal sections of the two
prisms.

This phenomenon depends on the fact that a plane polarized ray of
light can be decomposed, in passing a section of a bi-refracting crystal
like selenite or mica, into two rays, polarized at right angles and differing in phase.

This fact is illustrated by passing a polarized ray (from a Nicol prism)
through a very thin crystallized plate of mica or gypsum (selenite)
obtained by cleavage. By the double refraction of the thin plate the po-

larized ray is separated into two, ordinary and extraordinary. The extraordinary, having to pass over a greater distance, joints the ordinary ray, after emergence, with a phase slightly different, the degree of difference depending on the nature of the lamina, the inclination of the incident ray, &c., but in every case this difference of phase can be easily calculated, and the resultant beam of light is said to be elliptically polarized. Each of the components of this ray enters the analyzer and is again resolved. One of its elements is suppressed in the Nicol and the other, consisting of vibrations in the principal plane, passes through. The result is two sets of vibrations in the same plane slightly different in phase, which are, therefore, in a condition to interfere and produce color. If the source of light be monochromatic, when the analyzer is rotated, only certain variations in luminous intensity will be observed; but if, on the other hand, white light be employed these variations in phase will give rise to a display of colors. In order that the field of vision be of a uniform tint it is necessary that the lamina of crystal be of uniform thickness. For ordinary use the selenite plate is ground to a thickness which will give green and red tints.

For crossed Nicols the colors of the selenite plate appear brightest when it is so placed that the plane of vibration in the crystal forms an angle of 45° with the plane of vibrations of the polarized incident ray. If the selenite plate is rotated in its own plane, the color appears in the four quadrants at its maximum and disappears at intervals of 90°.

If the planes of the two Nicols are parallel, the same order of phenomena appear as before, except that the positions of maximum and minimum are reversed.

If the analyzer be rotated and the selenite plate and polarizer remain stationary there is no effect produced, when the principal section of the selenite is parallel or perpendicular to the polarizing plane of the under Nicol. But if this plane is inclined less than 45° to that of the polarizer, then the selenite plate in a complete revolution of the analyzer will appear four times brightly colored and four times colorless. In adjoining quadrants the colors will be complementary. When the Nicols are so placed as to produce the maximum intensity of color, if small bi-refracting crystals be introduced at random into the field of vision, they will, in general, have the same effect on the plane polarized ray as the selenite plate. Since the axes of these crystals may have any accidental position with reference to the planes of the Nicols, it follows that the field of vision, which before appeared of a uniform tint, will now become variegated, the color disappearing in some cases and becoming more intense in others.

When a bi-refracting crystal is cut into laminæ normal to its axis, of appropriate thickness, it gives some peculiar phenomena when examined with polarized light. When the analyzer is perpendicular to the polarizer, there is seen in the ordinary image a black cross, the existence of which can be explained by the mathematical theory of polarization. The arms of this cross are parallel and perpendicular to the primitive plane of polarization. Between the arms are generally to be found rings which present the successive tints of the fringes of interference. In the extraordinary image the order of the phenomenon is entirely reversed.

Having now briefly described the more important optical phenomenon which forms the basis of the examination of butters with polarized light, I will next say something of the nature of the substances to be examined.

The expressions "fats" and "oils" designate those natural products of animals and vegetables known as glycerides. Chemically considered they are the normal propenyl ethers of the fatty acids, or, in other words, compounds of the triad alcohol, glycerine, with the fatty acids. The term "fat" is applied to such bodies when they are solid at ordinary temperatures, and "oil" when they are semi-solid or liquid. Those which are most important are:

Tri-stearin, $C_3H_5(C_{18}H_{35}O_2)_3$, occurs in natural fats. It may be obtained in a considerable degree of purity by repeated crystallizations from ether. It crystallizes in plates of a pearly luster. Its melting point is 55° C.

Tri-palmitin, $C_3H_5(C_{16}H_{31}O_2)_3$, is found in animal fats and palm oil. It crystallizes with a pearly luster from ether. The crystals have a melting point of from 50° to 66° C.

Tri-butyrin, $C_3H_5(C_4H_7O_2)_3$, occurs chiefly in butter. At ordinary temperature it is liquid, and has a distinct and peculiar odor and taste.

Tri-olein, $C_3H_5(C_{18}H_{33}O_2)_3$, occurs in animal fats and in almond and olive oil. At ordinary temperatures it is liquid, is neutral to test papers, and has neither taste nor smell.

Minute quantities of tri-myristin, caprin, caprylin, and caproin are also found in butter.

Pure butter fat is supposed to contain—

	Per cent.
Tri-olein, about	42.5
Tri-stearin, about	51.0
Tri-butyrin, about	6.3
Other glycerides, about	.2
	100.00

Olive oil is composed chiefly of tri-palmitin and olein.

Tri-stearin is the chief constituent of mutton fat, it having only small quantities of olein and palmitin.

Beef fat has somewhat more palmitin and stearin than mutton tallow. Lard has more olein.

It is thus seen that in dealing with butter fats and their substitutes we have to consider chiefly tri-olein and stearin, and, in smaller quantities, tri-palmitin, butyrin, &c. It follows, therefore, that the chief differences in the several substances will be due to the different proportions in which these glycerides are mixed and to such other physical differ-ences as the various sources of the substances under examination would produce. These differences, however, prove greater when subjected to physical and chemical analysis than the foregoing résumé of their chemical constitution would indicate. Advantage has been taken of these differences of physical structure to discriminate between fats and oils of different origins. The specific gravity and the melting point furnish two valuable points of discrimination, but both of these are perhaps inferior in value to the evidence afforded by the crystalline structure of the fats. The observation with the microscope of the crystals obtained in various ways furnishes valuable data for discrim-ination, and if the light employed be plane polarized or elliptically. polarized by a selenite plate, these data become still more valuable.

The first account of the use of the selenite plate in such examinations was given by Dr. J. Campbell Brown in the Chemical News, vol. 28, pages 1, *et seq.* He gives the following directions for the polaro-micro-scopic work :

Examine several portions of the original sample by means of a good microscope, using a one-fourth or one-fifth inch object-glass. In butter made from milk or cream nothing is seen except the characteristic globules, and the granular masses of curd and the cubical crystals of salt. The hard fats of butter are present in the globules in a state of solution, and are not recognizable in a separate form.

If stearic acid, stearin, or palmitin be present in separate form, they will be recog-nizable by simple fusiform crystals, or starlike aggregations of acicular crystals. They indicate the presence of melted fats.

Other substances, such as starch flour, palm oil, corpuscles, Irish moss, coloring matter, &c., may also be distinguished by the microscope as distinct from butter or fats.

Examine the same portions with the same object-glass, together with a polariscope, consisting of two Nicol's prisms and a selenite plate. The crystals referred to polarize light, and when viewed by the polariscope are distinctly defined. Particles of suet and other fats which have not been melted may also be distinguished by their action on polarized light, by their amorphous form, and by their membranes.

The value of this deportment of fresh-butter fat with elliptically po-larized light did not meet with the appreciation its merits deserved un-til attention was again called to it by Prof. Thomas Taylor, of the De-partment of Agriculture.

Any fat or oil which is homogeneous and non crystalline will present the same phenomena when viewed with polarized light and selenite plate; in other words will have no effect on the appearance of the field of vision. It is only, therefore, fats which are in a crystalline or semi-crystalline state that can thus be distinguished from fresh, amorphous butter. Naturally it follows that a butter which has been melted and cooled, or butter which has stood a long time, would impart a mottled appearance to the field of vision. For a simple preliminary test, how-ever, the procedure is worthy of more attention than its discoverer, Dr. J. Campbell Brown, accorded to it.

FORMS OF FAT CRYSTALS.

The forms of fat crystals differ greatly with the kinds of fat and the proportions in which they are mixed. It would be idle to attempt a description of all these modifications.

Husson[1] has published an illustrated description of some of the more important fat crystals. Suet crystals, according to Husson, are very characteristic of stearin. They are small, rounded, or elliptical masses formed by stiff, needle-like crystals, and resemble a sea urchin or hedge hog.

In lard are seen polyhedral cells arising from the compression of the fatty globules. In impure lard are also seen the remains of cells and adipose tissue. Fresh butter shows some long and delicate needles of margarine (?) united in bundles and grouped in various ways. When the butter is melted these needles diminish in length and become grouped round a central point. I have mentioned these descriptions especially for the purpose of calling attention to the fact, that, in the illustrations of the microscopic appearance of butter and other fats, emphasis is often given to one particular phenomenon, and the real appearance as seen in the microscope is not reproduced.

The only reliable representation is found in the actual photo-micrograph or its exact graphic reproduction.

When the crystals of certain fats are prepared in a special way they show, with polarized light, a distinct cross, the existence of which is explained by the laws of elliptical polarization already mentioned.

This cross was first described by Messrs. Hehner and Angell in 1874 in the following words:

If some of a fat containing crystals be placed on a slide and a drop of castor or olive oil be applied and pressed out with a thin glass cover, the depolarization of light is much enhanced; a revolving black cross, not unlike that on some starch grains, is seen in great perfection. These crosses are most clearly defined in the crystals obtained from butter, and these thus mounted form a brilliant polariscopic object.

They add further:

Thus far and no farther, as it seems to us, can the microscope assist us in this matter; but even such indications are valuable, especially when subsequent analysis proves the sample to be an adulterated article. The microscopic evidence in such case frequently serves to clinch together the whole superstructure, and thus certainty is made doubly sure.

Dr. Thomas Taylor has further called attention to this phenomenon in a paper read before the American Society of Microscopists at its Cleveland meeting, August, 1885. On page 3 of the reprint of this paper he says:

Since the publication of that paper I have experimented largely with butter, and have made the discovery that when it is boiled and cooled slowly for a period of from twelve to twenty-four hours at a temperature of from 50 to 70 Fahr. it not only becomes crystallized, but, with proper mounting and the use of polarized light, it ex-

---

[1] Ann. d. Chem. et d. Pharm., vol. 5, pp. 12, 469.

hibits on each crystal a well-defined figure resembling what is known as the cross of Saint Andrew. In course of time, the period ranging from a few days to a few weeks according to the quality of the butter used and the temperature to which it is exposed, the crystals, which at first are globular, degenerate, giving way to numerous rosette-like forms peculiar to butter.

On page 5 he says:

About ten years ago, while making some experiments with boiled butter, I first observed it exhibited small crystals somewhat stellar in form, but gave no further attention to the fact until May last. For the purpose of determining the real form of the crystal of boiled butter I procured a sample of pure dairy butter from Ohio. I boiled it, and when cold examined it under a power of 75 diameters. To my surprise I found globular bodies. When I subjected them to polarized light a cross consisting of arms of equal length was observed on each crystal. On rotating the polarizer the cross of each crystal rotated. On rotating the glass on which the specimen of butter was mounted the crosses remained stationary, thus showing that the appearance of the cross depends, probably, on the fact that the crystals are (1) globular, (2) polarizing bodies, (3) translucent, and (4) comparatively smooth. Were they opaque or non-polarized or did they consist of long spines, causing great divergence of the rays of light, no image of the cross would be visible; showing that the appearance of the cross under polarized light and the conditions stated is not due to any physical structure of the fatty crystals themselves. But from whatever cause the appearance of the cross on the butter crystals arises, its constant appearance on new butter under the conditions above described is a fact beyond any question; and, as far as my experience goes, the better the quality of the butter the more clearly defined is the cross; it is black, large, and well defined. When these crystals are under polarized light and a selenite plate combined they exhibit the prismatic colors, but the cross proper is not visible in this case, although the crystals are still divided into four equal parts and are exceedingly interesting objects.

Dr. Taylor having thus directed the attention of scientists to these important phenomena, it has not taken long to show that there is little reason for the rather mean opinion of European chemists of the value of the microscope in detecting adulterations of butter. In several cases of prosecution before the District authorities the offenders have been convicted solely on the microscopical evidence and have admitted the justice of the sentence. If only fresh butters were exposed for sale, and all adulterants were certainly once melted and slowly cooled, but little more than this qualitative examination would be necessary.

Prof. H. A. Weber, of Columbus, Ohio, has made some interesting experiments with the microscope on fats, which in the main bear out the conclusions of Messrs. Brown, Hehner and Angell, and Taylor. As was to be expected, however, he has shown that the appearance of the cross on a crystal of natural fat does not show that it is derived from pure butter. He says, in Bulletin No. 13 of the Ohio Experimental Station, Experiments 7, 8, 9, and 10:

Experiment 7.—The difference between the behavior of the tallow fats in Experiment 3 and the last three experiments could only be ascribed to a difference of conditions. It is well known that table butter normally contains 4 to 6 per cent. of salt and 5 to 20 per cent. of water. These ingredients constitute the most marked difference between butter and the rendered animal fats as tallow and lard. In order to test the effect of this mixture upon the tallow fats, about half an ounce of the oleo oil used in Experiment 3 was mixed in a porcelain mortar with a small quantity of salt and eight or ten drops of water. After the water was thoroughly incorporated, the mass was transferred to a test tube and boiled for 1 minute as in the case of butter. It was then poured into a wooden pill-box and allowed to cool as before. The cooled mass presented quite a marked difference in appearance from that obtained from the same substance in Experiment 3. It retained to a great extent the yellow color of the oleo oil, was of a more granular nature, and in fact resembled boiled butter in every respect. When a small particle was stirred up with olive oil on a glass slide it separated readily. When covered and viewed with a pocket lens it revealed a mass of globules resembling insect eggs. Under the microscope these globules exhibited essentially the same characteristics as those obtained from butter in Experiment 1. The crystalline mass of the oleo globule seemed somewhat coarser, and to this condition was ascribed the fact that the cross, as well as the colors produced by the selenite plate, were less sharply defined than in the globules obtained from butter. The slides prepared from this material were remarkably free from the small detached crystals of fat observed in Experiment 3.

Experiment 8.—Having thus discovered that these globular masses may be obtained from pure tallow fat by simply observing the conditions which obtain in butter making, the following test was made: Nine grams of oleo oil and 1 gram of lard were placed in a small beaker glass and eight or ten drops of a saturated solution of salt in water added. The mixture was then gently heated to melt the fats. After shaking violently for a few moments to mix the salt solution with the fats, the mixture was boiled gently for 1 minute and then allowed to cool as before in a wooden pill-box. The microscopic examination of this preparation revealed globular masses which could in no wise be distinguished from those obtained from pure butter. The crystalline texture was dense, the cross of St. Andrew's plainly marked, and the colors produced by the selenite sharply defined.

Experiment 9.—A mixture of one part of lard to five parts of oleo oil was treated as in the last experiment with like results.

Experiment 10.—In this test a mixture consisting of 20 per cent. of lard and 80 per cent. of oleo oil was employed. Whether the consistency of this mixture was peculiarly adapted to the formation of the globules, or whether possible variations of conditions in manipulation were more favorable, the writer is unable to judge from a single experiment, but the fact is that in this case the individual "butter crystals" were exceedingly large and characteristic.

The use of polarized light in photo-micrography is also valuable in enabling the photographer to print the light-colored crystals on a dark background. To illustrate some of the forms of crystals of butter and its substitutes as they appear under polarized light a large number of microscopic samples were prepared and photographed by Messrs. Richards and Richardson. Results of some of the more interesting of these photographs are herewith transmitted. In all cases the figures are magnified 40 diameters, unless otherwise stated.

DESCRIPTION OF PLATES.

PLATE I.

FIG. 1.—Fresh butter boiled.

FIG. 2.—Fresh butter made in the laboratory without the use of salt, melted, filtered, and boiled. A small sample of the butter was taken and boiled for one minute in a test tube over the naked flame, then set aside and allowed to cool slowly for twenty-four hours. A suitable quantity was then taken, sufficient to make a slide for the microscope, thinned with olive oil, and pressed out on the cover.

PLATE II.

FIG. 3.—Fresh Virginia butter boiled and let stand for seven days. Specimen prepared by Dr. T. Taylor, March 11, 1886.

FIG. 4.—Fresh Virginia butter boiled. Specimen prepared by Dr. T. Taylor March 11, 1886.

PLATE III.

FIG. 5.—Fresh Kentucky butter boiled. Specimen prepared by Dr. T. Taylor March 11, 1886.

FIG. 6.—Fresh butter boiled. Specimen prepared by Dr. T. Taylor March 15, 1886.

PLATE IV.

FIG. 7.—Filtered butter fat dissolved in boiling alcohol and allowed to cool slowly.

FIG. 8.—Filtered butter fat dissolved in boiling ether and allowed to cool slowly. The fresh butter was melted and filtered through a jacketed filter, thus getting rid of the water, curd, and salt; allowed to cool and prepared as above.

PLATE V.

FIG. 9.—Beef suet fat. Not boiled. The suet fat was cut up into fine pieces and melted in the water bath at a low heat and filtered; allowed to cool slowly. Specimen was taken several days after the sample was prepared.

FIG. 10.—Beef suet fat boiled with the addition of salt and cooled slowly.

PLATE VI.

FIG. 11.—Beef suet fat, "oleo oil," dissolved in boiling ether and allowed to cool slowly.

FIG. 12.—Beef suet fat, "oleo oil," dissolved in boiling alcohol and allowed to cool slowly.

PLATE VII.

FIG. 13.—Leaf lard. Not boiled. Specimen taken direct from can as purchased in the open market. Magnified 160 diameters.

FIG. 14.—Lard dissolved in boiling ether and allowed to cool slowly.

PLATE VIII.

FIG. 15.—Beef fat, "oleo oil," and lard, "neutral," boiled with salt and water and allowed to cool slowly.

FIG. 16.—Butterine, from Armour & Co., Chicago. Boiled and allowed to cool slowly.

Plate IX.

Fig. 17.—Butterine, from Armour & Co., Chicago. Not boiled. Specimen taken direct from tub as received July, 1886. Magnified 160 diameters.

Fig. 18.—Butterine, from Armour & Co., Chicago. Melted, filtered, and boiled.

Plate X.

Fig. 19.—Butterine, from Armour & Co., Chicago. Dissolved in boiling ether and allowed to cool slowly.

Fig. 20.—Oleo oil, from Armour & Co., Chicago. Melted, filtered, and boiled. Allowed to stand four days under cover glass.

Plate XI.

Fig. 21.—Oleomargarine, from Armour & Co., Chicago. Not boiled. Specimen taken direct from tub as received July, 1886. Magnified 160 diameters.

Fig. 22.—Oleomargarine, from Armour & Co., Chicago. Boiled with salt and water and allowed to cool slowly.

Plate XII.

Fig. 23.—Same as Fig. 22.

Fig. 24.—Same as Fig. 22.

PLATE I

Fig 1

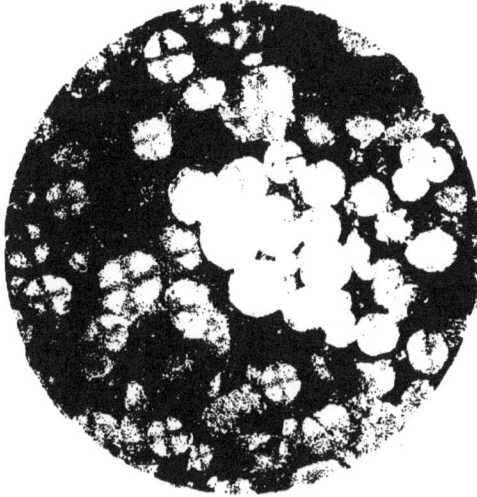

BUTTER x·40

Fig 2

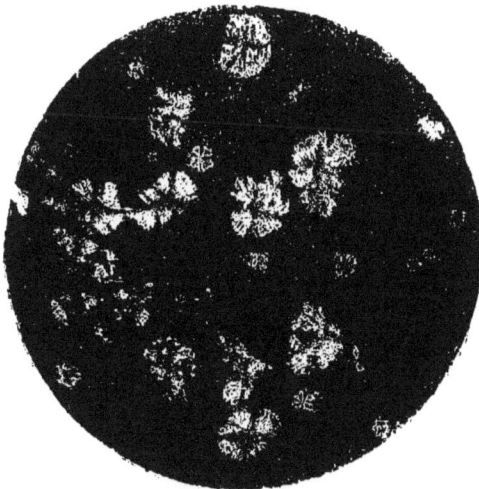

BUTTER x·40

Photo by Clifford Richardson

A Hoen & Co Heliocaustic Baltimore

Fig 3

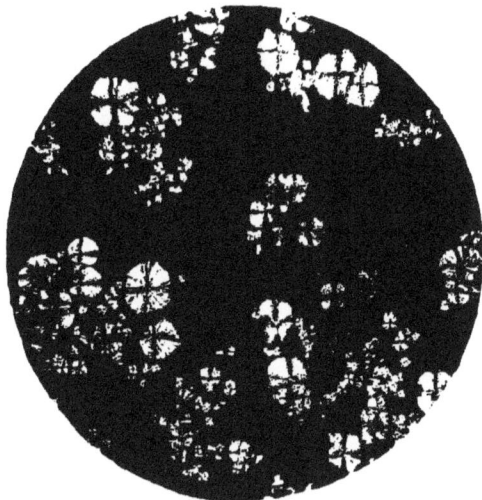

BUTTER x40

Fig 4

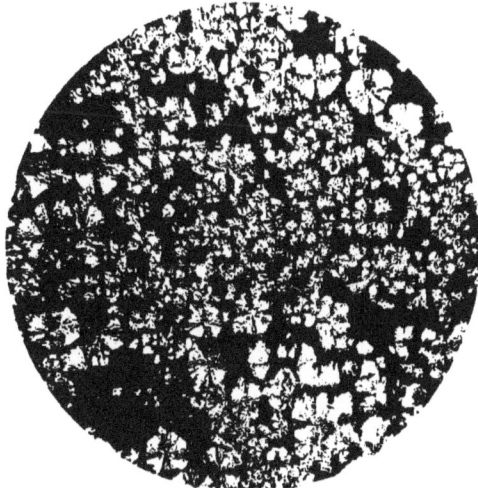

BUTTER x40

Photo by Clifford Richardson   A Hoen & Co. Heliochastic Baltimore

PLATE III

Fig 5

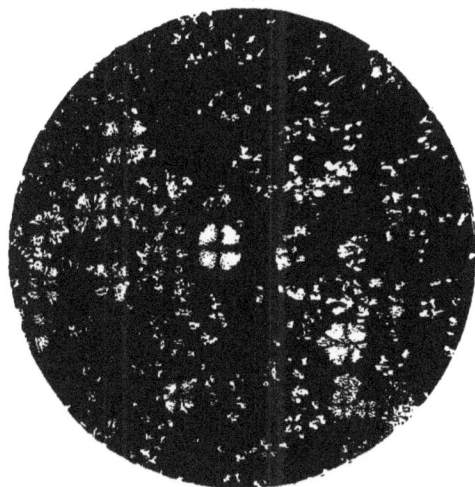

BUTTER x40

Fig 6

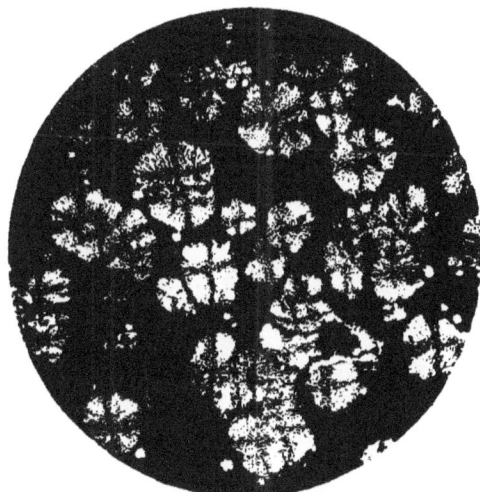

BUTTER x40

Photo by Clifford Richardson

Fig 7

BUTTER x40

Fig 8

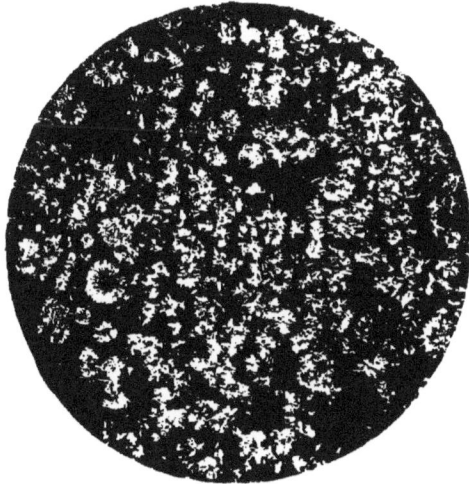

BUTTER x40

Photo by Clifford Richardson   A Hoen & Co Heliocaustic Baltimore

Fig 9

BEEF FAT x 40

Fig 10

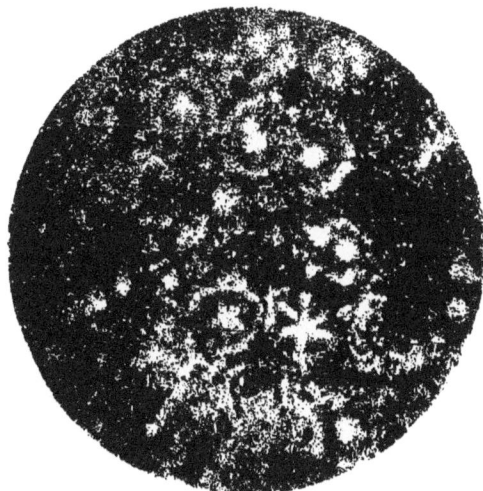

BEEF FAT x 40

Photo. by Clifford Richardson.   A. Hoen & Co. Heliocaustic. Baltimore

PLATE VI

Fig 11

BEEF FAT x 40

Fig 12

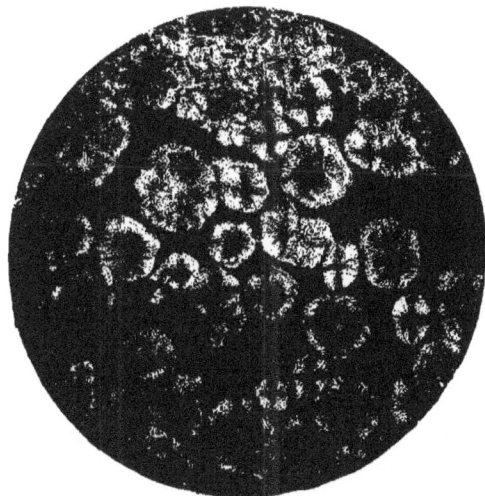

BEEF FAT x 40

Photo by Clifford Richardson.

Fig 13

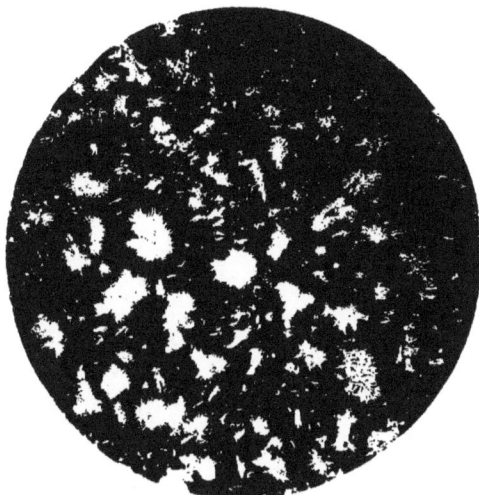

LARD ×160

Fig 14

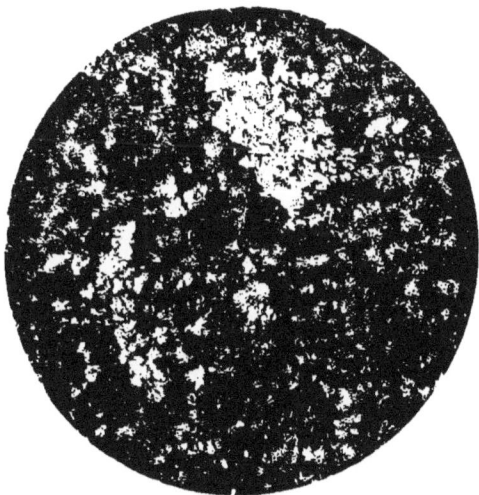

LARD ×40

Fig 15

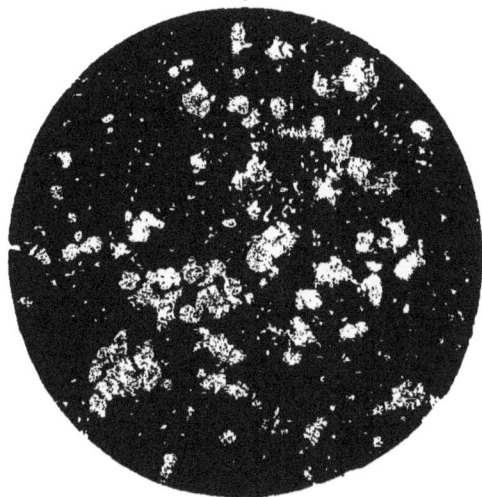

BEEF FAT & LARD x 40

Fig 16

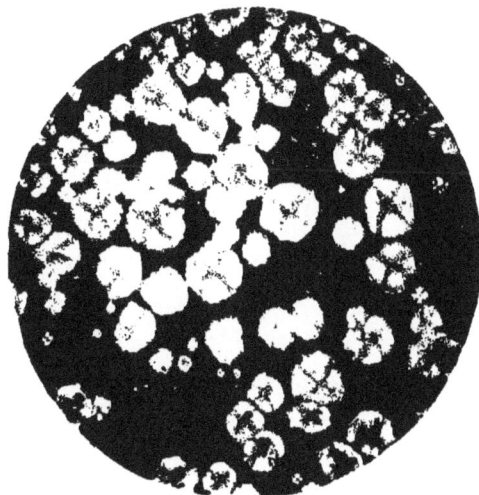

BUTTERINE x 40

Photo by Clifford Richardson　　　　　　　　A Hoen & Co. Heliocausic Baltimore

Fig 17

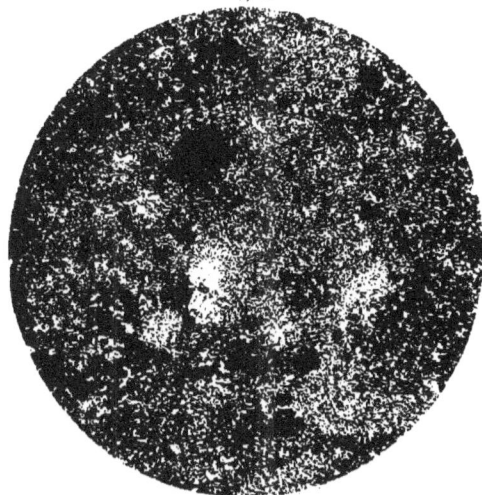

BUTTERINE x160

Fig 18

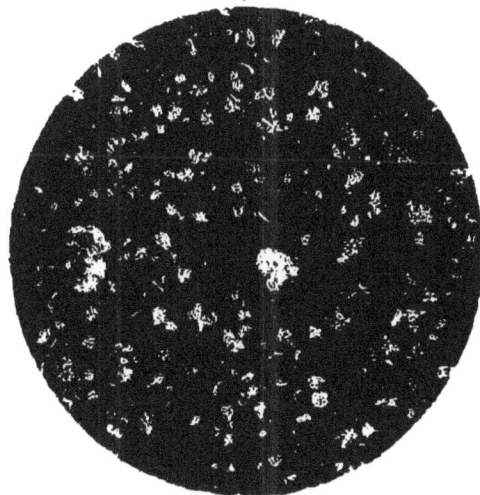

BUTTERINE x40

Fig 19

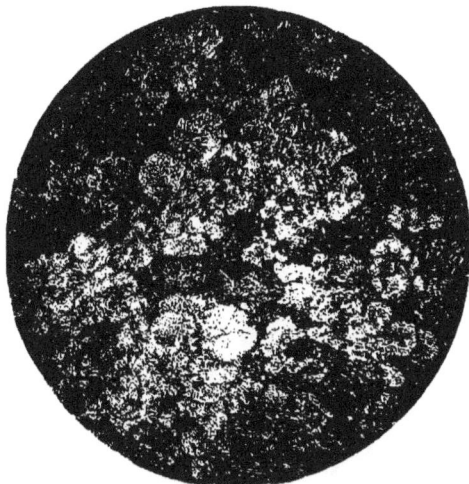

BUTTERINE x40

Fig 20

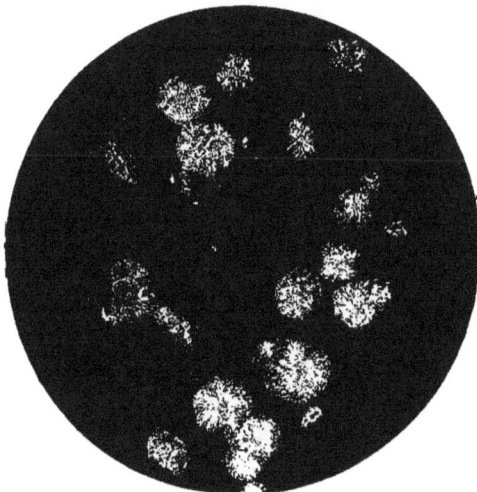

BEEF FAT x40

PLATE XI

Fig 21

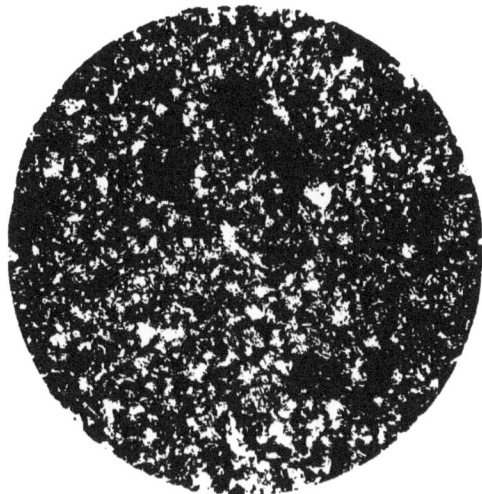

OLEOMARGARINE x160

Fig 22

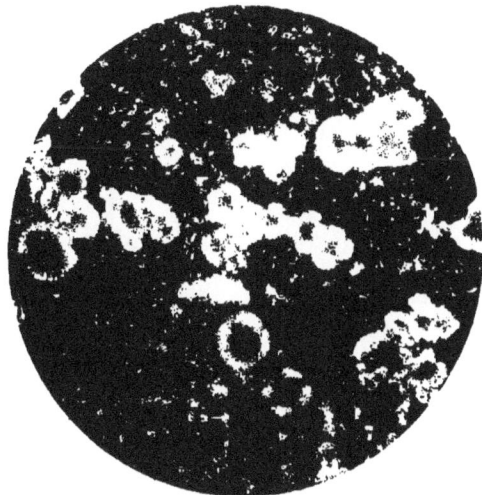

OLEOMARGARINE x40

Photo by Clifford Richardson

A Hoen & Co Heliocaustic, Baltimore

Fig 23

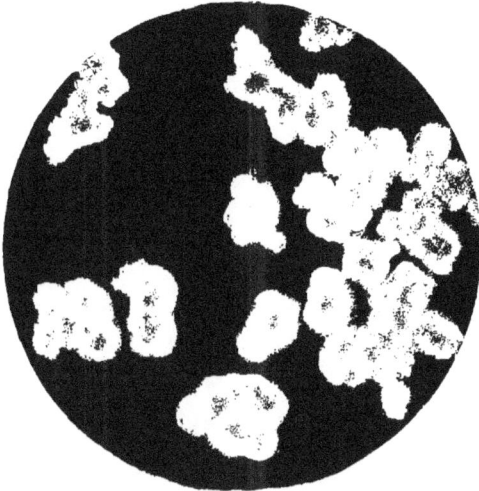

OLEOMARGARINE   ×40

Fig 24

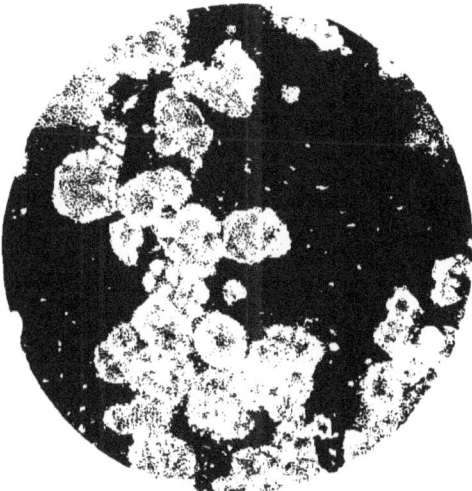

OLEOMARGARINE   ×40

A careful study of these illustrations will show that the microscope and polarized light are most valuable and reasonably certain means whereby a qualitative examination of butters can be made. The approximate amount of added fat can only be determined by a chemical analysis of the suspected sample, taken in connection with some of its further physical characteristics.

I have given above all the really valuable points heretofore established in respect of the use of polarized light in butter and fat analyses.[1]

The use of the microscope in butter examinations has not commanded as much attention among analysts as its merits deserve. Sell says:[2]

Though investigations have shown that the differences in structure under the microscope are not in all cases sufficiently characteristic to determine a sharp distinction between two different fats, yet it must be admitted that the microscopic examination is able to prove the presence of foreign fats at the moment it succeeds in establishing the presence of molecular tissues in animal or vegetable parasites.

Leudtner and Hilger say :[3]

The use of the microscope in the examination of fats requires a still further development before it can become generally applicable.

Having written to the editor of the Analyst for some information on the subject of the use of the microscopic methods in England, he replied: "The whole subject has been studied over and there is nothing in it."

Dr. S. M. Babcock, chemist of the New York Experimental Station, says:[4]

At the time these butters were received there was considerable controversy regarding the efficiency of Dr. Taylor's method for the detection of adulterations in butter by means of the microscope. An excellent opportunity was offered in these samples for testing this method in an impartial manner, and a microscopical examination of them was made before the nature of the butters was revealed by other tests. The butters were examined directly with polarized light and a selenite plate, and afterwards the crystals from the melted butters were examined in the same way for the "Saint Andrew's cross."

The direct examination with polarized light and a selenite plate showed prismatic colors in all of the adulterated butters, and a uniform tint in all of the genuine butters, except No. 2, which appeared very much like the adulterated samples. The crystals from all of the butters, adulterated as well as genuine, gave a well-defined Saint Andrew's cross with polarized light. This was also the case with neutral lard (No. 14), in which the cross was sharply defined, though quite small. No. 15 consisted of stearine from the oleo-oil factories, and showed no cross when examined by itself, but when combined with a small quantity of butter fat the crystals formed had the same appearance as those from pure butter.

The method has also been quite unsatisfactory in trials made at the station with butters whose character was known. Whether these results were due to a lack of skill or to imperfect knowledge in the details of the work I do not know. The

[1] Notices of minor importance on the same subject can be found in Chem. News, vol. 4, pp. 230, 283, 309, 322 ; Zeit. Anal. Chem., 1872, p. 334 ; Journ. Royal Microscopical Society, 1878, p. 378 ; American Quarterly Microscopical Journal, 1878, p. 294 ; American Journal of Microscopy, October, 1878 ; Bied. Centralblatt, 1879, pp. 861-865 ; 1882, p. 345 ; 1882, p. 49 ; Amer. Chemist, vol. 2, p. 428.

[2] *Op. cit.,* p. 503.

[3] Ver. Bay. Vertreter d. Angewand. Chem., p. 222.

[4] Fifth Ann. Rept. Bd. Control N. Y. Exp. Sta., pp. 330, 331.

uncertain results of some skilled microscopists, however, would indicate that the difficulty is inherent in the method. It certainly is not simple, and is not calculated to supersede the chemical methods now in use.

Caldwell,[1] after references to the notices of the use of the microscope in the examination of butter published up to that time (1882), says, p. 519:

It is plain, therefore, that little dependence can be placed on any microscopic test of the genuineness of butter, at least so far as the observation of the crystalline forms of foreign fats is concerned, for neither does the absence of such forms prove that the butter does not contain oleomargarine, nor does their presence prove the adulteration.

On the other hand, Mylius[2] has shown that the polarization microscope may be used for the detection of minute quantities of foreign fats in butter. Pure butter gives with crossed Nicols a dark field, whereas crystals of foreign fat will appear bright. Skalweit[3] recommends this method highly, and affirms that even the kind of foreign fat present may be determined.

In spite of the generally unfavorable opinions I feel sure that the chemist who neglects to make a simple microscopic examination of a suspected butter with polarized light and a selenite plate loses a valuable qualitative indication of the character of the samples with which he has to work. The melting of the sample of butter and its slow cooling to secure good bi-refracting crystals I consider a much less valuable indication than the simple observations above described.

SPECIFIC GRAVITY.

The determination of the specific gravity of a butter fat gives a most valuable indication of its purity. The density of pure butter glycerides is distinctly greater than that of the common adulterants, with the exception of cotton-seed oil. While this difference is not great, it is nevertheless large enough to be easily detected by careful manipulation.

Manipulation.—The relative weight of the filtered and dried fat is to be determined in a picnometer. This flask should be carefully calibrated by weighing the pure distilled water it will contain at the temperature at which the subsequent determinations are to be made. The flask should be provided with a delicate thermometer, but this is not essential, since the temperature can be determined by an external thermometer.

The temperature at which the determinations should be made is evidently that at which all the common butter adulterants will be in a perfectly fluid state. Generally the temperature of 100° F. has been employed. Since, however, "neutral lard" may have a melting point as high as 40° C. or even a little above that I have uniformly taken the specific gravity at that degree. In case the fat should have a melting point a little above this the temperature can be raised until the fat is

[1] Second Ann. Rept. N. Y. S. Bd. of Health.
[2] Correspondensblatt des Vereins Anal. Chem., 1878, No. 3.
[3] *Ibid.*, 1879, Nos. 5 and 13.

fluid and can then be reduced to 40° C., without danger of solidification. The difference between the specific gravities expressed at 37° C. and 40° C. is not of very great magnitude.

Blyth[1] recommends the use of a picnometer of 50 to 100 grams capacity, with a thermometer stopper. This is filled with water at 35° C. and placed in a beaker of water at 43° C. When the water has reached a temperature of 37°.7 C. the flask is removed and weighed.

The fat whose density is to be determined is treated in the same manner and weighed at the same temperature.

Wigner[2] places the butter-fat in a wide tube where a bubble of the specific gravity of .896 is kept below the surface by the bulb of the thermometer. At a certain temperature the bubbles will slowly sink to the bottom. In butters of .911 density, above which a sample may be passed as pure, these beads will sink as follows :

Specific gravity of beads	.880	.8896
Temperature	62°.7 C.	55°.5 C.

If the beads sink at any temperature lower than these the butter will need further examination.

Estcourt[3] describes a method of taking specific gravity of fats as follows :

The bulb of a Westphal balance is suspended in a test-tube containing the fat, the test-tube being immersed in paraffin, in a water bath. The adjustment of the weights takes place at a temperature of 92°.2 C. This process has been modified by König.[4]

In König's process there are several water baths which are closed with the exception of a tube for carrying off the steam. In the cover of each bath are four openings for the reception of four test-tubes 1¼ inches in diameter and 8 to 9 inches long. These are fastened air-tight into the openings mentioned. Each tube stands one-half inch above the cover of the water bath. Each piece of apparatus when in use contains in one of the tubes a sample of pure butter and in the others the samples under examination.

The specific gravity is determined by small areometers 6 inches long and with a scale marked from .845 to .870. The numbers obtained at 100° C. were as follows : Pure butter, .867 ; artificial butter, .859 ; beef fat, .860 ; mutton fat, .860 ; lard, .861 ; horse fat, .861. Mixture of pure butter with other fats gave numbers between .859 and .865.

The process of König has been tested by the Board of Health at Berlin and found relatively useful.[5] The method has also been approved by Elsner ;[6] by Ambuhl and Dietzsch ;[7] and Meyer.[8]

[1] Foods, p. 295.
[2] Blyth, op. cit., p. 295.
[3] Chem. News, vol. 34, p. 254.
[4] Industrieblätter, 1879, p. 455.
[5] Sell, op. cit., p. 505.
[6] Die Praxis des Nahrungsmittelchemikers, 2d ed., p. 50.
[7] Rep. d. Ver. Anal. Chem., 1884, p. 359.
[8] Zeit. Anal. Chem., 1881, p. 376.

Jones[1] calls attention to the fact that the specific gravity of butter increases with age.

The specific gravities of several samples are compared in the following table, the numbers in second column being obtained after eighteen months :

Specific gravity at 37.7 C.

Sample.	1.	2.
1	.9123	.9083
2	.9105	.9114
3	.9110	.0185
4	.9112	.0165
5	.9125	.9155
6	.9133	.0132

In other samples there was a decrease in specific gravity. In five samples out of nine there was an increase and the percentage of soluble acids had also increased.

Since butters in general are obtained for analysis without having been long kept the observation of Jones does not have much practical importance.

Sendtner and Hilger[2] find that a filtered pure butter fat does not show a specific gravity less than .866 at 100° C. In the Erlangen University numerous experiments with twenty different samples of butter showed variations from .866 to .8685.

Allen[3] recommends Sprengel's tube for the determination of specific gravity of oils at the temperature of boiling water.

The weight of the Sprengel tube and that of water contained in it at 15°.5 C. being known, the tube should be completely filled with the oil by immersing one of the orifices in the liquid and gently sucking the air from the other orifice of the tube. The tube is then placed in the mouth of a conical flask containing water kept in a rapid ebullition, and the cover of a porcelain crucible placed over it. As the oil gets hot it expands and is expelled in drops from the horizontal capillary orifice of the tubes. When the expansion ceases any oil adhering to the orifice is removed by cautious application of filter paper, the tube removed from the bath, wiped dry, allowed to cool, and weighed. The weight of the contents divided by the weight of water at 15°.5 C. previously known to be contained by the tube will give the density of the oil at the temperature of the boiling water ; water at 15°.5 C. being taken as unity.

Bendikt[4] prefers the Sprengel tube to all the other methods of estimating the specific gravity of oils. He also recommends the Westphal balance as used by Bell and Walkenhaar.

[1] Analyst, 1879, p. 39.

[2] Vereinbarungen betreffs d. Untersuch. u. Beurteilung v. Nahrungs-Genussmitteln, pp. 221-2.

[3] Com. Organic Analysis, Vol. 2, 2d ed.. p. 15.

[4] Analyse der Fette, &c., p. 53.

Dr. Muter[1] gives the following table of the specific gravity of various oils at 37°.7 C.

Kind of oil.	Specific gravity.	Kind of oil.	Specific gravity.
Olive oil	907. 0	Linseed oil (boiled)	938. 0
Almond oil	905. 6	Castor oil	953. 8
Arachis oil	908. 5	Sperm oil	872. 4
Rape oil	906. 7	Whale oil	906. 0
Nut oil	908. 4	Seal oil	915. 0
Cotton-seed oil (brown)	917. 6	Codliver oil	917. 9
Cotton-seed oil (refined)	913. 6	Lard oil	907. 8
Poppy-seed oil	913. 4	Neat's-foot oil	907. 0
Hempseed oil	919. 3	Butterine	903 to 906. 0
Linseed oil (raw)	925. 2	Butter-fat	912 to 914. 0

METHOD EMPLOYED IN CHEMICAL DIVISION.

When convenient the determination of specific gravity is not made until a number of samples is on hand. Each determination is made in duplicate. The picnometers, holding about 25 grams, are filled with the filtered fat, at as low a temperature as possible, and placed in a flat dish filled with water as nearly to the tops of the flasks as possible. The picnometers used should all be of the same height. The stopper has a capillary perforation for the escape of the oil as the temperature rises. If the picnometers are not furnished with thermometers of their own, a delicate thermometer is suspended in the water surrounding them. The water-bath is slowly warmed and gently but constantly stirred until the temperature reaches 40° C. It is kept at this temperature for fifteen or twenty minutes, until the fat has taken on the same temperature as the water. The picnometers are then carefully cleaned and dried, and, after cooling to the temperature of the balance-room, are weighed. This method is somewhat tedious when only one determination is to be made, but where many samples are to be examined it is sufficiently speedy. In respect of accuracy it leaves nothing to be desired.

TEMPERATURE AT WHICH SPECIFIC GRAVITY IS STATED.

Different analysts select different temperatures for determining specific gravity. It would be well to have some agreement on this point to avoid confusion.

Since the specific gravity determined at any temperature can be easily calculated for any other given temperature, I suggest that it might be well to express all specific gravities in terms of water at 4° C.

THE MELTING POINT OF FATS.

The fats pass rather slowly from the semi-solid state, which is their natural condition at ordinary temperatures, to complete fluidity. It is, therefore, difficult to determine accurately the exact temperature at which they melt.

---

[1] Allen, *op. cit.*, p. 15, foot-note.

The value of the melting point in the examination of fats is at once apparent, provided it is possible to be assured that it represents a definite temperature which can be easily and accurately determined.

At a temperature of 40° C. pure butter fat has a specific gravity of .912, while the substitutes therefor, viz, lard, tallow, oleo-oil, neutral lard, &c., have specific gravities varying from .900 to .905. Yet even these small differences are extremely valuable in distinguishing the fats from each other.

The differences in melting points, when they can be accurately determined, will also prove helpful to the analyst. The usual methods employed to determine melting points have been based on the assumption that a fat becomes transparent at the moment it assumes the liquid state. Usually the fat is melted and placed in glass capillary tubes, and, after cooling, put into water near the bulb of a thermometer. The water is slowly warmed, and the moment the fat in the tube becomes transparent the reading of the thermometer is taken. A careful observer is able in this way to make multiple determinations which agree well together, but the readings of different persons are apt to vary greatly. Moreover, it is not the *melting* but the *transparent* point that is determined.

In 1883, at the Minneapolis meeting of the Association for the Advancement of Science, I described a method of determining the flowing point of a fat. The melted fat having been put into a small bent metallic tube, was, after cooling, placed in a bath of mercury. One arm of this U-tube was slightly longer than the other. The bent tube was immersed in the mercury until the longer arm was just below the surface. The fat in the tube was, therefore, subjected to a certain definite pressure from the mercury, due to the difference in length of the two arms. When the melted fat first appeared on the surface of the mercury, the thermometric reading was made. It is scarcely necessary to add that the bulb of the thermometer was wholly immersed in the mercury. Fairly good results were obtained by this method.

Another method, which gave rather good results, I tried at the same time. A thin film of fat was spread over the surface of the mercury and the temperature noted at which a platinum wire drawn through it left no trace. The solidifying point was determined in the same operation by observing where the wire left a mark. Various methods for determining the melting point of fats are given by Reichert.[1] The method preferred by him is a modification of Guichard's process,[2] in which the fat is forced out of the tube by a water pressure of a constant magnitude.

Dr. H. Krüss[3] describes an apparatus for estimating the melting point by the completion of an electric circuit dependent on the melting of the fat used as an insulating material. A platinum wire, bent into the

[1] Zeit. Anal. Chem., 1885, pp. 11 *et seq.*
[2] *Ibid.*, 1883, p. 70.
[3] Zeit. f. Instrumentenkunde, vol. 4, pp. 32, 33.

form of a small hook, is dipped into the melted fat, a portion of which adheres to it. This process is repeated until a sufficient insulation is produced. The fat-covered end of the wire is then dipped into a mercury cup, which contains also the bulb of the thermometer. The cup is placed in the electric circuit and the moment of contact is determined by the ringing of an electric bell. Thorough trial of this method convinced me that it was less accurate than any of those which have already been mentioned.

Realizing the importance of determining some definite point at which fats would assume a constant condition under the influence of temperature, I was led to select another physical aspect of fats, easily and certainly visible, which could be regarded as the melting point. This condition may be defined as the point at which the molecular attraction of the fat becomes greater than the molecular cohesion.

If a thin film of any fat be suspended in a liquid of equal specific gravity with it and this liquid be slowly warmed, a point will be reached at which the film will roll up and finally assume the form of a sphere. By imparting to the globule a gentle motion of rotation the observer is easily able to distinguish the moment when it becomes sensibly symmetrical. I use the following method and apparatus for applying this principle to the determination of the melting points of fats.[1] The apparatus consists of (1) an accurate thermometer for reading easily tenths of a degree; (2) a less accurate thermometer for measuring the temperature of water in the large beaker glass; (3) a tall beaker glass, 35cm. high and 10cm. in diameter; (4) a test tube 30cm. high and 3.5cm. in diameter; (5) a stand for supporting the apparatus; (6) some method of stirring the water in the beaker. I use a blowing bulb of rubber and a bent glass tube extending to near the bottom of the beaker; (7) a mixture of alcohol and water of the same specific gravity as the fat to be examined.

Manipulation.—The disks of the fat are prepared as follows: The melted and filtered fat is allowed to fall from a dropping tube from a height of 15 to 20cm. onto a smooth piece of ice floating in water. The disks thus formed are from 1 to 1½cm. in diameter and weigh about 200 milligrams. By pressing the ice under the water the disks are made to float on the surface, whence they are easily removed with a steel spatula.

The mixture of alcohol and water is prepared by boiling distilled water and 95 per cent. alcohol for ten minutes to remove the gases which they may hold in solution. While still hot the water is poured into the test-tube already described until it is nearly half full. The test tube is then filled with the hot alcohol. It should be poured in gently down the side of the inclined tube to avoid too much mixing. If the tube is not filled until the water has cooled the mixture will contain so many air bubbles as to be unfit for use. These bubbles will gather on

[1]Journal Anal. Chemistry, vol. 1, No. 1, pp. 39 *et seq.*

the disk of fat as the temperature rises and finally force it to the top of the mixture.

The test tube containing the alcohol and water is placed in a vessel containing cold water, and the whole cooled to below 10° C. The disk of fat is dropped into the tube from the spatula, and at once sinks until it reaches a part of the tube where the density of the alcohol-water is exactly equivalent to its own. Here it remains at rest and free from the action of any force save that inherent in its own molecules.

The delicate thermometer is placed in the test tube and lowered until the bulb is just above the disk. In order to secure an even temperature in all parts of the alcohol mixture in the vicinity of the disk the thermometer is moved from time to time in a circularly, pendulous manner. A tube prepared in this way will be suitable for use for several days, in fact, until the air bubbles begin to attach themselves to the disk of fat. In no case did the two liquids become so thoroughly mixed as to lose the property of holding the disk at a fixed point, even when they were kept for several weeks.

In practice, owing to the absorption of air, I have found it necessary to prepare new solutions every third or fourth day.

The disk having been placed in position, the water in the beaker glass is slowly heated and kept constantly stirred by means of the blowing apparatus already described.

When the temperature of the alcohol-water mixture rises to about 6 degrees below the melting point, the disk of fat begins to shrivel, and gradually rolls up into an irregular mass.

The thermometer is now lowered until the fat particle is even with the center of the bulb. The bulb of the thermometer should be small, so as to indicate only the temperature of the mixture near the fat. A gentle rotary movement should be given to the thermometer bulb, and I have thought it would be convenient to do this with a kind of clock-work, although I have not carried this idea into execution. The rise of temperature should be so regulated that the last 2 degrees of increment require about ten minutes. The mass of fat gradually approaches the form of a sphere, and when it is sensibly so the reading of the thermometer is to be made. As soon as the temperature is taken, the test tube is removed from the bath and placed again in the cooler. A second tube, containing alcohol and water, is at once placed in the bath. It is not necessary to cool the water in the bath. The test tube (I use ice water as a cooler) is of low enough temperature to cool the bath sufficiently. After the first determination, which should be only a trial, the temperature of the bath should be so regulated as to reach a maximum about 1°.5 above the melting point of the fat under examination.

Working thus with two tubes about three determinations can be made in an hour.

After the test tube has been cooled the globule of fat is removed with a small spoon attached to a wire before another disk of fat is put in.

Agreement of multiple determinations.

FILTERED BUTTER FAT.

	Degrees C.
No. 1, by one observer	33.5
No. 2, by another	33.5
No. 3, by a third	33.9
No. 4, by a third	32.4
No. 5, by a third	34.4

A second set of observations made with the same butter gave—

	Degrees C.
No. 1	33.7
No. 2	33.8
No. 3	33.5
No. 4	33.5

A different butter gave the following numbers:

	Degrees C.
No. 1	34.0
No. 2	33.7
No. 3	33.8
No. 4	34.0

Another butter, "Creamery Tub," gave the numbers below:

	Degrees C.
No. 1	33.7
No. 2	33.7
No. 3	33.6
No. 4	33.6

A neutral lard, from Armour & Co., Chicago, gave the following results:

	Degrees C.
No. 1	42.8
No. 2	42.4
No. 3	42.3
No. 4	42.6
No. 5	42.2
No. 6	42.0

An oleo oil, from Armour & Co., gave—

	Degrees C.
No. 1	29.4
No. 2	29.5
No. 3	29.5
No. 4	29.7
No. 5	30.0
No. 6	30.3
No. 7	29.7
No. 8	29.8

Another butter, shown by the microscope to be adulterated, gave—

	Degrees C.
No. 1	33.5
No. 2	33.7
No. 3	33.5

No. 1777, a doubtful butter gave—

	Degrees C.
No. 1	34.3
No. 2	34.5
No. 3	33.6
No. 4	34.0

No. 1779, also a doubtful butter, gave—

	Degrees C.
No. 1	34.2
No. 2	33.5
No. 3	33.0

These results show that the method is capable of general application. Collecting together the mean results obtained with butter-fats the following table is obtained:

TABLE No. 1.—*Melting points, etc., of genuine butter.*

Serial number.	Melting point.	Per cent. soluble acid.	Specific gravity at 40° C.
	° C.		
1745	34.5	5.48	.911
1766	34.3	4.52	.940
1768	34.2	5.21	.910
1769	33.7	3.05	.912
1772	34.0	5.26	.911
1785	32.0	4.48	.912
1786	34.7	4.32	.912
Mean	33.8	4.86	.911

TABLE No. 2.—*Melting points, &c., of butters of doubtful purity.*

Serial number.	Melting point.	Per cent. Soluble acid.	Specific gravity at 40° C.
	° C.		
1777	34.1	3.92	.910
1779	33.6	3.16	.909
1780	34.4	3.02	.910
1781	34.5	3.97	.910
Mean	34.1	3.51	.909

The above were all bought as pure butters. They are condemned on account of the low percentage of soluble acid, while by their specific gravity they appear to fall near the limit of purity. The soluble acid in the above was determined by washing out and not by Reichert's method.

Table No. 3.—*Melting point of substances sold as butter, but proved by analysis to be adulterated.*

Serial number.	Melting point.	Per cent. soluble acid.	Specific gravity at 40° C.
	° C.		
1755	39.0	1.53	.906
1778	33.6	0.21	.904
1787	34.6	0.09	.906
4594	35.3	0.09	.904
4595	37.8	0.90	.905

Table No. 4.—*Melting point, &c., of "oleo-oil" and "neutral lard" used as butter adulterants.*

Serial number.	Melting point.	Per cent. soluble acid.	Specific gravity at 40° C.
"Neutral lard":			
	° C.		
1754	42.4	0.10	.904
4507	42.4	....	....
"Oleo-oil:"			
1756	29.7	0.08	.903
4590	29.6	0.08	.903

Table No. 5.—*Melting point of mixtures made in laboratory as indicated.*

[The butter used had a melting point of 33°.1 C.; the "oleo-oil" of 29°.6 C.; and the "neutral lard" of 42°.4 C.]

No.	Composition of mixture.	Theoretical melting point.	Observed melting point.
		° C.	° C.
1....	2 parts butter, 1 part "neutral "	36.2	35.2
2....	1 part butter, 2 parts "neutral "......	39.3	39.6
3....	1 part butter, 1 part "neutral" and 1 part "oleo"	35.0	35.5
4....	2 parts butter, 1 part "oleo"	31.9	32.0
5....	1 part butter, 2 parts "oleo"	30.8	30.5

From the above it appears that the melting point of a mixture of two or more fats can be readily and accurately calculated from that of its constituents. The agreement, except in No. 1, is within the error of ordinary observation.

Remarks on preceding data.—The mean melting point of the butters examined is 33°.8 C., the maximum is 34°.7 C., and the minimum 32°.6 C. In general terms it may be said that a genuine butter will show a melting point falling within the limits of 33° and 34° C. Of butter adulterants the "neutral lard" has a comparatively high melting point and "oleo-oil" a low one. Unfortunately for analytical purposes it is easy for the fabricator to make an artificial butter whose melting point is sensibly the same as that of the genuine article. On the other hand it is seen that if a false butter be made of a genuine one and only one of the adulterants in common use, the variation of the melting point from the normal will be sufficiently great to call attention to the falsification.

19330—No. 13——4

EFFECT OF TIME ON MELTING POINT OF THE FAT DISKS.

By some variations in the melting point of fat disks of different ages my attention was directed to an investigation of the effect of time.

The following data will serve to measure the influence of age on the melting point:

BUTTERS.

Number.	Melting point.		Increase +; decrease−.
	Directly disk was made.	After 24 hours.	
	° C.	° C.	° C.
1..........	33.1	33.6	+0.5
2..........	34.3	34.7	+0.4
3..........	34.2	34.6	+0.4
4..........	34.5	35.2	+0.7
5..........	32.9	32.8	−0.1
6..........	33.1	34.5	+1.4

In every case except No. 5 in the above table it is seen that the melting point of the disks of butter was raised by standing on water at ordinary temperatures for twenty-four hours.

In one instance, a butter whose melting point was 34°.5 C. stood in the form of disks from May 27 until August 3. An attempt was made on this latter date to determine its melting point. At a temperature of 75° C. the disk had not assumed a spherical shape, and the temperature could be carried no higher on account of approaching the boiling point of the alcohol.

ADULTERATED BUTTERS.

Number.	Melting point directly disk was made.	Melting point after—	Increase.
	C.	C.	C.
1........	31.6	5 days ... 61.4	26.8
2........	32.9	18 hours .. 37.0	4.1
3........	38.1	24 hours ... 42.9	5.9
4........	35.3	46 hours ...35.3	0.0
5........	37.8	44 hours ...40.3	2.5

Again in every case but one a marked rise in the melting point.

"OLEO OIL."

	Melting point.
	C.
"Oleo," at once	29.6
"Oleo," after 42 hours	42.5
Increase	2.9

It would appear from the above results that adulterated butters and butter adulterants show a greater rise in melting points when the disks are a day or more old than pure butter. The analytical data, however, are too meager to permit a definite statement of this kind. Should it prove to be true, it would be a valuable indication in the discrimination between pure and adulterated butters. An examination of the old disks with the microscope did not reveal a crystalline structure, and this change, therefore, must be attributed to a molecular modification or superficial oxidation.

EFFECT OF THE PRELIMINARY HEATING OF THE FAT TO DIFFERENT TEMPERATURES.

A butter fat was melted at a low temperature and allowed to stand until the temperature had fallen to 30° C.; it was still perfectly fluid. The disks were formed by dropping on ice as usual. The melting point obtained was 33° C. The fat was now heated to 50° C. and treated as above; melting point, 33°.4 C. The temperature was then raised to 80° C.; melting point, 32°.8 C.

The above results, falling within the possible error of observation, show that the temperature to which the fat is subjected before the formation of the disks has no appreciable effect on the point at which the fat particle becomes a sphere.

EFFECT OF SUDDEN RISE OF TEMPERATURE.

A sudden rise of temperature tends to greatly lower the melting point. A fat which showed a melting point of 35°.3 C. when determined in the usual way, melted at once into a perfect sphere when dropped into the water-alcohol mixture having a temperature of 29° C. At 28°.5 C. the globule was irregular.

A disk of neutral lard, having by the usual method a melting point of 42°.4 C., became at once a sphere when dropped into the water-alcohol at 36°.2 C. Below that temperature the spheroidal shape was not symmetrical.

In all cases this phenomenon will appear. It may be suggested, therefore, with strict propriety, whether this may not be regarded as the proper melting point. Since the temperature at which the spheroidal state is assumed can be determined within one or two degrees by a preliminary trial, it would not be difficult to have a series of mixtures of water and alcohol arranged so as to show differences of temperature of 0°.5 C. By dropping the disks successively into these mixtures the instantaneous fusing point could be determined with accuracy.

The method set forth in the preceding pages has been proved by 165 determinations to be capable of giving agreeing results. Not only will the numbers obtained by the same observer be concordant, but also those of different analysts. This arises from the fact that the moment of the assumption of the spheroidal state is easily determined even by an unpracticed eye. I have also noticed that in this condition pure butter and oleo are quite transparent, while on the other hand neutral

rd and adulterated butters are still somewhat opalescent. From this
it is seen that the data obtained by the old method of determining the
temperature of transparency would differ somewhat from those obtained
by the proposed procedure. Since the age of the disk has a great deal
to do with its melting point, I suggest that all determinations be made
within fifteen minutes to two hours from the making of the disks.

The method can also be extended to such bodies as paraffine and
bees-wax. The melting point of a paraffine was found to be—

	Melting point.
	° C.
No. 1	53. 6
No. 2	55. 1
No. 3	55. 2
No. 4	53. 3

An interesting phenomenon was observed in determining the melting
point of the paraffine, which may be made to show, in a lecture experiment, the change of volume which bodies sometimes undergo in passing
from a solid to a liquid state. The same mixture of water and alcohol
used in the examination of fats, allowed the disk of paraffine to sink to
about the same point as the disk of fat. When the temperature rose,
however, to within one or two degrees of the melting point, there was a
sudden increase in volume. The pellet of paraffine rapidly rose to the
top of the tube. To avoid this and keep the globule within the liquid I
made a mixture of water-alcohol and absolute alcohol. With this
arrangement the rise of the paraffine was arrested in the upper third
of the tube occupied by the absolute alcohol, where its assumption of
the spheroidal state could be readily observed. On placing the tube in
a cooling bath the globule of paraffine rapidly sinks as it solidifies·
The disks of paraffine and bees-wax are quite irregular, but nevertheless
suitable for the process. The melting point of the one sample of bees-
wax examined was found to be 64°.2 C.

VISCOSITY.

The speed with which at identical temperatures and pressures different oils flow through an orifice may be used to distinguish them
from each other. For a description of the methods used in viscosimetry I refer to Allen's Com. Organic Analysis.[1] An ingenious and useful
apparatus for viscosimetry has been invented by Babcock.[2]

Babcock has applied his apparatus to the investigation of the viscos·
ity of butter soaps with promising results.[3]

[1] Vol. 2, 2d ed., pp. 194 et seq.
[2] Fifth Ann. Rept. Bd. Control N. Y. Exp. Sta., pp. 316 et seq.
[3] Ibid., pp. 338 et seq.

REFRACTIVE INDEX OF OILS.

The use of the refractometer of Abbé in the examination of butters has been proposed by Müller.[1] The principle of the use of this instrument is, that the fats of pure butter possess a less refractive power than the glycerides of a higher molecular weight.

This subject has also been treated by Skalweit.[2]

ESTIMATION OF SOLUBLE ACIDS IN BUTTER FATS.

Method of Hehner and Angell.[3]—Hehner and Angell, in June, 1874, published a pamphlet on butter analysis in which the details of their method were given.

The following is an abstract of this method :[4]

A weighed quantity, usually 3 grams, of the fat was saponified in a porcelain dish with caustic potash, with frequent stirrings with a glass rod. The clear butter soap was transferred to a flask or retort and decomposed by means of dilute sulphuric acid. This mixture, which contained sulphate of potash, glycerine, and the volatile acids in solution and the insoluble fatty acids floating on the top, was distilled, and the acidity of the distillate estimated by means of a soda solution of known strength. The practical difficulties of this method, such as the violent bumping of the boiling liquid and the impossibility of obtaining a distillate perfectly free from acid, led the authors to adopt a somewhat different method.

This modification is based upon the different percentages of the insoluble fatty acids in butter and other animal fats. The insoluble acids, after saponification, were collected on a moistened filter paper, washed with hot water, and when the soluble acid was washed out, dried and weighed.

They found the percentage of insoluble fats in butter to vary from 85.40 to 86.20, while in other animal fats the percentage of insoluble fatty acids was about 95.5. As will be shown further along, a small error is introduced into this method by washing the insoluble fatty acids on the filter. When this error is avoided, it is found that the percentage of the insoluble fatty acids in butter fat is considerably higher than the figure which has just been given. A detailed description of this part of the process will be given farther on. Turner[5] suggested the employment of alcohol, with the view to hasten the saponification of the fat; a modification of the process which has been almost universally adopted by analysts.

About 30 or 40cc. of spirits of wine are added to the butter in the porcelain dish and heated over the water bath to near the boiling-point.

---

[1] Archiv d. Pharm., 1886, p. 210.
[2] Rep. d. Ver. Anal., Chem., 1886, p. 181.
[3] Analyst, 1877, p. 147.
[4] Hassall, Food and its adulterations, p. 446.
[5] Ibid., p. 447.

About 5 grams of solid caustic potash are then added, and from time to time a few drops of water, to facilitate its solution, the liquid being stirred all the time. In this manner the butter becomes rapidly saponified. The clear yellowish solution is then freed from all alcohol over the water bath and the soap decomposed as already described. Care should be taken to remove all the alcohol, as a small quantity of the fatty acids might be held dissolved should any alcohol remain, and so lead to an erroneous result.

Hehner's method modified by Reichert.[1]—Weigh out 2½ grams of dried and filtered butter fat in an Erlenmeyer flask of 150cc. capacity; add 1 gram of solid potassium hydrate and 20cc. of 80 per cent. alcohol. This mixture is kept upon the water bath with constant shaking until the soap obtained no longer forms a foamy, greasy mass. Afterwards 50cc. of water are added to the flask, and the soap, after it has dissolved in water, is decomposed with 20cc. of dilute sulphuric acid (1cc. of pure sulphuric acid to 10cc. of water). The contents of the flask are now subjected to distillation, with the precaution of conducting through it a slow stream of air, in order to avoid bumping. It is also recommended to use a bulb tube with a wide opening, in order to avoid carrying over the sulphuric acid. The distillate, which, especially with fats poor in butter and by rapid distillation, always deposits a little of the solid fat acids, is filtered through a moistened filter paper and collected in a 50cc. flask. After 10 to 20cc. are passed over it is poured back into the flask and the distillation is now continued until the distillate amounts to exactly 50cc The distillate, which, when the distillation has gone on evenly, forms a water clear liquid, is immediately titrated with decinormal soda lye after the addition of 4 drops of litmus tincture. The titration is finished if the blue color of the litmus remains constant for some time. Six analyses of an artificial butter fat required 10.5cc. of decinormal soda lye to neutralize the acid in the distillate.

The genuine butter gave on three trials 14.50, 14.45, and 14.60cc., respectively, of the decinormal soda.

Two samples of cocoanut fat required 5.70 and 3.70cc. of soda lye.

Thirteen samples of pure butter required a mean of 13.97cc. of the decinormal soda.

All the other fats which are used in the adulteration of butter required a much smaller amount of the decinormal soda for the saturation of the distilled acid.

In artificial butters the proportion of pure butter and added fat may be calculated from the following formula:

$$B = a\,(n-b).$$

in which n represents the most probable value of the number representing the quantity of decinormal soda solution required either for pure butter or for the fat with which it may be adulterated. When B equals

[1] Zeit. Anal. Chem., 1879, pp. 68, et seq.

O, that is, when the substance contains no pure butter, the value of n may be taken at .30. We have, therefore,

$$O = a\,(0.30 - b)\ \text{from which}\ b = .30.$$

When B is equal to 100, that is, when the butter is pure, as has already been said, the most probable value of n, according to the thirteen analyses given, is 13.97, or in round numbers $14 \pm .45$, then we have the equation

$$100 = a\,(14.00 \pm 0.45 - 0.30)$$

and from this the value of

$$a = 7.30 \pm .24.$$

The above equations may therefore be condensed into B $= (7.30 \pm 0.24)\,(n - 30)$, that is, in order to find the probable butter content of a fat mixture subtract from the number of the cubic centimeters of decinormal soda lye used for titration .30 and multiply the remainder by 7.30. The probable error which will be met with by this estimation amounts to $\pm 0.24\,(n - 0.30)$.

Medicus and Scherer[1] examined the method of Reichert and found it to be quite exact. For pure butter they found the quantity of decinormal soda lye required should be 13cc.; a mixture of equal parts of butter fat and tallow required 7cc.

Two parts of butter fat and one of tallow required 9.1cc; three parts of butter fat and one of tallow required 10.1cc.

The authors call attention to the fact that melted butter fat slowly cooled may separate into portions requiring different quantities of the decinormal soda for the saturation of the distilled acid which they afford. Two and one-half to 3 pounds of pure butter fat were used. This was melted and allowed to cool with continued stirring in order to secure a perfectly homogeneous mass. $2\frac{1}{2}$ grams of this mixture, by Reichert's method, required 14cc. of decinormal soda. The fat was now again melted, poured into a large beaker glass, and uncovered allowed to cool without stirring. The solidification took place slowly. After solidification $2\frac{1}{2}$ grams from the upper layer required 13.3cc. of soda.

Allen[2] also highly recommends Reichert's method. He uses it as follows: Weigh out 25 grams of the clarified butter fat and saponify in a closed flask (a closed flask has been used in the work of the Chemical Division with butter since 1883) with 25cc. of approximately $\frac{N}{2}$ KOH.

Transfer the product to a porcelain basin and evaporate the alcohol at a steam heat. Dissolve the residue in water, add some fragments of pomace coiled round with platinum wire, and distil gently until 50cc. have passed over. Titrate the distillate with $\frac{N}{10}$ caustic alkali using phenol-phthalein as an indicator.

---

[1] Zeit. Anal. Chem., 1880, pp. 159 et seq.   [2] Analyst, 1885, p. 103, et seq.

Allen found that a genuine butter fat required not less than 12.5cc. $\frac{N}{10}$ alkali for neutralization of the acid in distillate and that this corresponds to 3.9 per cent. butyric acid distilled over, so that somewhat over 4 per cent. of volatile acids in terms of butyric may be considered to be yielded by the process. (Instead of 3.9 per cent. it should be 4.4 per cent. since 1cc. $\frac{N}{10}$ caustic alkali neutralizes .0088 grams butyric acid.)

Allen gives some comparative results with Reichert's method obtained by different chemists. In the conclusion of the paper Reichert's method is said to be more enlightening than Koettstorfer's for sorting butters.

Modification of Reichert's method by Dr. B. F. Davenport (communicated in MSS.)—Use only 10cc. of alcohol in the saponification; the advantage being that with this small quantity the saponification is almost immediate. In fact I begin to draw out the alcoholic vapor from the flask as soon as it comes to the boil, using a water pump; thus it takes only about fifteen minutes to complete the saponification and the mass evaporated down to a thick mass, free from any alcoholic vapors. My process is to melt the butter at about 80° C.; filter off the clean fat, stir it into a uniform mass as it solidifies. Weigh off two portions (for I work in duplicate) of the solid mass of 5 grams each upon counterpoised double filters of about the size of the scale pan, using double filters that there may be no chance of anything going through to the scale pan. Roll up the edges of the double filter over the butter upon them, and slip it all into an Erlenmeyer flask. It is easy to get the exact 5 grams upon the open filter, and by putting all into the flask there can be no loss in the transfer. Run off upon the butter in the flask 10cc. of 70 per cent. alcoholic solution, containing 2 grams of KOH. Saponify and get dry mass in about fifteen minutes, add to it 100cc. of water, dissolve, aided by heat, add 50cc. of dilute H_2SO_4 containing about one-tenth part of commercial H_2SO_4, add several pieces of rough pomace loaded with enough stout platinum wire to lie upon the bottom of the flask, and then distill off 100cc. directly into a sugar flask having a small funnel, and filter in its mouth.

I used at first after distilling off about 20cc. to pour it back into the flask and then distill off 100cc., but I soon learned that that made no difference, as also using a 50cc. sugar flask full of diluted H_2SO_4, instead of the directed 40cc., which was not quite so convenient a quantity to measure off. I leave the end of the bulb tube connecting the flask with the condenser long enough to enter the condenser so far that there is no need of any rubber connection between them, there being no escaping at the upper end of the condenser of any vapor or of scarcely any odor at all. The operation requires no transferring of the material from the beginning to end. Samples of known pure butter have by this method required an average of 28.8cc. of alkali to neutralize the 100cc.

of distillate. I use phenol-phthalein as an indicator instead of litmus. When the alcoholic KOH solution has been made for some time I make a blank saponification and distillation with that and discount the cubic centimeters of soda solution required by that for that required by the butters.

Reichert's method has also been tried and approved by Caldwell.[1] He says:

For foreign fats Reichert's method was followed with much satisfaction. When all the necessary solutions are once prepared the analysis is made with comparatively little trouble; with less, in fact, than is allowed even by those who praise it most. Its author says that a current of air must be passed through the liquid in the flask while the distillation is going in, to prevent bumping. and Ambuhl says that all attempts to dispense with this precaution by the use of pumice-stone, platinum scraps, and the like failed. Nevertheless, finding it very inconvenient to use the current of air, I ventured to try a combination of short spirals of platinum wire and pieces of pumice stone together, and with complete success; the ebullition continued from beginning to end as quietly as could be desired.

Meissel[2] has described a modification of Reichert's process as follows:

Five grams of the melted and filtered butter fat are treated in a 200cc. flask with 2 grams of stick alkali and 50cc. 70 per cent. alcohol. After complete saponification the alcohol is evaporated. The soap is dissolved in 100cc. water and decomposed with 40cc. one-tenth H_2SO_4. The flask is supplied with some pieces of pumice-stone and connected by means of a bulb with a condenser.

The distillation is continued until 110cc. are drawn over. After filtration 100cc. are titrated in presence of litmus with one-tenth N potash and the number of cubic centimeters required increased by one-tenth.

If less than 26cc. of the alkali solution are required in the titration the butter may be suspected of falsification.

Mode of procedure in Reichert's method (used by Dr. C. A. Crampton, Department of Agriculture).—About 2.5 grams of the melted butter fat are weighed out by means of a small pipette and beaker, which are weighed again after the sample has been taken out, and run into a bottle provided with a patent india rubber stopper; 25cc. of a solution of (approximately) semi-normal alcoholic potash is added, the bottle closed and placed in the steam bath until the contents are entirely saponified, facilitating the operation by occasional agitation. The bottle is then removed from the bath, allowed to stand a few moments until partially cooled off, when its contents are transferred to a porcelain evaporating dish, the bottle being rinsed with a little alcohol. The alcohol is then driven off as rapidly as possible, and when the mass of soap and alkali is nearly dry, it is dissolved up in 25cc. of water, and transferred to a suitable flask of about 200cc. capacity, which is fitted with a delivery tube and condenser; the delivery tube is carried up about 8 inches before it is bent to enter the condenser and a bulb is blown in it just below

---

[1] Second Ann. Rept. N. Y. S. Bd. of Health, p. 526.

[2] Ding. Poly. J., vol. 233, p. 229.

the elbow and filled with broken glass or glass wool. After the soap solution has been transferred to this flask, the evaporating dish is rinsed out with 25cc. more water, which is added to the contents of the flask, and the fatty acids are then set free by the addition of 20cc. of a solution of phosphoric acid,[1] making the liquid measure in all about 70cc. Heat is applied gently at first, and gradually increased until the distillate comes over regularly. When 50cc. have distilled off the operation is finished and the distillate is titrated with one-tenth alkali, using phenolphthalein as an indicator.

I have adopted phosphoric acid in preference to sulphuric for setting free the fatty acids, because it is not so liable to carry over as the latter; much greater care is necessary when sulphuric acid is used. Before the modification of the delivery tube was adopted, I frequently found H_2SO_4 in the distillate. Thus, before using the bulb, two blank experiments required 1.8 to 2.0cc., one-tenth alkali, for neutralization and gave a perceptible precipitate of $BaSO_4$. After adding the bulb I found blanks occasionally to require as much as .8cc. when the distillation had not been carefully watched. The following comparative results show that there is practically no difference which acid is used, when the operation is carried on with care. The processes used were identical, except that in the second, 20cc. of 10 per cent. sulphuric acid was substituted for the phosphoric acid. The results are for 2.5 grams of fat.

No. 1 { With phosphoric acid	12.7	12.6	12.7	
With sulphuric acid	12.7	12.7	12.6	
No. 2 { With phosphoric acid	15.8			
With sulphuric acid	15.3			
No. 3 { With phosphoric acid	13.1			
With sulphuric acid	13.2			
No. 4 { With phosphoric acid	15.3	14.1	14.5	
With sulphuric acid	14.8	14.6	14.9	14.5 15.0

Blanks should always be run, and will be generally found to require .1 to .3cc. of the deci-normal soda before they will show the color with the phenol indicator.

Koettstorfer's process [2] (*as used in this laboratory*).—About 2.5 grams butter fat (filtered and free from water) are weighed into a patent rubber-stoppered bottle and 2½cc. (approximately) semi-normal alcoholic potash added. The exact amount taken is determined by weighing a small pipette with the beaker of fat, running the fat into the bottle from the pipette and weighing beaker and pipette again. The alcoholic potash is measured always in the same pipette and uniformity further insured by always allowing it to drain the same length of time (thirty seconds). The bottle is then placed in the steam bath together with a blank, containing no fat. After saponification is complete, and the bottles cooled down, the contents are titrated with accurately semi normal hydro-

[1] Made by dissolving 200 grams of commercial glacial phosphoric acid in a litre of water; its specific gravity is 1.140.

[2] Zeit. Anal. Chem. 1879, p. 199; Analyst, 1879, p. 106.

chloric acid, using phenol-phthalein as an indicator. The number of
cubic centimeters of the acid used for the sample deducted from the
number required for the blank gives the number of cubic centimeters
which combines with the fat, and the saturation equivalent is calculated
by the following formula, in which W equals the weight of fat taken
in milligrams and N the number of cubic centimeters which has combined with the fat.

$$\text{Sat. Equiv.} = \frac{2\,W}{N}.$$

For pure butters the mean value of N is about 17 when 2.5 grams of
butter fat are taken, and the saturation equivalent may vary from 230
to 255. On the other hand for lards, tallows, and other fats commonly
used for adulterants the equivalent rises to 270 and 290. These numbers, therefore, give a fair idea of the purity of a butter, or if an adulteration has been practiced, of its extent.

ESTIMATION OF INSOLUBLE ACIDS IN BUTTER FAT.

Method of Hehner.[1]—This method consists in saponifying the fat with
alcoholic caustic potash, subsequent evaporation of the alcohol, decomposition of the soap with sulphuric or hydrochloric acid, and the determination of the insoluble acid gravimetrically.

The process as originally described by Hehner is carried on as follows:

The filtered butter fat is weighed in a beaker glass with a glass rod;
3 or 4 grams are taken out by means of the glass rod and put in an
evaporating dish about 5 inches in diameter; the glass rod with the fat
which remains on it is left in the evaporating dish. The beaker glass
is again weighed and the amount of butter fat determined from the
difference in weight. To the weighed fat are added 50cc. alcohol and 1 to
2 grams of pure caustic potash. The alcohol is warmed gradually upon
the water bath, by which the butter fat, especially when stirred with
the glass rod, easily dissolves to a clear yellow liquid, giving off a distinct odor of butyric ether. The heating is continued for about five
minutes and distilled water is then added drop by drop to the mass.
If this produces a cloudiness in the liquid, due to the separation of un-
decomposed fat, the heating is continued somewhat longer until finally
the further addition of water does not produce the least cloudiness.
Should, however, through the careless addition of water, some fat separate in the form of oily drops which do not again easily pass into the
solution in the diluted alcohol, the whole mass must be evaporated to
dryness and treated anew with alcohol, or the experiment be done over
again with some fresh fat.

The clear soap solution is now evaporated on the water bath to the
consistency of sirup in order to remove the alcohol, and the residue

[1] Zeit. Anal. Chem. 1877, pp. 145 et seq.

dissolved in 100 to 150cc. of water. To the clear liquid hydrochloric or sulphuric acid is added to a strongly acid reaction, in order to decompose the soap. The insoluble fat acids are now separated out as a cheesy mass, which for the most part quickly rise to the surface. The heating is continued for a half hour until the fat acids are melted to a clear oil and the acid aqueous liquid is almost completely clear. Meanwhile a thick Swedish filter paper of 4 or 5 inches in diameter has been dried in a water bath. The filter paper must be of the best quality and so thick that even hot water will only pass through it drop by drop. A small beaker glass is now weighed, afterwards a filter tube, and then the filter tube and the filter; in this way is obtained the weight of the filter and the beaker glass.

The weighed filter is now fitted to a funnel moistened and half filled with water. The aqueous liquid and the melted fat are then poured out of the evaporating-dish into the filter, and the dish and glass rod are washed with boiling water. There is no difficulty in bringing all of the fat on the filter, so that the evaporating dish does not appear in the least greasy. To make sure, however, the dish can be washed with ether and the liquid obtained added to the fatty acids.

The fatty acids are washed upon the filter with boiling water. The filter should be never more than two-thirds full. If the filtrate tested with sensitive litmus tincture does not appear acid, the rest of the water is allowed to run through, and the funnel is dipped into a beaker-glass filled with cold water, so that the surface of the liquids within and without the funnel are at the same level. As soon as the fatty acids have solidified the filter is taken out of the funnel, placed in the weighed beaker-glass, and dried in a water-bath to constant weight. The drying is continued for two hours and the filter paper is then weighed. It is again dried for two and a half hours and weighed a second time. It must be remembered that it is not a mineral substance which is under treatment, but an easily-oxidizable fat, so that an exact constant weight cannot be expected.

Butter fat gives between $86\frac{1}{2}$ and $87\frac{1}{2}$ per cent. of insoluble fatty acids, though in some cases the number may rise to 88 per cent. On the other hand, the animal fats give about $95\frac{1}{2}$ per cent. of insoluble fats.

It must be expected that the kind of food which cows receive influence considerably these numbers. In order to determine this important point, Dr. Turner had a cow fed for a long time exclusively on oil cake, with the object of raising the percentage of insoluble fat acids to the highest point. It is worthy of remark, however, that the butter so produced gave the unusually low percentage of 86.3.

Method of Muter.[1]—The total fatty acids. About 10 grams (or 150 grains) of the butter fat at 100° F. are weighed by difference from a suspended tube into a clean, dry 15-ounce flask, and 5 grams of potassium hydrate with 2 fluid ounces of rectified spirit are added. The flask is

[1] Analyst, 1-77, pp. 10, 11.

placed in a basin with hot water, and kept boiling for a considerable time, until on adding water not the faintest turbidity occurs. Ten ounces of water are added, the evaporation continued (just short of boiling) until all traces of alcohol are dissipated. The contents of the flask are then made up to 7 ounces with nearly boiling water, and a good-fitting cork having been introduced through which just passes a tube 2 feet long and ending in a small funnel, 5 grams of full strength sulphuric acid are poured in down the tube followed by some water. The whole is then agitated with a circular motion until the soap, which rises suddenly, is changed into a perfectly clear and transparent stratum of fatty acids. The flask and contents are then cooled down to 40° F., till a perfectly solid cake of fatty acid forms. A few drops of cold water are run in to wash the tube, and, the cork having been removed, a small piece of fine cambric is placed over the mouth of the flask, held *in situ* by an ordinary India-rubber ring. The fat cake is caused to detach itself from the sides of the flask by a gentle movement, and then the filtrate is decanted, without breaking the cake, into a litre test mixer with a good stopper. About an ounce of cold water is poured into the flask through the cambric, and the whole cake and flask rinsed out by gently turning round, and the washings added to the filtrate. Six ounces of water at 120° F. are now added through the muslin, which is then quickly detached, and the cork and tube inserted; the whole again heated, this time to 200° F., and kept constantly agitated with a circular but not a jerky motion for five minutes. This agitation so divides the fat that it almost forms an emulsion with the water, and is the only means of thoroughly and rapidly washing fatty acids without loss. In practice no butyric acid comes off at 200° F., but any trace that might do so is caught in the long tube. The cooling and filtering are then again proceeded with as above described (the filtrate being added to the contents of the test mixer), and the washings are repeated alternately, cold with 1 ounce, and hot with 6 ounces of water, until they do not give the slightest change to neutral litmus. After thoroughly draining the residual cake by letting the flasks stand upside down for some time, the cambric is removed and the flask is laid on its side in the drying oven, with a support under the neck, until the acids are thoroughly fused, when they are poured while hot into a tarred platinum capsule, dried and weighed. The film of fatty acid still remaining on the flask is rinsed out with ether and dried in a small weighed beaker, and the weight added to the whole. If any drops of water be observed under the fatty acids in the capsule after an hour's drying the addition of a few drops of absolute alcohol will quickly cause them to dry off. If any trace of fat is on the cambric it should be also dried and extracted with ether, but with care not to break the cake at the last pouring off this does not occur.

The process is absolutely accurate, and the merest tyro cannot make any loss so long as he does not deliberately shake the melted acids against the cork, which he could not do if he practiced a circular agitation while washing.

The filtrate in the test mixer is now made to a definite bulk of 1 litre, and in 200cc. the total acidity is taken with a weak solution of sodium hydrate. The solution I generally use represents .01 of NH_3 in each cubic centimeter, as it serves also for nitrogen combustions; but a useful strength would be decinormal soda, containing .004 NaOH in each cubic centimeter. The acidity found is multiplied by 5, calculated to H_2SO_4 and noted as "total acidity as H_2SO_4"; 100cc. are next taken, and precipitated with barium chloride in the presence of a strong acidulation, with hydrochloric acid, well boiled and washed by three decantations, boiling each time; and lastly on a filter, till every trace of soluble barium is removed. The precipitate is dried, ignited, and weighed as usual, multiplied by 10, and calculated to H_2SO_4 and noted as "total sulphuric acid." Lastly, 100cc. are evaporated to dryness over the water bath in a tarred platinum dish holding 120cc. and furnished with a cover of platinum foil, also tarred. When dry the dish is covered and heated over a Bunsen till all fumes cease, and, a fragment of pure ammonium carbonate having been added, the whole is again ignited and weighed. The amount of potassium sulphate found is multiplied by 10 and calculated to H_2SO_4 and noted as "combined sulphuric acid."

OTHER METHODS.

Liebschütz[1] has described a method for the examination of butter and oleomargarine, being a modification of David's process.[2]

The fatty acids are saponified by baryta in alcoholic solution. The alcohol is evaporated and the glycerine washed out. The excess of baryta is removed by exactly neutralizing with sulphuric acid and filtering. The residue, however, is not merely a mixture of glycerine and water. The addition of alcohol in excess throws down a considerable quantity of salts which have remained in solution. The alcohol is again evaporated and the glycerine obtained, dried, and weighed. Pure butter yields about 13.7 per cent. of glycerine in this way, while oleomargarine yields only 7 per cent. The glycerine from butter when ignited left about 5 per cent. ash (barium) while that from oleo left only .3 to .6 per cent.

RESULTS OF HANSSEN'S INVESTIGATIONS.

Dr. August Hanssen has made a comparative study of the more important methods of analysis mentioned in the foregoing pages and has reached the following conclusions:

(1) The determination of the melting-points of the different fats is to be strongly recommended.

[1] Analyst, 1885, p. 111, et seq.
[2] Compt. Rend., 1886, vol. XCIV, p. 1127.
[3] Studien über den chemischen Nachweis fremder Fette im Butterfette, p. 31.

(2) The elementary analysis of the fats gives no indication whether adulteration has been practiced or not.

(3) Butter fat is not easily decomposed by heat. With a rise of temperature the decomposition is at first, for the greater part, confined to the glycerides of the non-volatile acids.

(4) In the saponification of butter fat by Hehner's method there is no appreciable loss of ethers. There is also no loss of volatile acids in direct saponification in alcohol.

(5) For the detection of foreign fats in butter, the best method is that of Reichert-Meissel, and next that of Koettstorfer.

(6) For a comparative test of the various methods the mean for insoluble acid (Hehner) is taken at 87.50 per cent. ; for Koettstorfer's equivalent 227, and for Reichert-Meissel 28.8.

(7) The washing out of the soluble acids must not be carried too far ; for 2 to 2.5 grams of fat three litres of water seem best.

ABSORPTION OF BROMINE AND IODINE BY BUTTER FATS.

Oleic acid is capable of absorbing for each formula molecule one molecule of bromine or iodine. Stearic acid does not possess this property. Therefore it is easy to approximately determine the relative quantities of these two acids when present in the same fat by the quantity of the halogen absorbed.

Thus (stearic acid) $C_{18}H_{36}O_2$ does not absorb bromine and iodine, while (oleic acid) does.

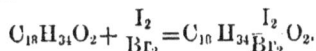

$$C_{18}H_{34}O_2 + \frac{I_2}{Br_2} = C_{18}H_{34}\frac{I_2}{Br_2}O_2.$$

The glycerides of the above acids, i. e., the natural fats, have the same absorptive power as the acids themselves.

Mills, Snodgrass & Akitt[1] have determined the quantities of bromine absorbed by various fixed oils. The method employed is as follows :

The weight of dry oil taken is about .1 gram; this is dissolved in a stoppered bottle of 100cc. volume by 50cc. dry CCl_4. To this is now added a solution of about 8 grams per litre of bromine dissolved in CCl_4. The addition of this reagent is continued until a permanent coloration is produced at the end of fifteen minutes.

If greater accuracy is required an excess of bromine may be added, afterwards treated with a solution of KI and some starch, and titrated with a standard solution of sodium thiosulphate.

The excess of bromine may also be determined by titration with a standard solution of β-naphthol in CCl_4

Hübl[2] has described the reactions of fats with iodine.

The reagents employed are an alcoholic solution of iodine and $HgCl_2$, in the proportion I_2: $HgCl_2$.

The iodine is dissolved (25 grams) in absolute alcohol (500cc.) The mercuric chloride is also dissolved (30 grams) in nearly absolute alcohol

[1] Journ. Soc. Chem. Industry, vol. 2, p. 435, and vol. 3, p. 366.

[2] Ding. Poly. J., vol. 243, p. 281.

(500cc.). After filtering it is added to the solution of iodine. After standing twelve hours its iodine strength is determined by titration with decinormal solutions of sodium thiosulphate. From .8 to 1 gram of the fat is dissolved in 10cc. chloroform. To this, in a stoppered bottle, is added the solution of iodo-mercuric chloride (20 to 30cc.) After standing for two hours the solution must still be brown.

Add now 10 to 15cc. 10 per cent. water solution of KI and dilute with water to 150cc. The free iodine is then determined by standard thiosulphate of sodium. The compound formed when pure oleic acid is treated as above is chloro-iodo-oleic acid ($C_{19}H_{34}IClO_2$).

Moore[1] has tried Hübl's method and finds it valuable.

The fat of butter containing less oleic-glycerides than the fats ordinarily used as adulterants for butter shows, consequently, less bromine or iodine absorption :

Kind of fat.	Absorption of bromine.	Absorption of iodine.
	Per cent.	Per cent.
Butter fat	24.5 to 27.9	26. to 35.
Lard.................	37.3	59. 61.9
Tallow		40.
Cotton-seed oil......	50.	105. 109.
Cocoanut oil	5.7	8.9

The method is therefore of value in determining the nature of the fat under examination.

If there be a mixture of two fats the methods will also give a fairly good approximation of the percentages of each.

Thus, let x be the percentage of one fat and y of the other. Then—

$$x + y = 100$$

Let m be the representative of the iodine absorption of x and n of y, and let A be the number found for the mixture. Then—

$$x = \frac{100 (A - n)}{m - n}$$

Jones[2] points out the changes which butter fats undergo when kept for a long while at a high temperature. He notices in a few hours that the specific gravity of such a fat kept at 100° F. increased from 912.1 to 912.6. He uses the following method of estimating the insoluble fatty acids :

REAGENTS.

(a) Twenty-eight grams roughly weighed of the best potassium hydrate dissolved to a litre with alcohol, specific gravity .810.

(b) Twenty-five grams of strong sulphuric acid made up to a litre of distilled water.

(c) Decinormal soda solution of exact strength.

Saponification is carried on in flasks about 250cc. capacity. About 5 grams of butter fat are used for each saponification. The alcoholic

[1] Am. Chem. Jour., vol. 6, p. 416.

[2] Analyst, 1878, pp. 19 et seq.

potash is measured by 50cc. pipette, which is allowed to drain into each flask for exactly the same length of time. The flasks are closed with glass marbles, placed upon the water bath and saponified at a tempera. ture of about 50° C. After perfect solution has taken place they are allowed to remain for an hour or two and then diluted with slightly warmed distilled water. Into each flask and likewise into two beakers containing 50cc. of the alcoholic potash are now run about 1cc. of the approximately semi-normal acid more than is necessary to neutralize the 50cc. of alcoholic potash. The excess of the acid over the potash is afterwards determined by the decinormal soda. The flasks after the addition of the acid are nearly filled with water and gently agitated, then placed on the water bath until the fatty acids form a clear stratum. They are then allowed to cool and stand over night. On the following morning the solutions from the cakes of fat are poured into a filter. When the whole solution is on the filter the flasks are rinsed with 15 to 20cc. of cold distilled water, and when this is poured off about 150cc. of hot water are added and the flasks briskly shaken for a minute or two. Two good washings with hot water are believed to be enough. The filtrates are now treated with the decinormal soda, the amount for the excess of sulphuric acid deducted, the remainder being the index of the soluble acids of the butter, which are calculated as butyric acid.

The insoluble fatty acids in the flasks and the small amount that may have passed on to the filter paper are allowed to remain until the following day, by which time the latter become air-dried and in a fit state to rinse with ether. The fat in the flasks is then melted and poured, together with the rinsings of the ether, into counterpoised dishes with perpendicular sides, about 3 inches across and 1½ inches deep, and the filter papers are also thoroughly washed with ether, the funnels being covered during the process. After the evaporation of the ether a little absolute alcohol is added, the dishes dried in the water-bath for half an hour, cooled, and weighed. Afterwards they are again dried for twenty minutes and reweighed.

For a more convenient method of manipulating fatty acids, Blyth [1] has recommended the following:

The flask in which the saponification is made should be of 300 to 400cc. capacity, with a rather long and narrow neck, furnished with an accurately fitting stopper, through which two tubes pass, one provided with a stop-cock to let out the liquid, and therefore terminating on a level with the interior surface of the stopper, the other to let in the air, prolonged to nearly the bottom of the flask and externally bent siphon-like. The fat is saponified in the flask and the soap decomposed in the usual way; when this is effected, the stopper is inserted, and the flask is turned upside down and kept in that position during the entire washing process. Directly the whole of the fat has risen to the surface the lower liquid is run off, whilst hot or cold water is introduced by opening

---

[1] Analyst, 1878, p. 112.

the stopper under the water and simultaneously sucking at the syphon. Thus all waiting for the fat to cool is discarded, and reasonable quantity of water can be rapidly used to thoroughly wash the fatty acids, and a filter is not required.

DETERMINATION OF SOLUBLE AND INSOLUBLE FAT ACIDS.

METHOD ADOPTED BY ALLEN.[1]

(a). Dissolve 14 grams of good stick-potash in 500cc. of rectified spirit, or methylated spirit which has been redistilled with caustic alkali, and allow the liquid to stand till clear. This solution will be approximately seminormal.

(b). A standard hydrochloric or sulphuric acid of approximately seminormal strength.

(c). Accurately prepared decinormal caustic soda. Each 1.0cc. contains .0040 grams of NaOH and neutralizes, .0088 grams of butyric acid, $C_4H_8O_2$.

A quantity of the butter fat (separated from water, curd, and salt, as described on page 152) is melted in a small beaker, a small glass rod introduced, and the whole allowed to cool, and then weighed. It is remelted, stirred thoroughly, and about 5 grams poured into a strong 6-ounce bottle. The exact weight of fat taken is ascertained by reweighing the beaker containing the residual fat.

By means of a fast-delivering pipette 50cc. measure of the alcoholic potash (solution a), is run into the bottle, and the pipette drained exactly thirty seconds. At the same time another quantity of 50cc. is measured off in an exactly similar manner into an empty flask.

The bottle is fitted with an india-rubber stopper, which is tightly wired down, and is placed in the water-oven, and from to time removed and agitated, avoiding contact between the liquid and the stopper. In about half an hour the liquid will appear perfectly homogeneous, and when this is the case the saponification is complete, and the bottle may be removed. When sufficiently cool, the stopper is removed, and the contents of the bottle rinsed with boiling water into a flask of about 250cc. capacity, which is placed over a steam bath, together with the flask containing merely alcoholic potash, until the alcohol has evaporated.

Into each of the two flasks is now run about 1cc. more seminormal acid (solution b) than is required to neutralize the potash, and the quantity used accurately noted. The flask containing the decomposed butter fat is nearly filled with boiling water, a cork with a long upright tube fitted to it, and the whole allowed to stand on the water-bath until the separated fatty acids form a clear stratum on the surface of the liquid. When this occurs the flask and contents are allowed to become perfectly cold.

Meanwhile the blank experiment is completed by carefully titrating the contents of the flask with the decinormal soda, a few drops of an alcoholic solution of phenol-phthalein being added to indicate the point of neutrality.

The fatty acids having quite solidified, the resultant cake is detached by gently agitating the flask, so as to allow the liquid to be poured out, but avoiding fracture of the cake. The liquid is passed through a filter to catch any flakes of fatty acids, and is collected in a capacious flask. If any genuine butter be contained in the sample, the filtrate will have a marked odor of butyric acid, especially on warming.

Boiling water is next poured into the flask containing the fatty acids, a cork and long glass tube attached, and the liquid cautiously heated till it begins to boil, when the flask is removed and strongly agitated till the melted fatty acids form a sort of emulsion with the water. When the fatty acids have again separated as an oily layer, the contents of the flask should be thoroughly cooled, the cake of fatty acids detached,

---

[1] Commercial Organic Analysis, vol. 2, 2d ed., pp. 156 et seq.

and the liquid filtered as before. This process of alternate washings in the flask by agitation with boiling water, followed by cooling, and filtration of the wash-water, is repeated three times, the washings being added to the first filtrate. It is often difficult or impossible to obtain the wash-water wholly free from acid reaction, but when the operation is judged to be complete the washings may be collected separately and titrated with decinormal soda. If the measure of this solution required for neutralization does not exceed 0.2cc. further washing of the fatty acids is unnecessary.

The mixed washings and filtrate are next made up to 1,000cc., or some other definite measure, and an aliquot part carefully titrated with decinormal soda (solution c). The volume required is calculated to the whole liquid. The number so obtained represents the measure of decinormal soda neutralized by the soluble fatty acids of the butter fat taken, plus that corresponding to the excess of standard acid used. This last will have been previously ascertained by the blank experiment. The amount of soda employed in this is deducted from the total amount required by the butter fat quantity, when the difference is the number of cubic centimeters of standard soda corresponding to the soluble fatty acids. This volume multiplied by the factor 0.0088 gives the butyric acid in the weight of butter fat employed.[1]

The flask containing the cake of insoluble fatty acids is thoroughly drained and then placed on the water-bath to melt the contents, which are poured as completely as possible into the (wet) filter, through which the aqueous liquid was previously passed. The fatty acids are then washed on the filter with boiling water, to remove the last traces of sparingly soluble acids. The filter is then placed in a small dry beaker and treated in the manner described on page 88, the main quantity of fatty acids and the supplementary portion subsequently dissolved out of the flask and filter being weighed separately.[2]

When it is only required to determine the insoluble acids of butter fat the foregoing tedious mode of operating may be avoided by diluting the soap solution obtained by saponifying 5 grams of the fat till it measures about 300cc. The large excess of alkali is then neutralized by cautious addition of hydrochloric acid, and the hot solution treated with a slight excess of barium chloride or magnesium sulphate. The precipitated barium or magnesium soap is well washed with hot water, and then rinsed off the filter into a separator, where it is decomposed by dilute hydrochloric acid. The resultant layer of insoluble fatty acids is washed by agitation several times with warm water, and is then treated as directed on page 88.

In the analysis of butter fat, the sum of the insoluble fatty acids by weight and of the soluble fatty acids, calculated as butyric acid, should always amount to fully 94 per cent. of the fat taken. In the author's own experience the sum more frequently approaches or even exceeds 95 per cent., especially if the butter be adulterated.

The soluble fatty acids, calculated as butyric acid, should amount to at least 5 per cent., any notably smaller proportion being due to adulteration.[3] The insoluble fatty

[1] Thus, suppose an experiment to have given the following figures: Weight of butter fat taken, 5.120 grams; decinormal soda required in the blank experiment, 3.90cc.; decinormal soda required to neutralize one-fifth of the solution of the soluble fatty acids, 6.25cc.; then
$$\frac{.0088 \, (31.25 - 3.9) \times 100}{5.120} = 4.70 \text{ per cent.}$$

[2] Instead of weighing the insoluble fatty acids, W. F. Perkins has proposed to dissolve them in alcohol, and titrate with standard alkali in the manner described on page 76. The objection to this plan is the somewhat variable character of the fatty acids themselves. Calculating their neutralizing power on the assumption that they are wholly stearic acid, Perkins found 92.0 and 91.7 per cent. of insoluble acids in pure butter fat. Calculated to oleic acid these figures would not be materially modified, but their equivalents in palmitic acid are 88.3 and 83.0 per cent. respectively.

[3] According to J. Bell, the proportion of soluble acids calculated as butyric acid not unfrequently falls as low as 4.5, and the percentage of insoluble acids sometimes slightly exceeds 89.0.

acids from genuine butter fat rarely exceed 83½ per cent., occasionally reaching 80 per cent., but a sample ought scarcely to be regarded as certainly adulterated unless the insoluble acids exceed 89½ per cent. As a standard for calculation 88 per cent. of insoluble acids[1] may be regarded as a fair average, the soluble acids being taken at 5½ per cent.

Allen, in a later contribution to the literature of Reichert's method, says:[2]

A further experience in the employment of Reichert's process for examining fats has led me to abandon the expression of the results in terms of butyric acid, in favor of a statement of the weight of caustic potash neutralized by the distillation from 100 grams of the oil. This is obtainable by multiplying the volume of decinormal alkali neutralized by the distillate from 2.5 grams by the factor 0.2244.[3]

The following table contains a number of results expressed in both ways:

	C. C. of $\frac{N}{10}$ alkali required by 2.5 grams.	KOH required by 100 parts of oil.	Observer.
Butter or milk fat;			
Cow's	12.5 to 15.2	2.80 to 3.41	Reichert, Caldwell, Moore, Allen, &c.
Ewe's	13.7	3.07	Schmitt.
Goat's	13.6	3.05	Do.
Porpoise's	11.3	2.51	Allen.
Cocoanut oil	3.5 to 3.7	0.78 to 0.83	Reichert, Moore, Allen.
Palm-nut oil	2.4	0.54	Allen.
Palm oil	0.8	0.18	Moore.
Cacao butter	1.6	0.36	Do.
Butterine and oleomargarine	0.2 to 1.6	0.04 to 0.36	Caldwell, Moore, Allen.
Whale oil	3.7	0.83	Allen.
Do	12.5	2.80	Do.
Porpoise oil	11.0 to 12.0	2.47 to 2.69	Do.
Sperm oil	1.3	0.29	Do.
Bottle-nose oil	1.4	0.31	Do.
Menhaden oil	1.2	0.27	Do.
Cod-liver oil	1.1 to 2.1	0.24 to 0.47	Do.
Sesame oil	2.2	0.48	Do.
Cotton-seed oil	0.3	0.07	Moore.
Castor oil	1.4	0.31	Allen.

From these results it is evident that the fats of different kinds of milk (butter fats) are sharply distinguished from nearly all other fats by the large proportion of soluble volatile fatty acids they yield by Reichert's process. The most remarkable exception is presented by porpoise oil and some samples of whale oil. In porpoise oil I have found 5 per cent. of valeric acid, and Chevreul obtained as much as 9.63 per cent. In a recent paper I pointed out that in porpoise butter the glyceride of valeric acid appeared to replace the butyrin characteristic of the butter of terrestrial mammals.

Some of the chemists who have employed Reichert's process take the precaution to filter the distillate before titrating it, so as to get rid of any volatile acids which may be insoluble or very sparingly soluble in water. This plan may sometimes be adopted with great advantage. Thus when the solution of the soap obtained by saponifying cocoanut or palm-nut oil is acidulated and distilled, a notable proportion of lauric acid passes over and solidifies in the condenser or on the surface of the distillate; and

---

[1] The percentage of adulterant in a butter fat may be calculated from the following formula, in which F. is the percentage of foreign fat and I that of the insoluble fatty acids: $F = (1-88) \times 13.3$. Or each 0.1 per cent. of soluble acids above 0.5 may be regarded as showing the presence of 2 per cent. of butter fat.

[2] Analyst, 1887, pp. 11 et seq.

[3] 1 cc. of $\frac{N}{10}$ alkali contains 0.00561 gram of KOH; and $\frac{.00561 \times 100}{2.5} = .2244$

by adding water to the contents of the retort, again distilling, and repeating this process several times, a very considerable proportion of volatile fatty acids can be obtained from cocoanut oil. In assaying butter, the appearance of insoluble acids in the distillate would furnish a valuable indication of the presence of cocoanut oil, and they should be removed by filtration, or the distillate will be found to neutralize so large a volume of alkali as considerably to diminish the practical value of the process as a means of distinguishing butter from butter substitutes, as has been pointed out by Moore and others. Latterly, I have adopted the plan of filtering the distillate in all cases, washing the filter with cold water, and then immersing the filter, with any adhering insoluble acids, in alcohol, which is then titrated with decinormal alkali and phenol-phthalein. In the case of ordinary butters and butter substitutes the insoluble volatile acids only neutralize about 0.2cc. of decinormal alkali.

The question having recently been raised, the following experiments were made at my request by Mr. William Barraclough on a sample of butter fat, in order to ascertain the variation in the results of Reichert's process produced by modifications in the methods of conducting the saponification and distillation:

(1) Two and a half cubic centimeters of butter fat was saponified by alcoholic potash in an open basin, the alcohol evaporated off completely at a steam heat, the residual soap dissolved in water, the solution acidulated with sulphuric acid in slight excess, diluted to 75cc. and distilled gently in a globular flask with side tubulure adapted to a condenser until 50cc. had passed over. The flask held 460cc. up to the side tube, and some fragments of pumice-stone coiled round with platinum wire were added to the contents to promote evolution of vapor.

(2) An exact repetition of No. 1 experiment.

(3) Saponification was effected in a flask furnished with a long tube and heated by steam. The subsequent manipulations were the same as in experiment 1.

(4) Saponification was effected in a well-closed bottle placed in the water oven. Other manipulations unchanged.

(5) Manipulation exactly as in experiment 3, except that the distillation was conducted in a flask fitted to the condenser by a cork and bent tube.

(6) Conducted as in experiment 3, except that the distillation was conducted in a retort.

(7) Blank experiment with the alcoholic potash employed in the previous experiments, the manipulation being that in experiment 3. The alcoholic potash was brown and not very recently prepared.

Experiments.

	Decinormal alkali for 2.5 grams.
	cc.
No. 1	11.80
No. 2	11.85
No. 3	12.40
No. 4	12.50
No. 5	12.40
No. 6	12.45
No. 7	0.25

These results show that a sensible loss occurs if the saponification be conducted in an open basin, doubtless owing to the formation of butyric ether. On the other hand, the exact nature of the distilling apparatus appears to be of little importance. This latter conclusion is not in accordance with the experience of some other chemists.

Zulkowsky and Groger[1] have studied and modified Haussman's method[2] of volumetric fat analysis. This method is based on the fact

[1] Ber. Chem. Gesel., vol. 16, p. 1140.
[2] Ding. Poly., J., vol. 244, p. 303, and vol. 246, p. 286.

that an alcoholic solution of a fat acid is immediately saponified by the addition of alcoholic potash, while a neutral fat requires time and heat to secure complete saponification.

When, therefore, an alcoholic solution of fat acids and neutral fats to which phenol-phthalein has been added is titrated with caustic potash, the red color only appears when the fat acids are saponified, and only comes permanently when all the fats are saponified. When the red color appears an excess of caustic potash is added and the whole boiled for half an hour to saponify all the neutral fats and retitrated, whereby the amount of caustic potash required to effect the saponification of all the fats is ascertained, and the quantity of potash required for each titration represents the relative proportion of fat acids and neutral fats in the mixture operated on. When a neutral fat is saponified the following reaction takes place:

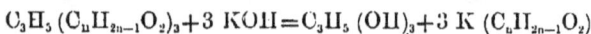

$$C_3H_5 (C_nH_{2n-1}O_2)_3 + 3\ KOH = C_3H_5 (OH)_3 + 3\ K\ (C_nH_{2n-1}O_2)$$

and therefore every litre of normal potash splits up one-third equivalent of glycerine, i. e., 30.667 grams. One cubic centimeter normal potash is therefore equivalent to 0.030667 gram glycerine. The theoretical yield of fat acids could also be calculated by the following formula:

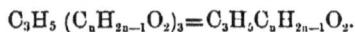

$$C_3H_5 (C_nH_{2n-1}O_2)_3 = C_3H_5C_nH_{2n-1}O_2.$$

Then one litre normal potash represents one-third equivalent of glycerine residue, or 12.667 grams. If 5cc. normal potash have been employed the weight of the glycerine residue would be .012667 × 5.

F. W. A. Woll[1] gives the results of his studies with butter and artificial butter.

Mixtures of pure butter with "oleo oil" were made and examined by the methods of Koettstorfer and Reichert, and the results compared with theory. The following numbers were obtained:

Per cent. butter.	Koettstorfer.			Reichert.		
	Calculated.	Found.	Difference.	Calculated.	Found.	Difference.
	mg.	mg.	mg.	cc.		cc.
20..............	200.8	201.4	+0.6	2.98	3.11	+0.13
40..............	206.2	207.3	+1.1	5.81	6.39	+0.58
50..............	208.5	209.0	+0.5	6.55	7.08	+0.53
60..............	211.5	212.7	+1.2	8.65	9.06	+0.41
80..............	217.7	215.6	−2.1	10.37	11.56	+1.19
Means ...	....	....	1.1	....	....	0.57

NOTE.—It is very easy to get exact results by the above method of mixture. Butter and an oil are used whose behavior with the reagents employed was determined by preliminary experiment. The case is very different when the analyst is called on to examine an *unknown* sample. The butter in an unknown sample may have quite a different per cent. of volatile acid from that used in the samples given. The value of this method, therefore, is seriously impaired for determining the extent of adulterations in case where the separate examination of the constituents is impossible.

[1] Zeit. Anal. Chem., 1884, p. 28, and Am. Chem. Jour., vol. 9, p. 62.

The author gives a table of the analyses of 37 samples of butter and butter substitutes giving the percentage of water, the specific gravity at 37°.7 C., the melting point determined by the method of Blyth, the milligrams of KOH required in Koettstorfer's method and of cubic centimeters by Reichert's method.[1]

The author concludes that the melting point is of no value in discriminating between pure and false butters, but the specific gravity, the saponification process, and the distillation of the volatile acid are sufficient to distinguish at once between the true and the false.

The oleo oil employed had a mean specific gravity at 37°.7 C. of 0.90369 and its melting point was 27°.6 C. The "neutral" had a specific gravity of 0.9053 and a melting point of 38°.1 C.

BEHAVIOR OF COCOANUT OIL WITH SOME OF THE METHODS USED IN ANALYSIS OF BUTTER FATS.

R. W. Moore, in a paper read before the American Chemical Society, September 18, 1885,[2] calls attention to cocoanut oil as a substitute for butter. He gives its fusing point at 24°.2 C. to 24°.3 C., and calls attention to the fact that its specific gravity is higher than that of butter fat. It is also noticed that the insoluble acids in butter fats may sometimes amount to as much as 90 per cent.[3]

The author has found that cocoanut oil yielded 86.43 per cent. insoluble acids,[4] and thus infers that it could be mixed with other fats and escape detection by this method, calling attention to the fact, however, that if the soluble acids be estimated according to the method of Dupré[5] the sophistications might at once appear.

The low figures obtained are ascribed to the volatility of lauric acid which escapes on drying the insoluble fats. By Koettstorfer's process the number of milligrams potash necessary to saponify one gram cocoanut oil was found to be 257.3 to 258.3[6] the large quantity required being due to the presence of lauric, caproic, caprylic, and capric acids. It is, therefore, possible to mix oleomargarine and cocoanut oil in such a manner as to produce results similar to those given by pure butter. This is shown by the following figures:

Cocoanut oil.	Oleomargarine.	
Per cent.	Per cent.	Milligrams.
49.3+	50.7 required of KOH	220.0
70.2+	29.8 required of KOH	234.9
53.1+	46.9 required of KOH	223.6
75.9+	24.1 required of KOH	234.9

[1] Op. cit., pp. 31, 62, 63.
[2] Analyst, 1885, p. 224 et seq.
[3] Fleischmann and Veith, Zeit. Anal. Chem., 1878, p. 287; Kretschmar, Ber. Chem. Gesel., vol. 10, p. 2091; Kuleschoff, Wag. Jahresbericht, 1878, p. 999; Jehn, Archiv der Pharm., vol. 9, p. 335; De la Source, Ibid., vol. 12, p. 920.
[4] Chem. News, vol. 50, p. 263.
[5] Analyst, 1877, pp. 87 and 114.
[6] Valenta, Ding, Poly. J., vol. 249, p. 270; Moore, Chem. News, loc. cit.

The oleomargarine used required 193.5 milligrams KOH per gram.[1] The iodine method of Hübl[2] was also tried with a mixture of cocoanut oil and oleomargarine, &c., and numbers obtained which come within the limits for pure butter.

Thus oleomargarine 55 per cent. + cocoanut oil 45 per cent. required 35.5 of iodine per 100 grams, and lard 40 per cent. + cocoanut oil 60 per cent. required 32.2 of iodine. In samples of butter the iodine numbers found by Hübl varied from 26.8 to 35.1.

By Reichert's method, however,[3] the presence of cocoanut oil mixed with butter and oleo is at once detected. Thus a mixture of 50 per cent. butter, 27.5 per cent. oleomargarine, and 33.5 cocoanut oil gave by Hebner's method 89.50 per cent. insoluble acids; by Koettstorfer's method, 227.5 mg. KOH; by Hübl's method, 35.4 per cent. iodine factor; by Reichert's method, 8.7cc. $\frac{N}{10}$ soda solution.

Pure butter requires by Reichert's method about 13cc., $\frac{N}{10}$ alkali to neutralize the volatile acids distilled over, while cocoanut oil in similar circumstances requires only 3.7cc. Little evidence is forthcoming in respect of the use of cocoanut oil as an adulterant of butter. It has been mentioned as an adulterant of lard[4] and Dietszch[5] mentions it as a compound of "Schmalzbutter." In attempts to use it as an adulterant of butter no great success was secured, since the oil not having been properly purified made the butter unpalatable. The smell and taste of the oil can be removed by a patent process of Jeserich and Meinert[6] which consists in treating the oil with superheated steam and saponifying any free fatty acids by calcined magnesia. The author closes his paper by recommending Reichert's process as superior to all others in examining for the purity of butters.

USE OF COTTON-SEED OIL AS A BUTTER ADULTERANT.

Cotton-seed oil is used largely as an adulterant for lard and butter. It has saponification equivalent of 285 to 296 and specific gravity at 99° C. .872, pure butter fat at the same temperature being .868.

Its further properties are thus described by Allen:[7]

The oil as expressed from the seeds contains in solution, often to the extent of 1 per cent., a peculiar coloring matter, which is characteristic of this oil and its seed, and which gives the oil a ruby-red color, sometimes so intense as to cause the oil to appear nearly black. Crude cotton-seed oil gives a very bright red coloration with strong sulphuric acid (page 59). When boiled with an alkaline solution, alcoholic potash being preferable for laboratory experiments, crude cotton-seed oil is saponified, and the resultant soap rapidly oxidizes on exposure to air, with production of a fine pur-

[1] Moore, Am. Chem. J., vol. 6, p. 416.   [5] Nahrüngsmittel und Getränke, p. 212.
[2] Ding, Poly. J., vol. 253, p. 281.   [6] Wag. Jahresbericht, 1882, p. 932.
[3] Zeit. Anal. Chem. 1880, p. 68.   [7] Op. cit., 2d ed., p. 112.
[4] Analyst, 1882, p. 193.

ple or violet blue coloration.[1] This reaction is characteristic of crude cotton-seed oil. The coloring matter causes crude cotton-seed oil to produce stains, and hence is removed by a process of refining. This is usually effected by agitating the crude oil at the ordinary temperature with 10 to 15 per cent. of solution of caustic soda of 1.060 specific gravity, when the alkali combines with the coloring matter and saponifies a portion of the oil. The mixture becomes filled with black flocks which deposit on standing[2] and leave the oil but slightly colored. The loss in refining is usually from 4 to 7½ per cent., but occasionally amounts to 12 or 15. Hence it is desirable, before purchasing crude cotton-seed oil for refining, to ascertain, by a laboratory experiment, what the percentage of loss is likely to be. Frequently the treatment with alkali is only carried far enough to remove the major part of the coloring matter, the oil being then boiled with a solution of bleaching powder, and subsequently treated with dilute sulphuric acid.[3]

Refined cotton-seed oil is of a straw or golden-yellow color, or, occasionaly, nearly colorless. The density ranges from .922 to .926, and the solidifying point from 1° to 10° C. By subjection to cold and pressure a certain proportion of stearine is separated, the melting point of the residual oil being correspondingly lowered. Refined cotton-seed oil is usually very free from acid, and when properly prepared is of pleasant taste and admirably adapted for edible and culinary purposes, for which it is now extensively employed, both with and without its nature being acknowledged. It is now substituted for olive oil in some of the liniments of the United States Pharmacopœia, but its principal applications are in soap making and the manufacture of factitious butter.

ESTIMATION OF SALT.

The method employed in this laboratory since 1883 has continued to give satisfaction, and can be recommended as the best in use.

From 10 to 20 grams of the well-mixed butter or butter substitute are placed in a separatory bulb provided with a closely fitting glass stopper. Add 25 to 50cc. hot distilled water, and after shaking well allow to stand for a few minutes. The water, which has dissolved most of the salt, is now drawn off through the stoppered tube of the apparatus. Fresh hot water is added and this operation repeated until the

---

[1] "Cotton-seed blue" is stated by Kuhlmann to have the composition of $C_{17}H_{24}O_4$. It is amorphous, readily destroyed by oxidizing agents, insoluble in water, diluted acids, and alkalies, sparingly soluble in carbon disulphide and chloroform, but more readily in alcohol and ether, and dissolves with purple color in strong sulphuric acid. The unoxidized coloring matter of cotton-seed oil has been recently examined by J. Longmore, who, in a communication to the author, states that it is a pungent golden-yellow product, insoluble in water, but soluble in alcohol and alkaline solutions, and precipitated from the latter on addition of acids. It dyes well and perfectly fast on both wool and silk.

[2] The deposit thus formed, consisting of coloring and albuminous matters, alkali, and partially saponified oil, is technically called "mucilage." It is decomposed with a slight excess of acid, and the resulting dark-colored grease is heated to a temperature of 120° C. (=250°F.) with concentrated sulphuric acid, which renders insoluble the coloring matters, &c., while the impure fatty acids rise to the surface. On distilling these with superheated steam, a mixture of fatty acids is obtained, which is separated into stearic and oleic acids by pressure. The "cotton-seed stearine" thus obtained is employed for making soap and composite candles, as also for adulterating tallow, &c.

[3] This method of treatment is economical, but causes the oil to acquire an unpleasant taste and smell, which cannot be removed.

volume of the wash water amounts to 250 to 500cc. By this time all the salt has been dissolved and separated from the butter.

Chromate of potassium is now added to the salt solution, and the titration is accomplished by a standard silver nitrate solution.

The amount of NaCl in butter is also determined by dissolving the fat with ether or light petroleum, and after incineration of the curd, weighing the residual ash, which is taken as the amount of salt present. This method is not to be recommended since it includes the salt found in the other mineral constituents.

Sell[1] gives the following method : Ten grams of butter are weighed into a porcelain crucible and dried at $100°$ C. for six hours. The melted fat, &c., is now filtered, and crucible and filter are washed with ether. The filter with its contents is then incinerated. The ash is extracted with water, filtered, and the NaCl estimated volumetrically in the filtrate.

ESTIMATION OF CURD.

The methods of estimating curd depend on the principle of first drying a weighed portion of the butter, and afterwards extracting the fat with ether or petroleum. The residual mass is then weighed and the curd determined by loss on ignition. This process is carried on in this laboratory as follows :

Five to ten grams of butter are dried at $100°$ C. for a few hours in a porcelain dish. The dried fat, &c., are filtered through a Gooch crucicle, the contents of the dish all brought into the crucible and well washed with ether or light petroleum. The filter crucible is dried for two hours and weighed. The curd is then determined by loss of weight on ignition. A number of experiments have also been made to convert the curd directly into an ammonium compound by Kjeldahl's process. This method has not met with sufficient success to merit a recommendation to general use. This method was first tried in the laboratory in 1884.

Babcock finds this method more satisfactory.[2] Ten grams of the fat are treated with light petroleum, and after the fat solution has been decanted the treatment is repeated. The purified curd is then treated by Kjeldahl's process.

QUALITATIVE TESTS.

The qualitative tests employed in the detection of artificial butter are the following :

(1) Microscopic examination. This method has already been sufficiently described.

(2) Solubility in a mixture of amyl-alcohol and ether.

---

[1] *Op cit.*, p. 527.
[2] Fifth Ann. Rept. Bd. Control N. Y. Exp. Sta., p. 345.

The quantity of stearin in butter fat is small compared with that in lard, tallow, &c. On this difference of constitution Professor Scheffer[1] has based a method of analysis.

A mixture is made containing 40 volumes of rectified amyl-alcohol and 60 volumes ether of .725 specific gravity at 15° C. One gram of butter fat is dissolved in 3cc. of this mixture at 26° to 28° C. On the other hand, 1 gram lard requires 16cc. of the solvent, 1 gram tallow 50cc., and 1 gram stearin 350cc.

For the experiment take a test tube of 12cc. capacity and place in it 1 gram fat, add 3cc. of the amyl-alcohol ether mixture. After tightly corking the tube put it in a water bath of 18° C. and with frequent shaking bringing the temperature to 28° C. If the butter is pure the solution becomes perfectly clear at this temperature. If not clear more of the solution can be run in out of a burette and the additional quantity required will be some indication of the quantity or quality of the adulterant which has been used.

According to Scheffer, mixtures of pure butter and lard gave the following data:

Butter.	Lard.	Quantity of mixture required.
Gram.	Gram.	CC.
.1	....	3.0
.9	.1	3.9
.8	.2	4.8
.7	.3	5.7
.6	.4	6.5
.1	.9	14.4

A trial of this method has shown that it is capable of giving valuable qualitative indications in respect of the purity of the sample under examination. I believe it is the best simple test aside from the microscopic examination capable of general application which has been proposed.

The easiest method to secure a certain weight of fats is to melt them and measure out from a pipette 1 cubic centimeter of each. The fats which do not melt easily should be stirred up thoroughly with a wire, while the temperature is raised from 18° to 28° C.

(3) Odor of the burning grease.[2]

(4) The insolubility of the stearate of potash in alkaline solutions.[3]

(5) Insolubility of tallow, lard, &c., in petroleum ether of .69 specific gravity.[4]

(6) The relative solubility of butter fats and substitutes therefor in a mixture of 50 per cent. alcohol and 66 per cent. ether.[5]

[1] Pharm. Rundsch., 1886, p. 248.

[2] Kunstmann. Pharm. Centralh., 1875, No. 9.

[3] Gatehouse, Chem. News, vol. 32, p. 297.

[4] Zeit. Anal. Chem., 1872, p. 334.

[5] Husson Zeit. Anal. Chem., 1880, p. 236; Filsinger, Pharm. Centralh., 1878, p. 260.

(7) Crook[1] warms half a gram of the filtered fat in a test tube to 66° C., and adds 1.5cc. phenol, shakes and warms in water bath until the liquid is clear. On standing pure butter gives a homogeneous solution· Tallow and lard appear, however, in distinct layers.

A method somewhat similar to this was proposed in 1877 by Bach.[2]

The apparatus required consists of a test tube and a thermometer. The reagent is a mixture of 3 volumes ether and 1 volume alcohol of 95 per cent. and 1 gram of the butter or tallow and put in the test tube with 20cc. of the above mixture, and this is placed in water at 20° C. At this temperature pure butter is completely dissolved. Butter, however, containing lard, beef, or mutton tallow remains undissolved.

(8) Horsely[3] calls attention to the perfect solubility of pure butter in ether, and that it is not precipitated from this solution by methyl-alcohol, while other common fats are thus separated at 20° C.

Lenz[4] confirms the general results of the foregoing process.

(9) Belfield[5] allows the fats dissolved in ether to crystallize, and distinguishes between them by their crystalline form.

(10) Paillat[6] has found that pure butter when mixed with copper oxide in ammonia gives a turquois blue color, while a butter adulterated with margarine (?) gives a greenish tint.

(11) Dubois and Padé[7] point out that the addition of any considerable quantity of foreign fats to butter not only changes the melting point of the fatty acids obtained, but also diminishes their solubility in alcohol.

(12) Wolkenhaar[8] distinguishes between the different fats by means of nitric acid, which gives to cotton seed oil, palm oil, lard, sesame oil, and several others a red brown color.

For a fuller discussion of most of these qualitative tests, consult either the original articles or Sell.[9]

(13) Method of Mayer.[10] This test is made as follows:

About 0.6 gram of butter fat is placed in a test tube with 12cc. water made slightly alkaline by a few drops of a solution of 2 per cent. soda, or two drops of 6 per cent. ammonia-water. The tube closed by the thumb is then well shaken, afterwards carried to a temperature of 37° C. to 40° C., with frequent shaking. The emulsion thus formed is poured into a separatory funnel. The fat is now washed several times with water at 37° C. to 40° C., the wash-water being drawn off by the stop-cock so as to maintain a constant level in the funnel. The fatty matter having thus been placed in contact with about 400cc. water, the stop-cock is so

[1] Analyst, 1879, p. 111.
[2] Pharm. Centralh., 1877, p. 166.
[3] Chem. News, vol. 30, p. 135 and 154.
[4] Zeit. Anal. Chem., 1880, p. 370.
[5] Rep. d. Ver. Anal. Chem., vol. 3, p. 383.
[6] L'Année Scientifique par Louis Figuier, 29th year, 1885.
[7] Bul. Soc. Chim., vol. 44, p. 602.
[8] Rep. d. Ver. Anal. Chem., vol. 3, p. 103.
[9] Op. cit., pp. 505–509.
[10] Jour. de Pharm. et de Chim., vol. 15, p. 97.

adjusted as to allow the removal of the wash-water as completely as possible. After cooling, the fatty matter remaining on the sides of the funnel is examined. If the butter be pure, there will be seen only a finely-divided mass, but the addition of a small portion of other fats will be revealed by greasy drops, which can be seen even during the progress of the washing. Natural butters made in summer require a lower temperature for the washing, viz, 35° C. to 37° C.

In most cases the microscopic test with polarized light and selenite plate combined with the solubility of the fat in the ether amyl-alcohol solutions will be found sufficient for the qualitative examination of a suspected butter.

RESULTS OF ANALYSES OF GENUINE AND SUSPECTED BUTTERS AND BUTTER ADULTERANTS.

TABLE No. 6.—*Analyses of butter.*

Serial number.	Specific gravity at 40° C.	Water.	Insoluble acid.	Soluble acid, by washing out.	Soluble acid, by distillation.	Salt, NaCl.	Albuminoids.	Curd.	Koettstorfer's equivalent.	Vol. $\frac{N}{10}$ soda for 2,5 grams.
		Pr. ct.	Pr. ct.	Pr. ct.	Pr. ct.	Pr. ct.	Pr. ct.	Pr. ct.		
1742	.91046	13.33	88.64	4.01	4.50	2.64	.7875	1.46	254.20	12.50
1743	.91119	8.53	87.85	4.14	4.57	3.01	.8312	1.31	250.60	13.10
1744	.91032	8.57	88.65	3.52	4.78	2.81	.8750	1.30	268.50	13.50
1745	.91067	8.14	88.08	3.68	5.48	2.04	.5688	1.25	264.50	15.30
1746	.91029	16.62	88.91	3.00	4.56	3.79	.7438	1.56	252.70	12.00
1747	.91244	4.50	86.60	5.02	5.51	3.41	.5250	.83	244.30	15.60
1749	.91165	11.46	87.50	5.49	4.61	1.48	.8312	1.14	250.10	13.10
1752	.91004	17.38	88.07	3.70	4.54	0.00	.4375	0.68	238.60	12.80
1759	.91013	13.95	87.47	4.73	4.80	0.00	.4375	0 81	249.70	13.60
1760	.91063	22.12	87.84	4.98	4.70	0.00	.1750	0.49	248.70	13.40
1761	.91067	23.46	87.47	5.27	4.99	0.00	.1750	0.59	243.00	11.10
1762	.91089	21.02	87.38	5.15	4.93	0.00	.2188	1.01	248.80	14.10
1763	.91073	11.89	87.71	4.69	4.98	2.61	.2625	1.30	244.90	14.10
1764	.91155	21.96	86.65	5.34	4.74	0.00	.4375	1.21	244.00	13.20
1765	.90958	31.55	88.00	4.45	5.02	0.57	.6125	1.83	252 00	14.30
1766	.91042	11.17	......	5.31	4.52	2.56	.4375	1.11	247.00	12.80
1768	.90995	7.68	87.24	5.08	5.21	5.62	.2625	0.71	247.00	14.80
1769	.91183	9.68	87.30	5.94	5.05	4.09	.5250	1.37	244.10	14.30
1770	.91060	7.35	88.14	5.05	4.47	5.28	.1375	0.91	252.10	12.70
1771	.91079	12.28	87.60	5.37	4.93	3.69	.4813	1.08	246.49	14.00
1772	.91093	8.89	87.21	5.47	5.26	3.18	.3063	1.03	215.10	14.90
1773	.91064	18.75	86.68	4.75	4.63	0.00	.7000	1.41	200.70	11.40
1775	.91034	9.87	87.58	5.17	4.56	4.83	.4375	1.12	251.80	12.90
1776	.91239	10.84	86.61	5.42	4.45	3.12	.4375	0.97	250.90	12.70
1777	.91031	12.28	88.48	4.66	3.92	5.79	.7438	1.43	236.50	11.10
1781	.91010	7.26	......	3.97	......	6.42	.4375	1.43	247.10	13.20
1782	.91112	12.32	87.23	4.24	......	6.53	.5250	2.02	245.40	13.60
1783	.91082	6.93	87.59	3.92	......	3.92	.4375	1.33	248.40	12.50
1785	.91186	8.29	87.10	4.48	......	5.11	.4375	1.16	247.50	14.50
1789	.91061	8.44	87.73	3.91	......	3.15	.7000	1.42	246.60	12.60
1790	.91080	4.44	87.85	4.41	......	1.81	.7000	1.02	251.50	13.90
1792	.91106	13.67	88.25	3.47	......	7.10	.4375	3.10	240.20	12.30
1795	.91136	8.22	87.75	4.18	......	4.37	.5125	1.34	240.70	14.50

TABLE No. 7.—*Analyses of doubtful butters.*[1]

1748	.90968	7.45	89.45	3.61	4.60	2.64	.7443	1.41	252.80	13.10
1757	.90964	11.30	89.44	3.54	4.25	5.28	.5688	1.63	253.60	12.10
1758	.90987	12.12	87.60	4.71	4.54	0.60	.4375	0.93	251.50	12.90
1767	.90974	10.90	88.68	4.73	4.45	2.16	.4813	1.33	249.70	12.60
1774	.90972	29.84	87.82	4.84	4.27	0.00	.9625	1.86	260.10	12.10
1779	.90947	11.59	88.01	3.16	......	5.00	.8750	1.56	250.60	12.50
1780	.90964	10.66	88.42	3.02	......	5.40	.8750	1.58	250.70	11.00
1793	.90938	8.50	88.00	3.31	......	13.00	......	1.12	253.50	12.30
1794	.90965	9.06	88.50	3.44	......	2.84	.4375	0.98	252.00	11.70

[1] These samples were bought for pure butter, but, on analysis, proved to contain adulterants.

TABLE No. 8.—*Analyses of butter substitutes.*

Serial number.		Specific gravity at 40° C.	Water.	Insoluble acid.	Soluble acid, by washing out.	Soluble acid, by distillation.	Salt, NaCl.	Albuminoids.	Curd.	Koettstorfer's equivalent.	Vol. N 10 soda for 2.5 grams.
			Pr. ct.	Pr. ct.	Pr. ct.	Pr. ct.	Pr. ct.	Pr. ct.	Pr. ct.		
1750	Lard	.90558	0. 00	92. 59	0. 41	0. 08	0. 00	.0875	Trace.	294. 30	0. 20
1751	Beef suet........	.90158	0. 00	92. 59	0. 22	0. 04	0. 00	....	0. 01	296. 90	0. 10
1753	Oleomargarine ...	.90490	9. 34	93. 50	0. 12	0. 25	0. 84	.3500	0. 63	274. 00	0. 70
1754	Neutral lard......	.90309	7. 42	90. 00	0. 20	0. 10	0. 49	....	0. 02	270. 50	0. 30
1755	Creamery butter-ine[1]	.90569	11. 69	92. 90	1. 16	1. 53	2. 39	.3063	0. 74	274. 80	4. 30
1756	Oleo fat[2]	.90267	14. 23	93. 35	0. 10	0. 08	0. 97	....	0. 00	286. 00	0. 20
1787	Country print....	.90561	14. 45	93. 72	0. 09	....	2. 42	.8750	1. 82	281. 10	1. 90

[1] 40 butter fat, 15 oleo fat, 30 neutral lard.
[2] Average 40 pounds per fat steer.

ANALYTICAL RESULTS.

The butters in table No. 6 were bought in open market and accepted as genuine on the results of the analysis. Some of these, however, ought justly to be classed in Table No. 7, as of doubtful purity. In quite a number of cases the number of cubic centimeters of decinormal alkali required to neutralize the distillate from 2.5 grams of the fat was less than 13. Nos. 1742, 1746, 1752, 1766, 1770, 1773, 1775, 1776, 1777, 1783, 1789, and 1792 come under this category. In all these cases, however, except 1765 and 1768, the specific gravity is above .910 at 40° C., and it would not be safe to condemn a butter as adulterated which had that specific gravity, unless the microscope should reveal crystals of foreign fat. In these samples such was not the case.

In the two cases mentioned, where the specific gravity fell below .910, there are other reasons for thinking the samples pure. In 1765 the percentage of soluble acid, by Reichert's method, is high, viz, 5.02. In 1768 it is still higher, viz, 5.21. With such proportions of soluble acid it would not be possible to condemn the samples as adulterated on the evidence of the specific gravity alone

On the other hand, when the percentage of soluble acid is low, as in 1777, the specific gravity and saponification equivalent prevent the classification of the sample among the doubtful butters. Nevertheless, should such a sample show with polarized light and a selenite plate bi-refractive crystals, it would be a strong presumptive evidence of adulteration. In any case, such a sample as 1777 would present numerous difficulties to the analyst, especially if he were called to testify in respect to its purity.

In Table No. 7 similar difficulties are encountered. The specific gravities are uniformly low. On the other hand, the percentage of insoluble acids are only suspiciously high in two instances, viz, 1748 and 1757. In the first of these instances, however, the soluble acid is above the limit of suspicion. The saturation equivalent is uniformly rather high, but not above the range of pure butters. While the butters are classed for convenience as "doubtful," they could not be so proved before a court on the chemical evidence alone.

In Table No. 8 we have plain sailing. All analytical data show the fats of the samples examined are not butter. Since the adulteration of butters with less than 30 per cent. of a cheaper fat could scarcely prove profitable, the chemist should be careful not to condemn a suspicious sample, if its purity be attested by any one of the processes employed in the examination, unless some one test shows it to be undoubtedly adulterated.

In the foregoing study of methods of analysis I have not attempted to give a complete citation of all the papers which have been written on this subject. A very complete bibliography of the subject up to 1882 is given by Caldwell,[1] and in the work of Sell.[2]

The probability of the detection of an adulterated butter by the physical and chemical processes described in the foregoing pages is very great.

In the order of value the quantitative processes employed may be arranged as follows: (1) Determination of volatile acids by distillation. (2) Determination of specific gravity. (3) Determination of the saponification equivalent. (4) Determination of the insoluble acids. (5) Determination of the melting point.

---

[1] Second Ann. Rept. N. Y. S. Bd. of Health, pp. 544–7.
[2] Arbeit a. d. Kaiserlichen Gesundheitsamte.

EXAMINATION OF MILK.

The adulteration of milk in this country consists usually either in the removal of cream or the addition of water.

Without making any attempt whatever to notice the prolific literature of this subject, which has accumulated during the past few years, such portions thereof as seem to be most helpful in the work of analysis will be cited. Those who care to study the subject in greater detail are referred to the periodical literature, especially to the "Analyst" and " Milch Zeitung."

The constituents of milk which are to be determined by analysis are (1) water; (2) sugar; (3) nitrogenous constituents; (4) ash, and (5) fat.

Water.—The simplest method for estimating water in milk consists in evaporating one or two grams in a flat platinum dish. The larger the diameter of the dish the quicker and more accurate will be the results.

If larger quantities of milk be used or the dish have not a flat bottom, the film which forms over the surface of the milk during evaporation will prevent complete desiccation. To avoid this many plans have been proposed. The milk may be mixed with gypsum, and then a larger surface be exposed and more rapid and complete drying secured.

Instead of gypsum, sulphate of barium, pure quartz sand, sulphate of strontium, and powdered glass have been used. All of these methods are capable of giving fairly accurate results when properly conducted.

The addition of acetic acid or alcohol to coagulate the albuminous matter before desiccation has been largely practiced, but Gerber and Radenhausen have shown[1] this treatment is without influence on the results. Jenks has also shown[2] that simple evaporation without any treatment whatever gives results which agree well with those obtained by using sand.

In fifty determinations the maximum and minimum difference between the two methods was only .14 per cent. and the mean difference .003 per cent.

Babcock[3] has proposed an ingenious and accurate method of determining the water in milk :

About two grams of rather coarse asbestos are placed in a platinum evaporator of 30cc. capacity, ignited and weighed. Five cubic centimeters of milk from the pipette,

[1] Bied. Centralblatt, 1876, p. 22.
[2] Chem. Centralblatt, 1882, p. 13.
[3] Second Ann. Rept. Bd. Control N. Y. Exp. Sta., pp. 167–8.

previously weighed, is run into the evaporator and the pipette weighed again. The milk in the evaporator is then dried at 100° C., until the weights taken one-half hour apart do not vary more than a milligram from each other.

The asbestos serves as an absorbent of the milk and presents a large surface which greatly facilitates the drying. For this purpose asbestos is much to be preferred to sand or any fine powder which requires frequent stirring for complete desiccation. When a number of analyses are to be made in succession, a second portion of milk may be dried in the same asbestos with advantage. In the series of analyses made during the feeding experiments the morning's and evening's milk were dried together in this way. The dried residue may be ignited for ash.

The figures given for solids in all analyses made during the year have been determined in the above manner. The solids may, however, be found with equal accuracy and in much less time by the method given below.

In the bottom of a perforated test-tube, such as is used in the estimation of the fat in fodders, is placed a tuft of clean cotton. The tube is then filled three-quarters full of ignited asbestos and a plug of cotton inserted to prevent the escape of loose fibers of asbestos. The asbestos must be slightly pressed together so as to leave no large spaces. The tube and contents are weighed, the plug of cotton carefully removed, and five grams of milk, from the weighed pipette, described before, run into it and the plug of cotton replaced. The tube, connected at its lower end by a rubber tube and adapter with a filter pump, is placed in a drying oven at 100° C. and a slow current of dry air drawn through it till the water is completely expelled, which in no case requires more than two hours.

Since the publication of the method of Adams for the estimation of fat, which will be given further on, I have made some attempts to estimate the water by drying the milk on long strips of asbestos paper, which are rolled up while still hot and weighed after cooling in a dessiccator. I have not yet secured an asbestos paper sufficiently bibulous to make this method completely successful. But it has the advantage of being very speedy, since on so large a surface exposed for two or three minutes to a temperature of 100° to 105° C. over a sand bath the water is completely evaporated.

An indirect method of estimating the water from the specific gravity has been prepared by Behrend and Morgen [1] by the formula—

$$S^2 = \frac{S\,(V-A)}{V - S^1}$$

in which S = specific gravity of the milk, S^2 = specific gravity of the milk free of fat, S^1 = specific gravity of the milk fat = .94, and V = volume taken = 100cc.

Numerous tables are given by the authors to show the agreement between the calculated percentage of fat and total solids obtained by the above formula and the gravimetric determinations.

Another indirect method of determining the quantity of water in milk consists in measuring the quantity of finely-pulverized common salt a given volume of it will dissolve.

This procedure was proposed by Reichelt. [2]

The apparatus consists of a glass vessel 24cm. high. The upper part has a diameter of 2.5cm. and the lower of 8mm. On the under side is a

[1] Jour. Landw., 1879, p. 249.
[2] Bayerish Kunst und Gewerbeblatt, 1860, p. 706.

scale marked to 45° C. The principle of the apparatus is based on the fact that at 30° to 35° C., 100 parts of water will dissolve 36 parts of salt. The operation is carried on as follows : Mix 62.5 grams of milk with 20.25 grams of salt and add 15 grams of litmus tincture, saturated with salt, to color the milk. Raise the temperature to 30° to 35° C., shake thoroughly, and then place the apparatus so that all the undissolved salt will fall into the under-graduated stem of the apparatus. Each degree of the scale corresponds to 62.5mgr. of the salt. The part undissolved subtracted from the total quantity will give the quantity dissolved, from which the quantity of water is easily calculated.

The lactometer of Geissler[1] is too complicated for ordinary use, and the method of estimating the water content of milk by measuring the volume of whey filtered from the coagulated albumens proposed by Zenneck[2] does not afford sufficiently exact results to merit further description.

SPECIFIC GRAVITY.

The specific gravity of a milk diminishes as its content of fat increases, and hence within certain limits it may be a valuable index of the character of the sample under examination.

When the cream has been removed, however, the specific gravity may be reduced to that of normal milk by the addition of water, and then the determination of the specific gravity alone is not a certain method of detecting adulteration, yet it is a valuable indication and should always be determined.

This determination may be made by any of the methods already denoted for fats and oils or by a hydrometer. Since the use of this latter instrument (lactometer, lactodensimeter) is easy and speedy, it is generally employed instead of the slower but more exact procedure with a picnometer.

Martin[3] found the average specific gravity of the milk from fifty cows from E. B. Brady's farm, Westchester, N. Y., to be 1.03101. From another lot of thirty one cows, farm of Peter Knox, it was 1.03149; from sixteen cows, farm of George Nelson, 1.03175.

Jenkins[4] makes the following observations respecting the values of the specific gravity determination :

A consideration of the observations noticed above brings us to the following conclusions with regard to the value of *total solids*, and of *specific gravity*, as criteria for judging of the quality of milk.

We have seen that pure herd-milk shows very wide variations in its content of solids and fat, and varaitions less striking in its specific gravity. No instance appears to be on record where a competent observer has found for the mixed milk of a number of healthy cows a specific gravity less than 1.029, and we may conclude with certainty that milk which falls below that density has been watered.

[1] Ber. Chem. Gesel., Vol. 10, p. 1272.
[2] Vieth, Milchprüfungsmethoden, p. 87.
[3] Fourth Ann. Rept., N. Y. State Bd. of Health, pp. 429 *et seq.*
[4] Rept. Conn. Exp. Sta., Vol. 10, pp. 88, 89.

As evidence of watering simply, specific gravity furnishes by far the most satisfactory test, and if 1.029 is adopted as a minimum, no pure milk will be condemned. In some cases moderately watered milk may escape detection.

If we will establish a minimum limit for the percentage of solids and fat which shall in no case condemn pure milk in any locality, we shall have to make it absurdly low, and thus offer a premium on watering milk of good quality.

QUANTITY OF WATER OR DRY SOLIDS IN MILK.

The law of Massachusetts fixes the legal maximum of water in milk at 87 per cent. The quantity, however, varies within large limits, and it is manifestly unjust to condemn a milk as adulterated when it has more than 87 per cent. water.

The chief factors which cause a healthy milk to vary in its percentage of solids are length of time the cow has been in milk, the season of the year, and consequently the character of the food of the animal. On this point the Report of the Massachusetts State Board of Health[1] makes the following observations:

The statutes prescribe a fixed and definite standard for commercial milk. Milk not containing 13 per cent. of solids is deemed to be adulterated under the law. It is often urged that, under such a standard, milk as obtained direct from the animal does not always conform to the requirements of the law. While this is true, it is also evident that a standard established at the minimum of quality, or that of the poorest milk obtained under the worst conditions, would admit of the sale of a very large quantity of adulterated milk.

It is possible to produce from inferior animals, under unfavorable conditions, such as impoverished diet, bad care, extreme age or youth, milk somewhat below the legal requirement. This ought not to be an argument for the reduction of the standard to include occasional cases of the lowest quality.

Mixed milk contains a greater amount of solids than its minimum constituents. Hence, the milk producer or dealer will find it a safe rule to sell mixed milk only, especially when his herd contains one or more animals producing milk of a poor quality. In the 40-quart cans of the Housatonic Valley, filled for the New York market, the milk must necessarily be a mixture from several animals, but in the case of the usual 2-gallon can, so largely in use throughout the larger part of this State, the contents may be often that of two or three animals only, and it occasionally may represent a single animal.

Under the Massachusetts law a rigid inspection of the milk sold in all the large cities is made, and the character of the milk is described in the following summary of the report of Dr. Harrington, milk inspector for Boston.[2]

During the year just ended I have received from the inspectors of the board, and from other sources, 1,759 samples of milk, which number includes samples from all of the cities and many of the towns of Eastern Massachusetts. They have been arranged in classes, according to their respective sources, to wit: (a) Samples from shops; (b) samples from wagons; (c) samples from producers (direct); (d) samples from unknown sources; (e) samples of known purity.

Among such a number, taken in most cases at random, there must necessarily be very many which, on inspection alone, are evidently pure, and which, on analysis, would yield figures above the standard fixed by law. The employment of the lactodensimeter, together with the Feser lactoscope, will, after a little practice, enable one to separate the good from the indifferent and poor samples, and in this way the good samples may, unless there be some reason for a full analysis—such, for instance, as unusual richness, averages, &c.—be passed on inspection. More than half of the samples submitted to me were good samples, and of the whole number 569 were passed as above, leaving 1,190 which were subjected to analysis. Of these latter there were 391 which were above, and 799 which were below, the statute standard.

Considering as above the standard the 569 samples which were passed on inspection, we have 960 above and 799 below, which is a very decided improvement over the milk supply of a year ago. A large proportion of those below the standard were not what would be considered as of very inferior quality; nearly one-half of those below the standard of 13 per cent. of solids were above 12 per cent., which fact of itself is evidence of a great improvement in the general supply.

Dr. E. W. Martin [1] has made a thorough study of milk adulteration, of which I give the following abstract:

Having made from time to time analyses of milk from cows of all breeds and kept under all conditions, of various ages, and at different times of the year, I found the percentage of the maximum, minimum, and average constituents to be:

Constituent.	Maximum.	Minimum.	Average.
	Per cent.	Per cent.	Per cent.
Water...............	82.04	87.87	87.5
Fat.................	7.59	2.78	3.3
Sugar	5.39	4.60	4.4
Caseine	4.34	4.30	4.1
Salts	.71	.65	.7
Total solids	17.96	12.13	12.5
Solids not fat......	10.37	9.35	9.2

Of the minimum amount of fat given above, only three cows were found giving milk so poor in fat, and their food and surroundings were of the poorest kind.

During the year 1883 I made many analyses of milk taken from the cans while being shipped to market, and the average percentage of the constituents of the samples taken were:

	Per cent.
Water........................	87.5
Fat	3.2
Sugar	4.4
Caseine	4.1
Salts	.7
Total solids	12.5
Solids not fat.............	9.3

From the foregoing results it is fair to assume that in average milk we should have at least 3 per cent. of fat, 9.2 per cent. of solids not fat, and 12.2 per cent. of total solids.

The State Board of Health of New Jersey have fixed the minimum amount of total solids at 12 per cent. and the maximum amount of water at 88 per cent.

In Massachusetts the law fixes a chemical standard of purity; it reads: "In all cases of prosecution, if the milk shall be shown upon analysis to contain more than 87 per cent. of water or to contain less than 13 per cent. of milk solids it shall be deemed for the purpose of this act to be adulterated."

This standard has been fixed from analyses by Sharples, Babcock, and others, as follows:

Analysts.	No. of cows.	Total solids.
Sharples.............	22	14.49
Babcock	8	14.55
Vaughn	58	14.08
Newton.............	24	14.26

[1] Fourth Ann. Rept. N. Y. S. Bd. of Health, pp. 429 *et seq.*

Gravimetric.—The percentage of fat in milk is the best criterion of its purity, although it is not impossible to make an emulsion with an added fat or oil after the natural fat of a milk has been removed.

For determining the quantity of fat in a milk by weight it is necessary to evaporate the sample to dryness and dissolve the fat by ether or a light petroleum.

Since, if the milk be evaporated in bulk, portions of the fat will be occluded by the other solids, it is necessary, in order to secure a total solution of the fat, to distribute it over some inert substances. Those already mentioned used for determining water, may also be employed for the fat analyses.

We use thin glass dishes (schälchen), in which the milk is dried in a thin film, or on sand, gypsum, or asbestos. The dish and its contents are then rubbed up in a mortar and transferred to a continuous extraction apparatus. The one employed is a modification of the continuous extractor made by Mr. A. E. Knorr, in which the return siphon is placed wholly within the extraction tubes, thus making the apparatus more compact and less liable to get broken.

The different methods of manipulation heretofore employed for the gravimetric determination are so well known that I will not describe them further, but pass at once to the consideration of a new process, which I have already tried sufficiently to show its merits over all others.

ADAMS'S METHOD.

Adams's method of estimating fat in milk[1] differs from the ordinary gravimetric methods solely in the preparation of the fat for extraction. Instead of drying the fat in the usual way the milk is absorbed by bibulous paper. It is unnecessary to state that this paper must first be thoroughly exhausted by the solvent which is used to dissolve the fat.

The kind of paper and the method of using it first proposed by Adams, are as follows :

As for material, the only extra article is some stout white blotting-paper, known in the trade as "white demy blotting mill 428," weighing 38 pounds per ream. This should be in unfolded sheets, machine-cut into strips 2¼ inches wide and 22 inches long; each sheet in this manner cuts into seven strips.

I have tried other papers, but none have answered so well as this; it is very porous and just thick enough. Each of these strips is carefully rolled into a helical coil, for which purpose I use a little machine, made by myself, consisting of a stout double wire, cranked twice at right angles, and mounted in a simple frame. One end of the strip being thrust between the two wires, the handle is turned, and the coil made with great facility. This may be done, for the nonce, on a glass rod, the size of a cedar pencil. Two points have to be carefully attended to : the paper must not be broken, and the coil must be somewhat loose, the finished diameter being a little under an inch. I am in the habit of rolling up a considerable number at a time and

---

[1] Analyst., 1885, pp. 46 *et seq.*

placing each within a brass ring as it is rolled, inscribing on one corner with a lead pencil its own proper number.

These coils are next thoroughly dried, and I need hardly say the accuracy of the process depends upon this drying. This can be satisfactorily done in an ordinary air bath at 100° C., providing the bath be heated properly and the paper kept in it long enough. I found the common way of heating the thin bottom of the bath with a single jet not to answer. My bath is placed upon a stout iron surface, which is heated by a large ring of jets; in this way the heat is evenly distributed over the whole of the bottom of the bath, and the papers, which are put in a cage frame of tinned iron wire 5 by 2½ inches and divided into eight partitions, get evenly and completely dried, if allowed to remain in the bath all night, and weighed in a weighing tube next morning, and their weights having been registered according to their numbers, stored away ready for use, as follows:

The milk to be examined is shaken, and with a pipette 5cc. are discharged into a small beaker 2 inches high by 1¼ diameter, of a capacity of about 30cc. weighing about 12 grams. This charged beaker is first weighed, and then a paper coil gently thrust into the milk very nearly to the bottom. In a few minutes the paper sucks up nearly the whole of the milk. The paper is then carefully withdrawn by the dry extremity of the coil and gently reversed, and stood, dry end downwards, on a clean sheet of glass. With a little dexterity all but the last fraction of a drop can be removed from the beaker and got on the paper. The beaker is again weighed, and the milk taken got by difference. It is of importance to take up the whole of the milk from the beaker, as I am disposed to consider the paper has a selective action, removing the watery constituents of the milk by preference over the fat.

The charged paper is next placed in the water oven on the glass plate milk-end upwards, and rough-dried. Mismanagement may possibly cause a drop to pass down through the coil onto the glass. This accident ought never to occur; but if it does, it is revealed in a moment by inspection of the surface of the glass, and the experiment is thereby lost.

In about an hour it is rough-dried and in a suitable condition for the extraction of the fat.

The method of Adams has been thoroughly tried by the English chemists, and has received the approval of the English Society of Public Analysts. It gives uniformly about .2 per cent. more fat in normal milk than the ordinary gravimetric methods.

In this laboratory we use the following modification of the process:

The blotting paper is replaced by thick filtering paper cut into strips 2 feet long and 2.5 in. wide. These are thoroughly extracted by ether or petroleum.

One end of the strip of paper being held horizontally by a clamp or by an assistant, 5cc. milk is run out by a pipette from a weighing bottle along the middle of the strip of filtering paper, being careful not to let the milk get too near the ends of the paper, and to secure an even distribution of it over the whole length of the slip. The pipette is replaced in the weighing bottle and the whole reweighed, and thus the quantity of milk taken is accurately determined. The strip of paper is now hung up over a sand bath in an inclosed space high enough to receive it where the air has a temperature of 100° C. (circa). In two or three minutes the paper is thoroughly dry. It is at once, while still hot, rolled into a coil and placed before cooling in the extraction apparatus already described.

The fat is dissolved by ether or petroleum, collected in a weighed flask, and, after thorough drying, weighed. I have already mentioned that by the use of asbestos paper I had hoped to be able to estimate the moisture in milk, but so far have not achieved the success which I believe is possible.

Of all the methods for the gravimetric determinations of fat in milk, I do not hesitate to say that the Adams method, properly carried out, is the best.

SOXHLET'S AREOMETRIC METHOD OF ESTIMATING FAT IN MILK.[1]

Caldwell and Parr[2] call attention to the difficulty which is often experienced in using Soxhlet's areometric method for the estimation of fat in milk. They say, speaking of the determination of fat by the lactobutyrometer: "But in this case, while the butyrometer gave tolerable results, Soxhlet's method failed entirely; even after standing five hours the layer of ether fat solution in the mixing bottle, which should be over a centimeter thick, was hardly a millimeter thick."

This experience is so much in harmony with my own that I thought it would be of interest to call attention to some of the difficulties encountered in working with Soxhlet's method.

Soxhlet's original paper was published in "Zeitschrift des Land-wirthschaftlichen Vereins in Bayern," in 1880.

It rests upon the assumption that an alkaline milk shaken with ether will give all its fat to the ether, and this solution, being lighter than the rest of the mixture, will collect at the top, where it can be separated and its specific gravity determined.

The reagents used are ether saturated with water and a solution of caustic potash containing 400 grams to the litre.

The milk and reagents having been brought to a temperature of 17.5° C. are measured into a flask (I use an ordinary pint beer bottle), with pipettes furnished with the apparatus; 200cc. milk, 10cc. of potash solution, and 60cc. of the aqueous ether are the quantities to be employed. The milk is first placed in the flask and to this the potash solution added and shaken vigorously. Afterwards the ether is added and the shaking continued for one minute longer. The bottle is then put into water at a temperature of 17.5° C. and gently struck on the table in a vertical position at intervals of half a minute for fifteen or twenty minutes. At the end of this time the ether-fat solution has collected at the top, whence it is passed to the areometric cylinder by means of the rubber bulb blowing apparatus shown in figure 1.

Water is now added at a temperature of 16° C. to 18° C. to the outer cylinder, and after the temperature has become constant the density of the ethereal solution is read on the scale of the areometer. At the same time the temperature is read from the delicate thermometer attached

[1] H. W. Wiley, Journal of Analytical Chemistry, vol. 1, no. 2.
[2] Am. Chem. Jour., vol. 7, p. 245.

to the areometer. The areometric degree is to be increased or diminished by the difference between the observed temperature and 17.5° C. as the former is above or below the latter. The percentage of fat is taken from a table which gives the numbers representing it for all degrees of the Soxhlet's scale between 43 and 66 for whole milk, or 2.07 to 5.12 per cent.; and for skimmed milk from 21.1 to 43, or from 0.00 to 2.07 per cent. It is thus seen that the scale includes all percentages of fat from nothing to 5.12. If a milk contain more than the latter percentage of fat it must be treated with a certain proportion of water before it can be examined by the Soxhlet's method.

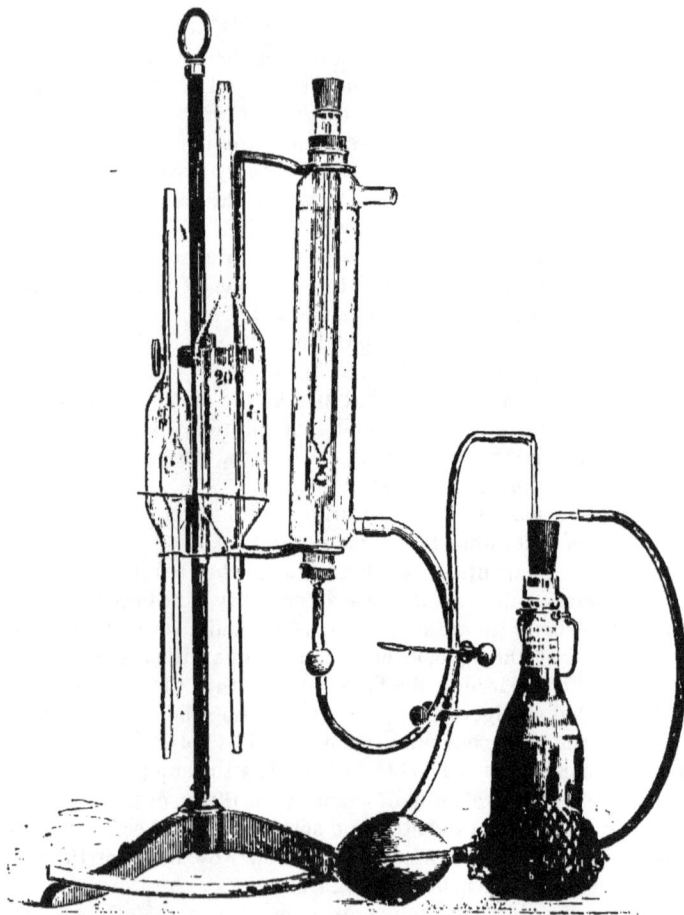

FIG. 1.

Both Soxhlet in his original paper and Liebermann[1] affirm that the ether retained in the form of an emulsion in the lower part of the liquid

[1] Zeit. Anal. Chem., 1884, p. 178,

in the flask does not contain a trace of fat. It is, therefore, necessary to assume that the emulsion has always the same proportion of ether, otherwise there would be variations in the density of the clear supernatant solution. This may be entirely true with those milks which permit the ether solution to separate readily, but where the separation is difficult and a great deal of time is required for it to take place, it is possible that this assumption may not hold good.

Liebermann, who having once condemned Soxhlet's method, on account of the slow separation of the ether solution, introduced a modification of gently shaking the mixture and then pronounced it successful. He says[1]: "Therefore the manner of making the first shaking with ether is not immaterial. The shaking must not be violent (Soxhlet says 'schüttteln eine halbe Minute kräftig),' but, nevertheless, always sufficiently so. The light vertical blows must also be skillfully applied. In fact, these are things which can only be attained by the skilled touch coming from experience."

It appears from the above, and my own experience fully convinces me of the truth of it, that in order to secure a proper separation of the ether fat solution, in all cases, one must be possessed of the art of legerdemain.

After giving the preference to his own volumetric method Liebermann ends his paper by the remark: "But if, on the contrary, the method of Soxhlet is employed, it will usually happen that a given milk must be examined twice, once to see whether the original method is applicable, and again, in case of failure, with the necessary modifications."

I think it will be readily agreed that such a method can find no place in the examination of the milk of individual cows for each sample of which a special modification of the method would have to be made.

Schmoeger[2] calls attention to the shortcomings of Soxhlet's method when milk poor in fat or skimmed milk is used. He says milk containing under 2 per cent. of fat must be evaporated with gypsum before it will give up its fat to ether. Yet it must not be forgotten that gypsum will give up something to ether, also. Schmoeger obtained from 20 grams of pure ignited gypsum 5mg. and from 20 grams sea sand 2mg. of extract. These facts must be taken into consideration when the gravimetric comparisons of fat per cents with the areometric results are made. Certain variations in the method of making these gravimetric determinations have lately come into use, which promise some improvement. Babcock[3] substitutes ignited asbestos for sand or gypsum. This, in my opinion, is a great improvement. Babcock[4] also dispenses with the evoprating dish and uses a tube open at both ends filled with as-

---

[1] Zeit. Anal. Chem., *loc. cit.*

[2] Bericht ueber die Thatigkeit des Milchwirthschaftlichen Instituts zu Proskau, as quoted in Zeit. Anal. Chem., 1885, p. 130.

[3] Second Ann. Rept. Bd. Control N. Y. Exp. Sta., p. 167.

[4] *Loc. cit.*

bestos, with a plug of cotton at each end. The milk is absorbed by the asbestos, the tube is then placed in a steam bath and a slow current of air drawn through it by an aspirator. In two hours the desiccation is complete. The method gives satisfactory results. It is inconvenient, however, to work a large number of samples at once by this method. After drying, the tube is placed in a continuous extractor and the fat removed by ether. I have used the following modification of the gravimetric method. The evaporation is made in a schälchen half filled with fine, pure asbestos. About 5 grams of milk are taken for each determination. The water is driven off at 100° C. and after the total solids have been noted by weighing, the asbestos is removed to the extraction tube. The schälchen is then finely ground in a mortar, transferred to the extraction tube and the mortar and pestle thoroughly washed with ether. The extraction is then made in the usual way.

Adams[1] proposes the use of blotting paper rolled into a helical coil as the absorbent of the milk for the purpose of drying and extraction of the fat. Johnstone[2] modifies this method by using disks of blotting paper held in a circular platinum dish. Dr. Vieth[3] hesitates to approve the blotting paper method on account of the fact that blotting paper itself gives up a considerable extract to ether.

Allen and Chattway[4] recommend certain modifications in Adams' method, consisting in a peculiar method of winding the coil of blotting paper.

Thompson[5] proposes the use of filtering paper instead of blotting paper. I have had this method tried in the laboratory by Mr. Knorr and with pleasing results. Care must be taken, however, to use only filtering paper which has been previously thoroughly extracted. It was found that the filtering paper necessary to absorb 5 grams of milk was afforded by a piece 24 inches in length by 2.5 inches in breadth. This paper extracted with ether gave the following residues:

	Milli-grams.
No. 1	11.4
No. 2	13.4
No. 3	12.0
No. 4	10.5
No. 6	12.2
No. 7	20.9
No. 8	15.5

Since the tables of the Soxhlet method are based on the old method of extraction they will have to be revised for the new data given by the Adams method.

One great advantage of the Adams method as modified by Thompson I have found to consist in the rapidity with which the preliminary dry-

[1] Analyst, 1885, p. 48.   [3] Ibid., 1885, p. 86.   [5] Ibid., 1886, p. 73.
[2] Ibid., 1885, p. 83.   [4] Ibid., 1886, p. 71.

ing is accomplished. I have been able to put 5cc. of milk on a strip of paper, hang it over a sand bath and have it rolled and in the extractor within five minutes.

I mention this to show that even in the matter of gravimetric determinations by which the areometric method is finally judged, there is still a certain limit of variability.

I will return now to the subject more immediately under discussion. Schmoeger further says[1] that with skimmed milk, buttermilk, and such milks as have stood twenty-four hours on ice the ether-fat solution separates difficultly or not at all. To avoid this he recommends, after the addition of the potash, fully five minutes shaking, in order to form butter of the fat. Then the ether is added and the process continued as usual. In this case the percentage obtained by the areometric method must be increased .1 per cent. in order to agree with the gravimetric determinations. Schmoeger further recommends that skimmed milk or sweet buttermilk after treatment with potash be shaken with 10 grams potassium sulphate until the latter is dissolved. But this method also influences the specific gravity of the ether-fat solution, and the corrections to be made are found in the table given.[2]

Soxhlet himself[3] has called attention to the fact that with skimmed milk the ether-fat solution does not readily separate. A special scale has been constructed for such fat-poor milks giving areometric readings from 21.1 to 43, with the corresponding percentages of fat. For such milks Soxhlet proposes the following treatment, viz : A soap solution is made by taking 15 grams of a stearine candle, adding to it 25cc. alcohol, and 10cc. of the potash solution of the strength before given. The stearine is saponified by heating the mixture, and after the solution has become clear it is made up to 100cc. with water. From .4 to .5cc. of this solution is added to the milk under examination, and after a good shaking the rest of the process is carried on in the usual way. After the first thorough shaking on the addition of the ether the light jolting must be continued for fifteen minutes at intervals of half a minute in order to have the ether solution collect at the top. At longest, the solution separated after three or four hours.

Halenke and Möslinger[4] call attention to the fact that if samples of milk are kept for some time, even on ice, the ether-fat solution will no longer separate. They prefer in such cases a modification of Liebermann's method, which they describe. In general I may say the areometric method has met with the approval of all analysts who have used it with exception of Preusse[5], but Soxhlet[6] has shown that Preusse did not understand how to use the apparatus.

---

[1] *Op. cit.*

[2] *Ibid.*, p. 132.

[3] Zeit. landw. Ver. Bayern, 1882, p. 18.

[4] Ver. Bay. Vertreter d Angewand. Chem., p. 110.

[5] Mittheil. Reichsgesundheitsamt, vol. I, p. 378.

[6] Zeit. landw. Ver. Bayern, 1881, p. 700.

The following chemists, in addition to those already mentioned, have given the method their entire approval: Egger, Kellner, Schrodt, Friedländer, Meissel, Fleischman, Hofmeister, Deitzell, Moser, Schreiner, Janke, Gerner, and Angström.

I will give now some of my own experiences with the areometric method :

The milk examined by me was mostly obtained from a neighboring dairy and was a mixture from forty cows. Samples were also bought from dealers in the city. The milk from the dairy mentioned was drawn at 5 p. m., and the examination made the following morning. This may partially account for the small success I had in securing a good separation of the ether-fat. The work extended from March 23 to May 7, 1886.

With the first series of samples in which the method of separation recommended by Soxhlet was followed ninety-three trials were made. In only four cases was the separation sufficiently good to get a reading within thirty minutes. A larger number of readings was obtained within an hour, and about half the number could be read at the end of three or four hours. Of the remainder about one-half could be read after twenty-four hours, and the rest did not separate at all. The results of reading the areometer at different times, however, showed that the density of the either-fat solution underwent quite a change. The following data will show the nature and extent of this change:

No.	Per cent. fat.		
	First results.	Results after 24 hours.	Difference.
1......	4. 16	4. 08	−0. 08
2......	3. 52	3. 83	0. 31
3......	3. 20	3. 52	0. 30
4......	3. 63	3. 68	0. 05
5......	5. 28	5. 28	0. 00
6......	4. 81	5. 13	0. 32
7......	4. 81	4. 71	−0. 10

From the above it is seen that there is no uniformity in the character of this change, but in the greater number of cases the areometer shows an increase in the percentage of fat on standing.

Attempts also to obtain a more perfect separation by varying the quantity of potash employed gave only conflicting results.

I was, therefore, forced to the conclusion that for general work Soxhlet's method would prove useless unless some method could be devised to secure a prompt and uniform separation of the ether-fat solution.

Various theories have been proposed to account for this peculiarity of milk in refusing to allow the ether solution to separate. Caldwell and Parr have supposed it to be due to the bran in the cow's food; Liebermann ascribes it to failure of manipulation ; Schmoeger that it is caused

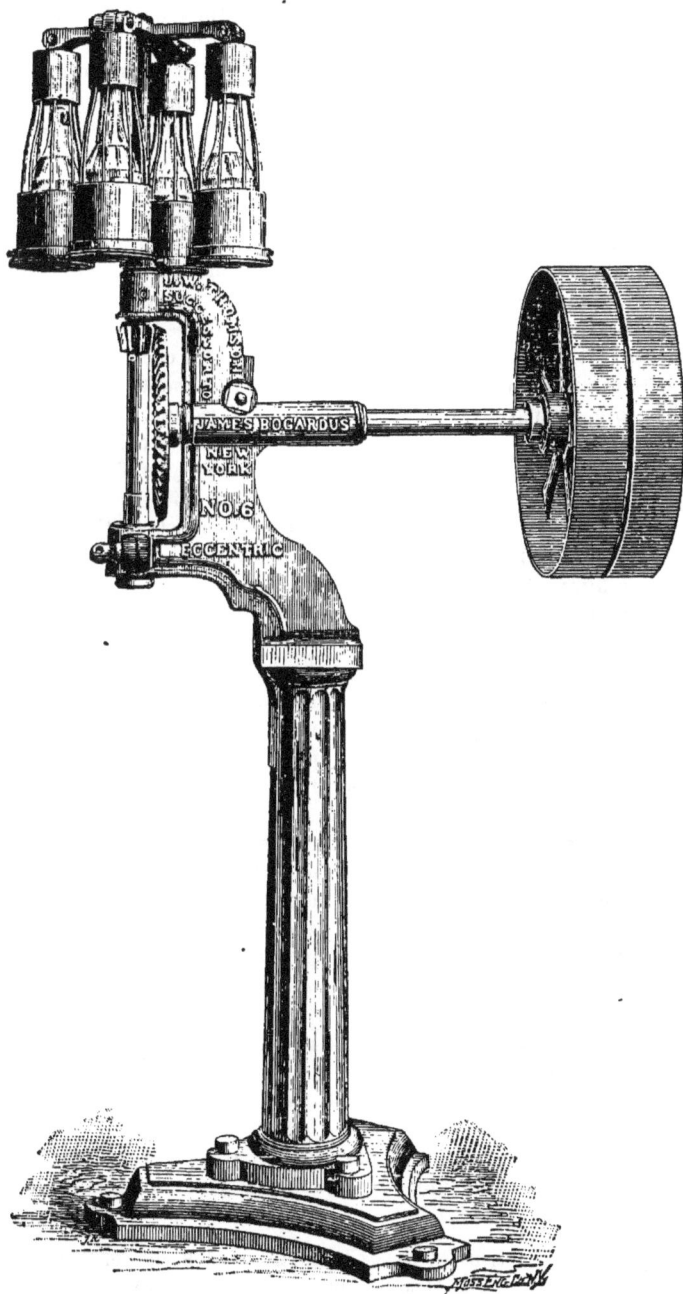

FIG. 2.

by the milk standing on ice; Soxhlet thinks it is the result of deficiency of fat; and others attribute it to differences in age and breed of the cows. The résumé which precedes shows that not only the actual volume of the ethereal solution, but also the time of the separation required, has a serious disturbing influence on the specific gravity of the ether-fat solution.

Therefore, the method, in order to be of general application, must be subjected to some radical modification.

In this direction were the attempts to secure a more prompt separation by varying the amounts of caustic-potash solution employed. These attempts, as the record has shown, were entirely unsuccessful. Even if the different kinds of milk would permit a prompt separation by varying the quantities of alkali employed, the amount for each sample could only be determined by numerous and tedious experiments.

I, therefore, turned my attention in another direction. It seemed to me that a centrifugal machine might be used to secure this separation, and accordingly I had a castaway drug-mill, formerly used in the laboratory, modified so as to serve for this purpose. The machine was so arranged as to hold four separatory flasks and impart to them a high speed of rotation. The form of the machine, with modifications made, is shown in figure 2.

At this point of my investigations this apparatus was finished and I immediately subjected it to a trial.[1]

Four samples which had not separated at all at the end of three hours were placed in the apparatus and whirled for ten minutes. At the end of this time three of them had completely separated, and the fourth nearly so. The apparatus was set in motion again for five minutes, at the end of which time the separation of the fourth sample was accomplished.

The number of revolutions per minute of the machine was about 350.

It will be seen from the above that the very first trial of the machine was completely successful, securing a perfect separation of the ether-fat solution in a few moments in samples which previous trial, by the usual method, had failed to separate in several hours.

The next determinations were made on a sample of milk purchased at the Department restaurant.

Duplicate flasks were treated in the usual way to secure the separation, and only at the end of two and a half hours was enough clear solution obtained to get a reading: No. 1 gave 2.40 per cent. fat; No. 2, 2.30 per cent. fat.

The first set of samples of the same milk separated by the centrifugal gave the percentages following: No. 1, 5.52 per cent. fat; No. 2, 2.32 per cent. fat.

---

[1] This apparatus was first described before the Chemical Society of Washington, May, 1886, and next at the Buffalo meeting of the A. A. A. S., August, 1886.

The separation took place perfectly in ten minutes, with a rate of revolution of about 300 per minute.

The second set of four samples was treated in the same way and separated completely in eight minutes. The following readings were obtained: No. 1 gave 2.36 per cent. fat; No. 2, 2.34 per cent. fat; No. 3, 2.31 per cent. fat; No. 4, 2.30 per cent. fat.

The third set of samples separated by the centrifugal showed the following percentages: No. 1 gave 2.23 per cent. fat; No. 2, 2.30 per cent. fat.

The volume of the clear ether-fat solution in each case was about 40cc.

The next trial was with milk also purchased in the Department restaurant. It proved to be one of the rare cases in which a reasonably prompt separation was secured by the old method. After thirty minutes about 25cc. of the ether solution had separated, which was enough to get a reading. Duplicate determinations were made: No. 1 gave 2.08 per cent. fat; No. 2, 2.04 per cent. fat.

Four separations of the same milk were also made with the centrifugal. Separation took place promptly in eight minutes at a speed of about 200 revolutions per minute, and the volume of ether-fat in each case was about 40cc.: No. 1 gave 2.01 per cent. fat; No. 2, 2.01 per cent. fat; No. 3, 2.00 per cent. fat; No. 4, 2.04 per cent. fat; which is an agreement as close as any one could expect.

Having thus shown that the centrifugal method was capable of making the areometric method applicable to almost every sample of milk, I undertook a new series of experiments. In all, 155 samples were subjected to treatment.

Of the 155 samples examined only 57 gave a good separation by the Soxhlet method in thirty minutes. Of the remaining 98, about half did not separate at all so as to permit a reading, and the other half only after several hours. Compare this with the centrifugal method, in which only 6 samples out of the whole lot required over fifteen minutes for separation and only one was abandoned as entirely inseparable, and the more general application of the process is at once apparent.

Of the 6 samples mentioned above, 3 were from the same cow, a grade Shorthorn, four years old, weight about 800 pounds, in milk since July 1, 1885. She gave 6 quarts of milk a day, was milked at 5 a. m. and 5 p. m. The samples of milk sent were taken at 5 p. m., on April 13, 17, and 22, respectively. The food received by this cow was the same as for all the others (36) from which samples were taken for analysis. They received at 5 a. m. 3 pounds of wheat bran, and the same of hominy chops, and then as much corn (maize) fodder as they could eat. The bran and chops were fed dry. In pleasant weather the cows were out until 3 p. m. They were then fed 10 pounds each of unthrashed oats. At 5 p. m. they got a half peck of chopped turnips and a repetition of the morning's feed of bran and chops.

The hominy chops used showed, on analysis, the following compo
sition :

	Per cent.
Water	7.13
Ash	2.53
Ether extracts	9.03
Carbohydrates	69.32
Crude fiber	2.36
Albuminoids	9.63

Two of the other samples were received April 27 and 30 from a thor-
oughbred Jersey, four years old, weight about 600 pounds, in milk since
July 1, 1885, giving at the time about 5 quarts daily. On the 29th of
April samples of milk were also treated from the same cow, but after
dilution the centrifugal separation, although more than usually difficult, did not require so long a time as on the occasion mentioned.

There is nothing shown by the analysis, by the breed of cow, nor by
the food which gives any definite idea of the cause of the peculiarity in
these milks which does not permit a speedy separation. It certainly
is not the quantity of fat present, for other milks having the same,
more or less, amounts of fat separated without difficulty. In the absence of any further evidence on this point we can only attribute the
phenomenon to bovine idiosyncrasy.

In all 90 samples were compared by the usual method of separation
and by the centrifugal. By the former method the mean percentage of
fat obtained was 4.01 and by the latter 3.88. It thus appears that the
numbers obtained by the centrifugal method must be increased by .13
in order to correspond to those of the old method. This discrepancy is
readily explained when it is remembered that by the centrifugal motion
the percentage of ether left in emulsion would naturally be less than
with the former process of separation. The ether-fat solution thus becomes more dilute and consequently has a lower specific gravity. When,
therefore, the percentage of fat in a milk determined areometrically, is
calculated by the tables given for the old method of separation, it should
be increased by .13 in order to represent the actual quantity present.

I think it safe to conclude from the data which have been obtained :

First, that the method of Soxhlet cannot be applied to the determination of fat in American milks, especially if they be from individual
animals. It works somewhat better on mixed milks from a large dairy,
but even in this case it is a rare thing to secure a prompt separation
and in most cases the method would be very difficult of application.

Second, that by the use of the centrifugal machine described a prompt
separation of the ether-fat solution can be obtained in all cases, even in
those in which after forty-eight hours no separation whatever takes
place by the usual method.

Third, that the estimation of the fat in milk by Soxhlet's areometer
can only be accurately secured when standard volumes of aqueous ether

and caustic potash are employed, when the volume of the ether-fat solution separated is sensibly constant and the time employed in separation sensibly the same. These conditions can only be secured by the use of the centrifugal machine described.

I propose to use a centrifugal apparatus also for assisting in the separation of the ether-fat solution in the lactobutyrometer; and it has already proved its usefulness in separating precipitates which subside very slowly.

I am of the opinion that such a machine would prove of great value in every chemical laboratory aside from its utility in determining the fats in milk.

Cronander[1] has proposed the following method of estimating the fat in milk:

A glass flask of 200 to 250cc. capacity, and two glass tubes constitute the chief parts of the apparatus. One of the tubes is furnished with a scale dividing it into ten equal parts. Below the last division the scale is expanded into a bulb, below which the tube extends for about 5cm. The other tube is bent to an obtuse angle and serves for the introduction of hot water into the flask to drive the fat into the measuring tube at the end of the operation. Both tubes are fastened to a cork stopper in such a manner as to have the measuring-tube end even with the under surface of the stopper, while the other extends almost to the bottom of the flask.

Of the milk to be analyzed 100cc. are taken at 17.5° C., 10cc. potash lye (200 grams to the litre) added and 30cc. aqueous ether. The flask is corked and thoroughly shaken. The ether-fat solution collects at the top (after one hour), and after evaporating the ether the residual fat is forced into the measuring tube by pouring water at 70° C. to 80° C. into the flask. The volume of the fat is thus determined and its per cent. can be calculated.

LIEBERMANN'S METHOD. [2]

This method, like that of Soxhlet's, depends on the separation of a fat from a mixture of milk and caustic potash by shaking. it with ether.

Apparatus.—(1) A glass cylinder with ground glass-stopper, 26cm. high and 3.5cm. diameter. (2) Burettes of the form shown in Figs. 3, 4. (3) A glass flask holding from 45 to 47cc., according to size of burette employed; neck 1cm. diameter, with edge ground accurately in a horizontal plane. (4) Four pipettes, two of 50cc. and one each of 20cc. and 5cc. Before beginning the operation the flask is graduated as follows:

The burette, Fig. 3, is filled to the zero-point with pure water at the temperature of the working room. The water is now run out of the

_____

[1] Milchzeitung, vol. 11, pp. 161-164.
[2] Zeit. Anal. Chem., 1883, p. 383; 1884, p. 476; 1884, p. 87.

burette into the flask (previously carefully cleaned and dried), until the meniscus at the ground edge of the neck passes from the concave to the convex form, a change which is effected by a single drop. When the flask is nearly full at least five minutes should be allowed for the water to settle in the burette. The cubical contents of the flask are now noted from the burette.

Reagents.—A solution of caustic potash having a specific gravity of 1.27. A solution of aqueous ether the same as is used in Soxhlet's method.

Manipulation.—Fifty cubic centimeters of the milk in the cylinder described above are treated with 5cc. of the potash solution, well shaken and allowed to stand for five minutes. This is next treated with 50cc. of the aqueous ether, and gently shaken for ten seconds. The cylinder is now allowed to stand for twenty minutes, receiving every half minute one or two light vertical blows. At the end of this time the separation of the clear ether layer is usually complete, yet it sometimes happens that some of the emulsion adheres to the under part of the flask in the form of a transparent covering. By means of a gentle rotating movement imparted to the cylinder this emulsion is collected and rapidly settles.

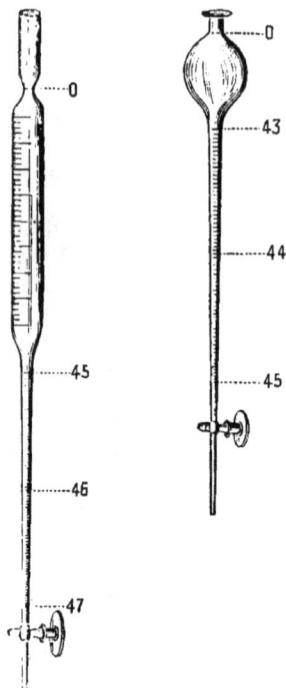

FIG. 3.   FIG. 4.

With a 20cc. pipette the clear ether solution is removed. Before this is allowed to flow into the flask that part of it which has been dipped into the solution is carefully wiped, so that no part of the potash liquid can drop into the flask. The ether solution is now evaporated, and the residue dried for at least half an hour at a temperature of 110° C., or what is still better, over a small flame until the odor of the decomposed butter is detected. The whole is now cooled in a dessiccator. It can now be weighed, if the weight of the flask is known, or it can be estimated volumetrically.

In case the estimation is made volumetrically, it must be carefully observed that the solidified fat contains no air bubbles. In case any air bubbles are noticed the fat must be again melted and warmed until they have all disappeared.

Into the flask containing the solidified butter fat water is again run out of the burette under the same conditions which obtained in determining the contents of the flask at first. It is of the greatest importance that all the measurements be made with the greatest exactitude, since a single drop too much or too little will influence the result.

In case some small particles of the butter fat are detached and swim about in the liquid no fear need be entertained that the results of the measurement will be influenced thereby.

It will appear at once that the difference between the volume of water originally held by the flask, and that which was necessary to fill it after the fat had been added, will represent the volume of the fat which was contained in the 20cc. of the ether solution. This number multiplied by 5 will give the volume per cent. of the fat at the temperature at which the experiment was made.

For converting volume per cent. into weight per cent. the following table is used:

Table for converting volume per cent. into weight per cent.

At temperature 15° C., volume per cent.×.91109=weight per cent.

16°	.90831
17°	.90642
18°	.90377
19°	.90170
20°	.90034
21°	.89857
22°	.89626
23°	.89216
24°	.88822
25°	.88703
26°	.87584
27°	.87463
28°	.87327
29°	.87191
30°	.87055

The following example will show the manner in which the above-described method of analysis may be reckoned.

The graduation of the flask shows a volume of 48cc. and 25cc. After the evaporation of the 20cc. of the ether solution 47.3cc. water was necessary to fill the flask. The volume of fat which was contained in the 20cc. of the ether solution is therefore 48.25—47.38=.95cc. This number multiplied by 5 gives 4.75cc. volume per cent. of fat. The temperature at which the estimation was made was 17° C.

Looking now in the table, opposite 17° C. we find the factor .90642 This number multiplied by 4.75 gives 4.3, which is equal to the per cent of fat by weight.

If it is wished to determine the per cent. by weight of butter per 100 grams, and not cubic centimeters as before, it is necessary to determine the specific gravity of the milk and to proceed according to the following formula:

$$P = \frac{p\ 1000}{S}$$

In this formula P denotes the number sought, p the quantity of fat found for 100 cubic centimeters, and S the specific gravity of the milk.

According to Wolff the percentage of fat obtained by the method ust mentioned is too high, because a part of the ether used for separating the fat remains dissolved in the alkaline milk and this part of the ether contains no fat. The result is that the ethereal solution of the fat contains more of this substance than it otherwise would if the whole of the ether was separated.

Wolff has therefore proposed the following changes in the quantities of the reagents to be used and claims thereby to have obtained results which wholly agree with the estimations of fat by weight. For 50cc. of milk he proposes 3cc. of potash lye of 1.145 specific gravity and 54cc. of the aqueous ether.

Liebermann, however, in a review of the methods proposed by Wolff, maintains that his original method gives entirely reliable results.

FLEISCHMAN AND MORGEN'S METHOD.[2]

Fleischman and Morgen describe a method of determining fat in milk when the specific gravity and total solids are known.

Fleischman[3] gives a more detailed study of this method.

The formulæ for the calculations are as follows:

$$(1) \qquad t = 1.2\,f\,2{,}665\,\frac{100S-100}{S}$$

$$(2) \qquad f = 0.833 - 2.22\,\frac{100S-100}{S}$$

In these formulæ t=per cent. total solids; f=per cent. fat in milk; S=specific gravity of the milk at 15° C.

The above formulæ may be simplified by putting

$$d = 100S - 100.$$

Tables are given to aid in the calculation of the results. By these formulæ when either the per cent. of fat or the total solids is known the other can be calculated with a high degree of accuracy.

ESTIMATION BY VOLUME OF CREAM.

The determination of the volume of cream gives a rough approximation of the percentage of fat in the milk.

The methods generally in use are based on the natural separation of the fat globules on standing and the estimation of the volume thereof in a graduated cylinder.

The creamometer of Chevalier[4] will serve as a type of all apparatus of this class. It is a cylinder 20cm. high and 40cm. diameter. The scale

[1] Pharm. Centralh., vol. 24, p. 435; Zeit. Anal. Chem., 1884, p. 87.
[2] Jour. Landw., 1882, pp. 293-301.
[3] Jour. Landw., 1885, pp. 251 et seq.
[4] Becke, Milchprüfungs-Methoden, p. 40.

begins at 5cm. from the top of the cylinder and is extended downwards. Each mark is one-hundredth of the whole volume. Being filled with milk to the zero point and allowed to stand twenty-four to forty-eight hours, the percentage of cream is read directly on the scale.

Since the volume of cream formed depends on the shape of the vessel the temperature, and the time, this method is not reliable. This error is reduced to a minimum by the use of a centrifugal machine for separating the cream. A machine for this purpose has been constructed by Lefeldt.[1]

In 1883 I saw a very convenient machine which had been constructed, in the laboratory of the University of Illinois at Champaign. The apparatus already described for separating the ether fat solution in Soxhlet's method I have used with success in separating cream. The centrifugals used in separating the cream from the milk in large dairies are constructed on the same principle.

For a comparison of the numbers obtained by these processes with those given by the gravimetric determination, I refer to Becke's monograph.[2]

The Lactocrite.—This name is given to an instrument invented by De Laval[3] designed to separate the fat in milk after appropriate chemical treatment.

The test vessels used in this apparatus are cylindrical boxes made of silvered metal, with accurately ground hollow silvered stoppers. These stoppers are expanded at the bottom, and at the top are contracted, and end in a small hole. They are joined to a glass tube of small internal diameter. This tube is furnished with a jacket by which it can be screwed onto the stopper, and this jacket carries two longitudinal slits, through which the divisions in the glass tube can be read. In the bottom of the jacket is a hole, so that the glass tube and metal stopper form a canal open at both ends.

The centrifugal machine consists of a steel revolving disk. In the upper part of this there is a circular cavity, extending from which, like radii, are 12 holes to receive the test apparatus above described. These holes dip slightly downward. The disk is incased with a jacket having a removable cover, which prevents a too rapid fall of temperature during the operation. By means of appropriate apparatus the disk can be driven at the rate of about 6,000 revolutions per minute.

Preparation of the milk.—In an ordinary test tube put equal portions of the milk to be tested and a mixture of 20 parts of concentrated acetic and one part of sulphuric acid. The test tube is closed with a cork in which is fixed a glass tube, shaken, and heated for ten to fifteen minutes in a water bath with frequent shaking.

[1] Becke, *op. cit.*, p. 43.
[2] *Op. cit.*, pp. 40–45.
[3] Ding. Poly. J., vol. 261, p. 219 ; Chem. Centralblatt, 1886, p. 798.

The cylindrical box above described is now filled from the test tube, the metal cork forced in, whereby the apparatus is entirely filled and the excess of milk forced out through the holes in the bottom of the jacket.

The disk having been warmed to 50° to 60° C. by hot water, is now filled with these samples and revolved for three to five minutes at the velocity already noted. The temperature of the disk should not be allowed to fall below 50° C.

At the end of this time the fat has completely separated and its volume can be read on the divisions of the glass tube. This division is so arranged as to represent .1 per cent.

Blyth [1] has made a comparison of the results furnished by the lactocrite with those obtained by Adams method. The results are given in the following table:

No.	Specific gravity.	Total solids.	Ash.	Fat.		
				Lactocrite.	Adams.	Difference.
1	1033. 0	12. 90	. 80	3. 40	3. 44	—. 04
2	1031. 0	14. 12	. 80	4. 55	4. 69	—. 14
3	1032. 0	13. 12	. 77	3. 60	3. 57	. 03
4	1030. 5	13. 07	. 74	3. 90	3. 99	—. 09
5	1032. 0	12. 98	. 76	3. 80	3. 76	. 04
6	1031. 5	14. 27	. 76	4. 90	4. 84	. 06
7	1032. 5	13. 84	. 78	4. 20	4 26	. 06
8	1060. 5	13. 00	. 76	3. 70	3. 69	. 01
9	1031. 0	13. 51	. 80	4. 05	4. 09	. 04
10	1034. 0	11. 76	. 76	2. 10	2. 07	. 03
11	1035. 0	9. 99	. 86	. 45	. 50	—. 05

The table shows the greatest differences between the two estimations to be .14 and the mean difference to be .05 per cent.

It is estimated that with the lactocrite 48 determinations of fat in milk can be made in an hour.

A further discussion of the merits of the lactocrite is given by Faber.[2] He says:

One great advantage of the lactocrite is the very simple way in which it is worked, so that no skill is necessary, but any dairyman may obtain as good results as the apparatus is able to yield. In order to illustrate this, I give below the results obtained by two persons at their first attempts: the first person is a dairyman used to heavy work. By way of a check I myself made some tests of the same milks:

By myself.	Dairyman.	
3. 1	3. 1	3. 2	3. 2
3. 2	Failed	3. 2	3. 2
3. 2	3 1	3. 3	3. 2
2. 65	2. 65	2. 6	2. 6
2 65	2. 65	2. 6	2. 65

These very favorable results are of importance as showing that in the lactocrite is at last found the long wished-for apparatus, possessing the two qualities not hither-

Analyst, 1887, p. 31.   Analyst, 1887, pp. 6 et seq.

to combined—simplicity of construction and working and sufficient correctness for all practical purposes.

The lactocrite will, no doubt, be found invaluable for butter dairies, or dairy factories buying milk from different farmers, by enabling them to carry out the system of paying for the milk according to the amount of butter-fat which is the only fair system. At present, both in England and in other countries, the farmer whose milk will make butter at a rate of 3 pounds per 100 pounds of milk gets the same price as the farmers whose milk is so rich as to give 5 pounds of butter per 100 pounds of milk, which of course is most unfair. When milk is paid for according to the fat contained in it, the temptation to skim it is done away with, and, besides, a great encouragement is given to the production of rich milk.

The lactocrite will also prove of use for analysts who have access to a separator stand, as it will give in short time a more exact determination of the amount of fat than any other apparatus. In this connection it will be of interest to know that a special construction of it has been adapted to fit Dr. De Laval's small hand separator, worked by hand and requiring no foundation.

Sebelien has published a comparison of the results obtained with the lactocrite and Cronander's method with the gravimetric methods.[1]

Cronander's method gave in general results slightly below those furnished by the gravimetric and Soxhlet's processes.

Dr. Cronander, to avoid this error, has introduced a slight modification into his process by adding a little alcohol to the mixture of potash, ether and milk. The principle of the separation of the fat thus becomes the same as in the lacobutyrometer of M. Chevreul. By using this modified process it was found possible to bring the results up near to those of the gravimetric method.

The results furnished by the lactocrite showed an almost perfect agreement with the gravimetric numbers, the differences being usually within 0.05 per cent.

Attention must be paid to keeping the test tube holding the milk and acids well shaken, especially before pouring its contents into the metal box, and that the rest of the apparatus be pressed in the box at once when the milk has been found. In proceeding in this way no separation of the different parts of the test liquid is possible, and thus a fair average sample is recovered in the test glass.

Concerning the question of the advantages of the lactocrite as compared with other forms of apparatus for estimating the fat in milk Sebelien is somewhat conservative, but seems to think that the matter will soon be determined by comparative trials.

LACTOBUTYROMETRIC METHOD.[2]

This volumetric method depends on the separation of the fat from the milk by a mixture of ether and alcohol. The method has been carefully studied by Caldwell and Parr.[3]

A mixture of 75 parts of pure ether, 100 of absolute alcohol, and 135 of water are employed. The instrument employed is made of moderately thick-walled tubing (about

[1] Landw. Versuchs-Stationen, vol. 33, pp. 393 et seq.
[2] Marchand, Instruction sur l'emploi du lactobutyrometer, Paris, 1856 and 1878.
[3] Am. Chem. Jour., vol 7, pp. 238 et seq.

1mm.); the stem is about 23cm., and the bulb about 8cm. long. It is important that the shoulder between the stem and the bulb should not be too abrupt. The bore of the stem is about 6mm., and it is graduated in $\frac{1}{10}$cc. The wider part of the tube has such a capacity that in passing from the lowest graduation on the stem to the inner end of the stopper in the lower mouth one passes from 5 to 33cc.; then the ether-fat solution will always come within the range of the graduation on the stem. This instrument differs from that originally given by Marchand only in being open at the bottom as well as at the top; this is a matter of some importance with reference to cleaning and drying it. The narrow stem in which the ether-fat solution collects makes more accurate readings possible than is the case with the wider tube with the same width of bore throughout, such as is now commonly used.

The manipulation is carried on as follows:

Closing the lower mouth with a good cork, 10cc. of the well-mixed sample of milk are delivered into the well-dried tube from a pipette, then 8cc. of ether (Squibbs's stronger) and 2cc. of 80 per cent. alcohol. Close the smaller mouth of the tube with a cork, and mix the liquids by thorough shaking, which, however, need not be either violent or prolonged. Both corks should be held in place by the fingers during this operation, and the upper one should be once or twice carefully removed to relieve the pressure within, otherwise it is liable to be forced out suddenly unless carefully watched, with consequent danger of loss of material. Lay the tube on its side for a few minutes and then shake it again, add 1cc. of ordinary ammonia diluted with about its volume of water, and mix as before by shaking; then add 10cc. of 80 per cent. alcohol, and mix again thoroughly by moderate shaking, and holding the tube from time to time in an inverted position while the lighter portion of the liquid rises to the surface.

Now put the tube in water kept at 40° to 45° C. till the ether-fat solution separates; this separation may be hastened by transferring the tube to cold water after it has stood in the warm water for a few minutes and then returning it to the warm water. Finally transfer the tube to water kept at about 20° C., and as the level of the liquid falls in the stem by the contraction of the main body of it in the bulb, gently tap the side of the tube below the ether-fat solution, to dislodge any flakes of solid matter that may adhere to the walls; then as this solution finally takes its permanent position in the tube, its volume will not be increased by the presence of such foreign matters. The readings are to be taken from the lowest part of the surface meniscus to the line of separation between the ether-fat solution and the liquid below it.

In this laboratory the use of the lactobutyrometer has been attended with the same difficulties, though to a less extent, which led to the modification of Soxhlet's method already noticed. The late improvements in both the volumetric and gravimetric determinations of fat in milk render a further discussion of the merits of the lactobutyrometer unnecessary.

OPTICAL METHODS OF ESTIMATING FAT IN MILK.

Since the white color of milk is due to the suspension of the fat globules, many devices have been contrived to determine the quantity of fat present by the opacity of the milk. The most convenient of these apparatus is the one designed by Feser.

It consists of a glass cylinder, in the lower part of which a smaller cylinder made of white glass is fixed. On this white glass are a few black lines. The outer cylinder carries a double scale, one set of numbers representing cubic centimeters and the other the percentage of fat.

Four cubic centimeters of milk are put in the cylinder and then water added until the black lines on the inner white cylinder become visible. The percentage of fat is then read from the top of the column of water in the large cylinder.

For a full description of the different forms of lactoscope the monograph of von der Becke may be consulted.[1] For sorting milks, the lactoscope in the hands of an experienced operator will give valuable indications in respect of the quantity of fat. A delicate lactometer, a good lactoscope, and an experienced operator will generally be able to determine whether a given sample of milk be whole or skimmed. The lactoscope, however, is of no value in determining with accuracy the percentage of fat present in a sample of milk.

ESTIMATION OF LACTOSE.

Chemical.—The chemical methods employed in estimating the sugar in milk will be fully discussed in another part of this bulletin devoted to the study of sugars and their adulterations.

Optical.—The optical method of determining the quantity of lactose in milk is both speedy and accurate when properly carried out. The principles which underlie this investigation and the proper method of carrying it out are given below.[2]

The usual method of determining milk sugar by evaporating the sample to dryness and extracting the sugar with alcohol after exhausting with ether requires a great deal of time and labor. If some reliable optical method could be devised the determination of the lactose in milk would be the work of only a few minutes. The difficulties which are encountered in seeking for such a method are numerous and serious, so much so that little credit has heretofore been given to any of the processes of optical analysis in use.

SPECIFIC ROTATORY POWER OF MILK SUGAR.

Crystallized milk sugar when first dissolved possesses a higher rotatory power than it has in the milk from which it was derived. This increased optical activity may be compared with the original by the ratio $8:5$, nearly. After the solution has stood for twelve to twenty hours, or immediately on boiling it, this extra rotatory power is lost. In estimating the specific rotatory power of milk sugar the numbers given always refer to the constant and not the transient gyratory property.

Among the earliest numbers assigned to the rotation of lactose are those of Poggiale $(a)_n = 54.2$ and Erdmann $(a)_n = 51.5$ [Sucrose $(a)_n = 66.5$]. Biot[3] places this number for lactose at 60.23, and Berthelot[4] at 59.3 for the transition tint $(a)_j$. Hoppe-Seyler, in his "Handbuch der physiologisch-chemischen Analyse," gives this number at $(a)_j = 58.2$. Since the

---

[1] *Op. cit.*, pp. 45 *et seq.*   [2] Am. Chem. Jour., vol. 6, pp. 289 *et seq.*
[3] Compt. Rend., vol. 42, p. 349.   [4] Würtz Dict. de Chim., vol. 2, 1st part, p. 188.

ratio of $(a)_v$ to $(a)_j$ is $1 : 1.1306$, the above numbers become for Biot $(a)_v =$ 53.27, for Berthelot $(a)_v = 52.47$, and Hoppe-Seyler $(a)_v = 51.48$. Hesse[1] observed the rotation number to be $(a)_v = 52.67$ when the solution contained 12 grams per 100cc. and the temperature was 15° C. On the other hand, when the concentration is only 2 grams per 100cc. the number assigned is $(a)_v = 53.63$. It appears from this that the specific rotation power of a solution of milk sugar diminishes with the increase of its concentration, and this view is adopted by Landolt, Tollens, and Schmidt.

The following general formula[2] is used to correct the reading of the polariscope for concentration of solution :

$$(a)_v = 54.54 - .5575c + .05475c^2 - .001774c^3,$$

in which $c =$ number grams sugar in 100cc. solution. These observations are contradicted by the work of Schmoeger,[3] who, in an elaborate series of experiments, using instruments of different construction and observing all necessary precautions, found the rotation number of lactose sensibly constant for all degrees of concentration up to the saturation point. In thirty-two series of investigations, in which the degree of concentration gradually increases from $c = 2.3554$ to $c = 36.0776$, and in which a constant temperature of 20° C. was maintained, the variations in the numbers obtained were always within the limits of error of observation. The mean of all these numbers fixes the value of $(a)_v$ at 52.53.

According to Schmoeger variations in temperature have far more to do with changes in rotatory power than differences of concentration. The value of $(a)_v$ falls as the temperature rises. Under 20° C. the disturbing influence of temperature is greater than above 20° C. At the latter degree $(a)_v$ varies inversely about .075 for each 1° C. change of temperature. Pellet and Biard,[4] as a result of their observations, fix the rotatory power of milk sugar at 53.94 for $(a)_j$ [δ. $(a)_v = 52.12$)].

After a careful review of the methods used in the above résumé and the numbers determined by them, I am inclined to accept the mean obtained by Schmoeger as the one entitled to the greatest credit. It also has the advantage of being almost the mean of all the various numbers which have been assigned as the specific rotating power of lactose, viz :

Poggiale	54.20
Erdmann	51.50
Biot	53.27
Berthelot	52.47
Hoppe-Seyler	51.48
Hesse	52.67
Hesse	53.63
Schmoeger	52.53
Pellet and Biard	52.12
Mean	52.65

[1] Anal. Chem. u. Pharm., vol. 176, p. 98.   [4] Bull. de l'Assoc. des Chimistes vol. 1,
[2] Tucker, Sugar Analysis, p. 91.   p. 171 et seq.
[3] Ber. chem. Gessell., vol. 12, p. 1922 et seq.

In the present state of our knowledge, therefore, the specific rotatory power of milk sugar should be taken at $(a)_v = 52.5$. I propose, at an early date, to make a careful study of this subject, in order to fix, if possible, an exact number for the expression of the rotating power, and to examine the conflicting evidence respecting the influence of the degree of concentration on the same. The estimation of lactose in milk by the polariscope is rendered difficult also by the presence in milk of various albumens—all of which turn the plane of polarization to the left. As will be seen by the data given further along, the ordinary method of removing these albumens, viz, by a solution of basic lead acetate, is far from being perfect. If, therefore, a portion of the albumen be left in the liquid submitted to polarization, the rotation to the right will be diminished by its presence.

Hoppe-Seyler[1] assigns as the rotation power of egg albumen $(a)_v = -35.5$, and for serum albumen $(a)'_v = -56$. Both acids and alkalies seem to increase the rotating power, which may with acetic acid reach $(a)_v = -71$.

Fredericq[2] gives the rotation number for blood serum for the rabbit, cow, and horse at $(a)_v = -57.3$, and for the dog at -44. Paraglobulin, according to the same author, has a rotation number $(a)_v = -47.8$.

Milk albumen[3] has the following numbers assigned to it:

Dissolved in $Mg.SO_4$ sol.	$(a)_D = -80$
Dissolved in dil. HCl.	$(a)_D = -87$
Dissolved in dil. NaOH sol.	$(a)_D = -76$
Dissolved in strong KOH sol.	$(a)_D = -91$

The hydrates of albumen[4] have rotation powers which vary from $(a)_v = -71.40$ to $(a)_v = -79.05$. From the chaotic state of knowledge concerning the specific rotating power of the various albumens, it is impossible to assign any number which will bear the test of criticism. For the purposes of this report, however, this number may be fixed at $(a)_v = -70$ for the albumens which remain in solution in the liquids polarized for milk sugar.

The phenomenon of "birotation" in milk sugar has already been noticed. The problem of analysis of this sugar is, however, still further complicated by the facts pointed out by Schmoeger[5] and Erdmann,[6] that when milk is rapidly evaporated in a plain dish the sugar is left in the anhydrous state, and that this sugar in fresh solutions exhibits the phenomenon of "half rotation." When such sugar is extracted with alcohol and re-evaporated, it, doubtless, is still anhydrous. But in the calculation of results this sugar is generally estimated as containing water of crystallization, and thus an error, which Schmoeger reckons at as much as .2 per cent., is introduced into the results. This

[1] Würtz, Dict. de Chimie, vol. 1, 1st part, p. 91.
[2] Compt. Rend., vol. 93, p. 465.
[3] Hoppe-Seyler in Handbook of the Polariscope, Landolt, p. 248.
[4] Kühne and Chittenden, Am. Chem. Jour. vol. 6, p. 45.
[5] Ber. chem. Gesell, vol. 12, 1915 et seq.; vol. 13, p. 212 et seq.
[6] Ber. chem. Gesell., vol. 12, p. 2180 et seq.

fact, not well recognized, combined with the knowledge that in the process of evaporation many particles of sugar must be occluded by the hardening caseine, tends to throw doubt upon the accuracy of estimating the sugar by the extraction method.

The work which I undertook had for its object the determination of the best method of preparing the milk-sugar solution for the polariscope, and a comparison of the numbers obtained by this instrument with those given by the ordinary process of extraction.

The reagents used for removing the albumens were:

(1) Saturated solution basic lead acetate, specific gravity 1.97.

(2) Nitric acid solution of mercuric nitrate diluted with an equal volume of water.

(3) Acetic acid, specific gravity 1.040, containing 29 per cent. $HC_2H_3O_2$.

(4) Nitric acid, specific gravity 1.197, containing 30 per cent. HNO_3.

(5) Sulphuric acid, specific gravity 1.255, containing 31 per cent. H_2SO_4.

(6) Saturated solution sodium chloride.

(7) Saturated solution magnesium sulphate.

(8) Solution of mercuric iodide in acetic acid; formula[1] KI, 33.2 grams Hg Cl₂, 13.5 grams. Strong $HC_2H_3O_2$, 20.0cc. Water, 64.0cc.

Alcohol, ether, and many solutions of mineral salts, hydrochloric, and other acids were also tried as precipitants for albumen, but none of them presented any advantages which would make a detailed account of the experiments of any interest.

Table No. 9 contains a record of the experiments which led to the adoption of 1cc. acetate of lead solution, or 1cc. acid mercuric nitrate, as the best amount of each for 50cc. of milk.

Nearly all the polarisations were made in a 400mm. tube. From two to four observations were made with each sample. An average of these readings was taken for each determination. In the calculations the value of $(a)_n$ was taken at 53 instead of 52.5, the number which subsequent investigations have led me to believe more exact. The instrument employed was a "Laurent Large Model" polariscope.

In all cases the volume of the solution was corrected for the volume of the precipitated caseine. The volume was assumed to occupy 2cc. for each 50cc. milk.

Since in the Laurent instrument the weight of sucrose in 100cc. to read even degrees on the scale is 16.19 grams $[(a)_n = 66.67]$, it follows that the weight of lactose in 100cc. to read one degree on the scale for each percent. lactose present would be 16.19: $x = 53$: 66.67; $x = 20.37$.

If 52.5 be taken as the value of $(a)_n$ for lactose, then $x = 20.56$.

In table No. 9, A indicates acetic acid, Pb basic acetate of lead, MR acid mercuric nitrate, &c. The letters C and H indicate the temperature; C denoting the ordinary temperature of the room, and H that the sample was heated to 100° C. and cooled before filtering.

The numbers obtained by extraction with alcohol are taken as the basis of comparison, not because I believe them to be more reliable, but because that method is the one generally employed in the estimation of milk sugar.

In the alcohol extraction the milk was evaporated to dryness in a thin glass capsule, the dish and dried residue pulverized in a mortar, washed with ether into a continuous extraction apparatus, exhausted with ether, and then with 80 per cent. alcohol for ten hours.

Duplicate analyses are indicated in the table by the small brackets.

TABLE No. 9.—*Percentage of milk sugar.*

Number.	Per cent. lactose extracted by alcohol.	Reagents employed in precipitating albumens.						
		Pb 1cc.	Pb 2cc.	Pb 3cc.	Pb 4cc.	Pb 5cc.	A 5cc.	Other reagents.
		Per cent. lactose.						
1	4.57				(10cc.)	3.67	4.23	
2	4.52				2.45	3.57	4.14	
3	4.46	4.48					3.57	
4	3.92	4.19				3.35		
5	4.35		3.55				4.32	
6	3.71	4.01					3.00	
7	4.10	{ 4.03 / 4.06 H					{ 4.44 / 4.68 H	
8	4.16	{ 4.29 / 4.33					{ 3.80 / 3.67 H	
9	4.48	{ 4.59 / 4.56 II					{ 4.04 / 4.12 II	H₂SO₄
10	4.10	4.12 II					3.47 II	
11	4.80	4.87 H			(4cc.)		4.44 H	4cc. 4.70 II 5cc. 4.76 H / 3cc 6cc. 4.76 II 8cc. 4.78H
12	4.77	5.02 H	4.62 II	4.50 H	4.31 II			
13	4.25	4.25	3.75	3.38	3.38		3.97	3.89 II / HNO₃
14	4.22	4.90 H	4.58 H					
15	3.14	{ 4.40 / 4.32 II					4.68 II	4.66 II 4.50 H
16	3.30	4.43 H					3.08	
17	4.72	4.45	4.18	3.87	3.65	3.26	3.96	{ 3.08 / 3.88 II 3.88
18	4.88	{ 4.87 / 4.87 II					{ 4.37 / 4.25	{ 4.27 / 4.43 II₂SO₄
19	4.31	{ 4.71 / 4.86 II					{ 4.43 / 4.43 H	(5cc.) { 4.51 / 4.70 II { 4.59 / 4.50 II
20	4.39	4.11						
21	4.70	4.17						
22	4.96	{ 4.93 / 4.97 II					{ 4.45 / 4.43 II	{ 4.60 / 4.07 H
23	4.60	{ 4.41 / 4.45					{ 3.86 / 3.86	{ 3.90 / 3.90 { 3.04 / 4.10
24	4.74	{ 4.41 / 4.45 II					{ 4.21 / 4.35 II	{ 4.32 / 4.44 II { 4.32 / 4.55 H
25	4.59	{ 4.33 / 4.37 II	{ NaCl 4.29 II	1cc. MR 4.29 II			{ 3.94 / 3.93 II	{ 4.03 / 4.10 II { 3.98 / 4.10 II
26	4.39							
27	4.60	4.18 II		4.06				
28	4.26	3.67 II		4.09				

Remarks on Table No. 9.—The results obtained by using various other reagents for the precipitation of the caseine, viz, MgSO₄, CuSO₄, HCl, &c., have not been entered in the table. In none of these cases was there sufficient encouragement to warrant an extended trial. In most cases the precipitation was slow or imperfect, and the filtration difficult.

One important fact should not be overlooked, viz, that any excess of basic plumbic acetate causes a rapid decrease in the rotatory power of the solution; whether this decrease is due to precipitation of the sugar or solution of the albumens does not clearly appear. Illustrations of this decrease are seen in analyses 2, 12, 13, and 17.

It seems to make little difference whether the precipatition is made hot or cold. The question of temperature is set forth in greater detail in the next table. From all the experiments made it clearly appeared that the best optical results are obtained by the use of a minimum quantity of basic lead acetate, or of either the acid mercuric nitrate or iodide. For 50cc. to 60cc. of milk, 1cc. of the lead acetate or mercuric nitrate solution of the strength noted, and 25cc. of the mercuric iodide solution are the proper quantities. It makes no difference, however, if a large excess of the two latter reagents is employed. Of the three the last is to be preferred.

In Table No. 10 will be found the results of the comparative determinations of milk sugar by extraction with alcohol, by precipitation with 1cc. basic lead acetate, and the same with 1cc. acid mercuric nitrate, hot and cold, to each 60cc. of milk.

In many of the analyses the large differences in results by the three methods show a fault of manipulation, but all the results have been given without selection.

TABLE No. 10.—*Percentage of milk sugar.*

No.	Extracted by alchohol.	C. Pb 1cc.	H. Pb 1cc.	C. MR1cc.	H. MR1cc.	No.	Extracted by alchohol.	C. Pb 1cc.	H. Pb 1cc.	C. MR1cc.	H. MR1cc.
	Per ct.	Per ct.	Per ct.	Per ct.	Per ct.		Per ct.	Per ct.	Per ct.	Per ct.	Per ct.
1	4.55	......	4.74	......	4.92	34	4.37	4.65	4.93	4.93	......
2	4.10	......	4.22	......	4.50	35	4.52	4.27	4.41	4.56	......
3	4.51	4.54	4.22	1.68	4.62	36	4.88	4.83	4.93	5.17	......
4	4.36	4.55	4.53	4.89	4.90	37	4.61	4.30	4.43	4.57	......
5	4.05	4.14	4.09	4.48	4.39	38	4.79	4.59	4.67	4.91	......
6	3.84	......	3.84	3.98	3.98	39	4.67	4.26	4.41	4.51	......
7	4.52	4.67	4.73	5.01	5.00	40	4.79	4.64	4.74	4.94	......
8	4.25	4.21	4.26	......	4.51	41	3.95	4.10	4.26	4.38	......
9	4.45	4.61	4.54	4.87	4.87	42	4.00	4.61	4.61	4.77	......
10	4.92	5.20	5.22	5.43	5.47	43	4.63	4.24	4.37	4.57	......
11	3.84	......	3.72	4.00	3.96	44	4.77	4.64	4.70	4.94	......
12	4.53	4.61	4.64	4.87	4.85	45	4.85	......	4.53	4.73	......
13	4.57	4.54	4.55	4.91	4.81	46	4.71	......	4.67	4.93	......
14	4.66	4.29	4.45	......	4.63	47	4.34	4.06	4.12	4.40	......
15	4.17	3.65	3.75	3.95	3.87	48	4.05	4.67	4.77	4.83	......
16	5.02	4.66	4.64	4.86	4.86	49	3.67	4.12	4.18	4.36	......
17	4.68	4.03	3.94	4.39	4.37	50	3.78	4.58	4.62	4.82	......
18	4.23	3.82	3.89	4.08	4.02	51	4.19	4.27	4.57	4.53	......
19	4.96	4.70	4.84	5.04	5.04	52	3.83	4.68	4.78	4.97	......
20	4.85	4.39	4.41	4.53	4.65	53	3.86	3.97	4.07	4.21	......
21	4.63	4.47	4.47	4.69	4.67	54	4.59	4.59	4.61	4.83	......
22	4.47	4.39	4.47	1.67	4.71	55	4.02	4.26	4.36	4.40	......
23	4.46	4.23	4.31	4.65	4.63	56	4.36	4.62	4.76	4.91	......
24	4.47	4.59	4.67	5.01	4.95	57	4.20	4.18	4.28	4.48	......
25	4.40	4.41	4.55	4.45	......	58	4.09	4.52	4.56	4.74	......
26	4.85	4.67	4.73	4.97	......	59	4.09	......	4.28	4.46	......
27	4.45	4.21	4.33	4.57	......	60	4.12	......	4.49	4.81	......
28	4.44	3.98	4.10	4.28	......	61	4.20	......	4.33	4.41	......
29	4.10	4.21	......	4.55	......	62	4.45	......	4.25	4.77	......
30	4.38	5.57	4.69	4.89	......	63	4.33	......	4.09	4.37	......
31	4.20	4.21	4.37	4.57	......	64	4.62	......	4.33	4.99	......
32	4.69	4.59	4.67	4.89	......	Av	4.33	4.34	4.38	4.58	4.63
33	4.52	4.27	4.41	4.41	......						

In the following table will be found the percentage of milk sugar obtained by using varying quantities of the mercuric iodide reagent, and a comparison of the results obtained with those given by the use of acid mercuric nitrate and basic plumbic acetate:

TABLE No. 11.—*Percentage of milk sugar.*

Number.	Pb.	MR.	Mercuric iodide.			
			20cc.	25cc.	30cc.	35cc.
	Per ct.	Per ct.	Per ct.	Per ct.	Per ct.	Per ct.
1	4.28	4.48	4.56	4.56	......	......
2	4.46	4.57	4.62	4.66	......	......
3	4.37	4.65	4.63	4.63	4.60	4.65
4	4.37	4.53	4.60	4.53	4.63	4.60
5	4.38	4.63	4.70	4.53	4.53	4.59
6	4.33	4.67	4.43	4.53	4.60	4.66
7	4.30	4.67	4.67	4.67	4.59	4.57
8	4.33	4.59	4.59	1.53	4.50	4.59
9	4.27	4.60	4.63	4.60	1.66	4.66
Av.	4.34	4.60	4.57	4.58	4.61	4.62

ALBUMEN REMAINING IN FILTRATE FROM LEAD ACETATE AND MERCURIC IODIDE SOLUTIONS.

From the fact that the polariscopic readings show that solutions of milk prepared with lead acetate have a lower rotating power than those prepared with mercury salts, it is to be inferred that the lead reagent either leaves certain soluble and transparent kinds of albumen in solution, or else dissolves a portion of those which are at first precipitated. To test the accuracy of this supposition a few analyses were made to determine the amount of albumen left in the filtrate from the lead and mercury reagents. At the same time different quantities of the mercuric iodide solution were used, in order to determine the amount which would give the best results. For 60cc. milk the quantity of mercuric iodide to be used should be 25cc. to 30cc.

In the following table will be found the percentages of albumen in the whey after precipitating with the reagents noted and filtering. Ten cubic centimeters of the filtrate were evaporated to dryness in a thin glass dish, and the dried residue (with the glass) burned with soda lime. The calculated nitrogen was then multiplied by 6.25 and the product taken as the percentage of albumen:

TABLE No. 12.—*Per cent. albumen in filtrate.*

From Pb.	From HgI2. 15cc.	From HgI2. 20cc.	From HgI2. 25cc.	From HgI2. 30cc.	From HgI2. 35cc.
.0865	.1950	.0865	.0865	.0562	.0865
.1130	.0674	.0865	.0865	.0865	.0865
.1130	.0674	.0562	.1130	.0562	.0312
.0865	.0674	.0562	.1130	.0562	.0562
.1130	.0674	.0562	.0312	.0865	.0562
.1130	.0090	.0865	.0300	.0865	.1412
.1130	....	.1412	.1130	.1412	.0562
.1950	....	.1412	.1130	.1412	.1412
.1130	....	.1412	.0865	.1412	.0865
.1412	....	.1130	.1412	.1130	.0865
.1130	....	.1362	.0090	....	....
....	....	.1250	....	....	....
....	....	.0090	....	....	....
....	....	.0090	....	....	....
Av.. .1182	.0789	.0868	.0839	.0964	.0828

In Table No. 13 will be found percentages of albumen remaining in fil-trate from lead acetate precipitation of forty-two samples taken from those represented in Table No. 10. From these two tables it is at once seen that the quantity of lævo-rotatory matter remaining in milk after treatment with basic lead acetate is much greater than in those samples treated with the two mercuric salts. This explains at once the higher per cent. of milk sugar obtained by using the last-named reagents, and shows that the use of lead acetate as a clarifying agent must be abandoned:

TABLE No. 13—*Per cent. albumen after precipitation by lead acetate.*

No.	Per cent.	No.	Per cent.	No.	Per cent.
1	.250	16	.237	31	.320
2	.306	17	.237	32	.305
3	.135	18	.169	33	.305
4	.272	19	.103	34	.237
5	.134	20	.271	35	.305
6	.239	21	.237	36	.339
7	.301	22	.271	37	.237
8	.305	23	.235	38	.374
9	.237	24	.271	39	.203
10	.339	25	.237	40	.373
11	.271	26	.237	41	.305
12	.305	27	.271	42	.339
13	.267	28	.330		
14	.237	29	.350	Av..	.278
15	.271	30	.374		

COMPARISON OF RESULTS OBTAINED BY EXTRACTION WITH ALCOHOL AND POLARIZA-TION.

By consulting Table No. 10, it will be seen that the percentage of sugar obtained by extraction with alcohol is practically the same as that got by polarization of the lead acetate filtrate.

Thus, the mean percentage of sugar by alcohol (65 analyses) is 4.32; by lead acetate, cold (53 analyses) is 4.34; by lead acetate, hot (64 anal-yses) is 4.38; by mercuric nitrate, cold (61 analyses) is 4.58; by mer-curic nitrate, hot (24 analyses) is 4.63.

If now the milk sugar, as has already been intimated, exists in an anhydrous state after extraction with alcohol, the percentage of it after the addition of the molecule of water would be increased. Thus molec-ular weight of anhydrous milk sugar, 342: molecular weight of the hydrous 360=4.38: x, whence the value of x=4.61. This agrees very nearly with the number obtained by acid mercuric nitrate.

By a study of Table No. 13 it is found that the mercuric iodide gives nearly the same rotatory power as mercuric nitrate, and also by com-bustion the filtrates from the milks clarified by lead acetate contain more albumen than those prepared with mercuric iodide. There is, therefore, every reason for believing that the numbers given by the mercury salts are nearer the truth than those from the lead.

It may be urged that the increased rotatory power observed by the mercury salts is due to the conversion by the dilute acids of a part of the lactose into galactose, which has a rotatory power greater than that of milk sugar. But when it is remembered that the quantity of acid introduced is extremely minute, that the samples need not be warmed, that they can be filtered and polarized within a few minutes of the time of the introduction of the reagents, the suggestion is seen to be of no force.

For example, in the acid mercuric nitrate it was found that the percentage of sugar was the same whether one, five, or ten cubic centimeters of the reagent were employed, and whether it was polarized immediately or after heating and cooling. It is evident that 1cc. of the reagent, containing less than a half cubic centimeter of nitric acid and diluted in 100cc. of liquid, could not exert any notable effect on the rotatory power of the solution.

In the mercuric iodide solution 20cc. of acetic acid are used for every 600cc. of the reagent.

Thirty cubic centimeters of this reagent contain, therefore, about 1cc. of acid. This in 100cc. of liquid, immediately filtered and polarized, could not affect in any marked degree the rotatory power.

Since combustion with soda-lime shows that the filtrate from the mercuric iodide sample is practically free from albumen, it is evident that the numbers obtained in this way must be a near approximation to the truth.

THE PROCESS OF ANALYSIS.

The reagents, apparatus, and manipulation necessary to give the most reliable results in milk sugar estimation are as follows:

Reagents.—(1) *Basic plumbic acetate*, specific gravity 1.97. Boil a saturated solution of sugar of lead with an excess of litharge, and make it of the strength indicated above. One cubic centimeter of this will precipitate the albumens in 50cc. to 60cc. of milk.

(2) *Acid mercuric nitrate*, dissolve mercury in double its weight of nitric acid, specific gravity 1.42. Add to the solution an equal volume of water. One cubic centimeter of this reagent is sufficient for the quantity of milk mentioned above. Larger quantities can be used without affecting the results of polarization.

(3) *Mercuric iodide with acetic acid* (composition already given).

Apparatus.—(1) Pipettes marked at 59.5cc., 60cc., and 60.5cc. (2) Sugar flasks marked at 102.4cc. (3) Filters, observation tubes, and polariscope. (4) Specific gravity spindle and cylinder. (5) Thermometers.

MANIPULATION.

(1) The room and milk should be kept at a constant temperature. It is not important that the temperature should be any given degree. The work can be carried on equally well at 15° C., 20° C., or 25° C. The slight variations in rotatory power within the above limits will not affect the result for analytical purposes. The temperature selected should be the one which is most easily kept constant.

(2) The specific gravity of milk is determined. For general work this is done by a delicate specific gravity spindle. Where greater accuracy is required use specific gravity flask.

(3) If the specific gravity be 1.026 or nearly so, measure out 60.5cc. into the sugar flask. Add 1cc. of mercuric nitrate solution or 30cc. mercuric iodide solution and fill to 102.4cc. mark. The precipitated albumen occupies a volume of about 2.4cc. Hence the milk solution is really 100cc. If the specific gravity is 1.030 use 60cc. of milk. If specific gravity is 1.034 use 59.5cc. of milk.

(4) Fill up to mark in 102.4cc. flask, shake well, filter, and polarize.

NOTES.

In the above method of analysis the specific rotatory power of milk sugar is taken at 52.5, and the weight of it in 100cc. solution to read 100 degrees in the cane sugar scale at 20.56 grams. This is for instruments requiring 16.19 grams sucrose to produce a rotation of 100 sugar degrees. It will be easy to calculate the number for milk sugar whatever instrument is employed.

Since the quality of milk taken is three times 20.56 grams, the polariscopic readings divided by 3 give at once the percentage of milk sugar when a 200mm. tube is used.

If a 400mm. tube is employed, divide reading by 6; if a 500mm tube is used, divide by 7.5.

Since it requires but little more time, it is advisable to make the analysis in duplicate, and take four readings for each tube. By following this method gross errors of observation are detected and avoided.

By using a flask graduated at 102.4 for 60cc. no correction for volume of precipitated caseine need be made. In no case is it necessary to heat the sample before polarizing.

ESTIMATION OF THE ALBUMINOIDS.

The albuminoids in milk are most easily estimated by combustion with soda-lime or by previous conversion into ammonic sulphate and subsequent distillation from an alkaline liquid.

(1) *Combustion with soda-lime*—From 4 to 5 grams of milk measured from a weighing flask are evaporated to dryness in a schälchen either alone or with sand, gypsum, pumice-stone or asbestos. When dry the whole is rubbed up in a mortar, transferred to a combustion tube, and burned in the usual way. The nitrogen calculated from the ammonia formed multiplied by 6.25 gives the total albuminoids.

(2) The estimation of the albuminoids by Kjeldahl's method is so well understood that it will not be necessary to describe it here.

Following are the results of the analyses of milks made in this laboratory.

In table No. 14 are the results of the daily analyses of milk from the Maythorpe Dairy.

In table No. 15 are the numbers obtained with milks from various sources.

In these analyses the fat was estimated by the modified Soxhlet method, the sugar by the optical method, and the albuminoids by combustion with soda-lime.

TABLE No. 14.—*Analyses of milk from Maythorpe Dairy.*

[All these samples were bought from D. M. Nesbit, College Station, Md.]

Number.	Specific gravity at 15° C.	Water.	Fat areometric.	Albuminoids.	Sugar.	Ash.	Total solids.
		Per ct.	Per ct.	Per ct.	Per ct.	Per ct.	Per ct.
1	1.0348	87.31	....	2.57	4.60	.73	12.69
2	1.0340	86.96	....	2.81	5.00	.74	13.04
3	1.0333	87.62	3.64	2.61	4.80	.73	12.38
4	1.0339	....	4.12	2.84	4.85	.72	....
5	1.0326	87.69	4.00	2.72	5.05	.72	....
6	1.0316	87.08	3.92	2.63	5.14	.72	12.92
7	1.0337	87.27	....	2.80	5.19	.72	12.73
8	1.0362	87.98	3.21	2.77	5.10	.74	12.02
9	1.0341	86.97	3.66	2.75	5.19	.72	13.03
10	1.0333	87.62	3.98	2.78	5.27	.71	12.38
11	1.0315	87.89	3.51	2.80	4.99	.66	12.11
12	1.0337	87.54	4.25	2.80	4.90	.73	12.46
13	1.0334	86.09	4.62	2.98	5.02	.77	13.91
14	1.0368	85.44	....	3.92	4.65	.85	14.56
15	1.0328	86.73	....	3.04	5.00	.72	13.27
16	1.0358	84.58	4.73	4.05	4.67	.94	15.42
17	1.0335	87.84	4.08	3.15	4.92	.73	12.16
18	1.0325	87.33	....	2.63	5.04	.71	12.67
19	1.0323	86.60	....	2.03	4.95	.71	13.40
20	1.0353	86.24	....	4.13	4.70	1.21	13.76
21	1.0328	88.56	4.06	2.98	4.75	.55	11.44
22	1.0368	84.03	....	4.51	4.55	1.15	15.97
23	1.0328	84.64	5.22	2.84	4.90	.61	15.36
24	1.0325	88.10	4.24	2.73	5.04	.72	11.90
25	1.0329	86.17	....	2.76	4.90	.74	13.83
26	1.0349	85.46	4.74	3.64	4.95	.86	14.54
27	1.0323	86.50	....	2.87	4.82	.64	13.41
28	1.0309	84.93	....	3.61	4.38	.81	15.07
29	1.0330	85.73	4.92	2.98	5.14	.58	14.27
30	1.0344	86.60	....	2.59	5.17	.68	13.40
31	1.0339	86.85	....	3.18	5.00	.62	13.15
32	1.0363	85.67	....	3.92	4.70	.85	14.33
33	1.0324	86.55	....	2.80	4.84	.70	13.45
34	1.0369	83.75	....	4.73	3.69	.84	16.25
35	1.0339	85.66	....	3.29	5.13	.68	14.34
36	1.0346	....	5.08	3.11	5.02	.64	....
37	1.0350	85.67	4.87	2.94	5.67	.74	14.33
38	1.0340	....	4.75	3.22	5.02	.68	....
39	1.0340	87.15	4.47	2.76	5.30	.70	12.85
40	1.0355	88.98	4.78	2.76	5.57	.63	11.02
41	1.0325	87.71	4.00	2.69	5.02	.56	12.29
42	1.0333	87.04	4.11	3.04	4.75	.64	12.96
43	1.0338	85.49	5.25	2.84	4.90	.80	14.51
44	1.0318	86.92	4.26	2.87	4.80	.70	13.08
45	1.0343	86.10	4.66	2.69	4.89	.70	14.90
46	1.0343	87.18	3.75	2.59	5.03	.66	12.82
47	1.0328	87.44	3.57	2.66	5.01	.72	12.56
48	1.0334	86.79	4.03	2.80	4.80	.65	13.21
49	1.0342	85.85	4.81	3.15	4.97	.75	14.15
50	1.0327	87.87	4.18	2.80	4.80	.72	12.13
51	1.0338	86.56	4.02	2.87	5.19	.61	13.44
52	1.0319	86.10	4.96	2.63	5.20	.63	13.90
53	1.0319	87.63	3.38	2.76	4.95	.70	12.37
54	1.0318	87.50	3.51	2.66	4.49	.81	12.50
55	1.0343	85.37	4.72	3.15	4.85	.80	14.63
56	1.0323	86.85	3.75	2.87	4.77	.71	13.15
57	1.0338	86.14	4.08	2.87	5.07	.73	13.86
58	1.0332	86.23	4.50	2.66	5.15	.77	13.77
59	1.0317	87.82	3.16	2.56	4.85	.68	12.18
60	1.0325	86.51	4.21	2.66	4.85	.60	13.49
61	1.0354	84.64	....	3.43	5.15	.84	15.36
62	1.0339	86.89	4.00	2.84	5.02	.78	13.11
63	1.0340	86.98	3.94	2.80	5.23	.69	13.02
64	1.0340	87.74	3.72	2.59	5.27	.69	12.26
65	1.0305	87.96	3.13	2.56	4.87	.66	12.04
66	1.0331	87.57	3.88	2.63	4.95	.73	12.43
67	1.0305	89.20	3.57	2.76	4.33	.73	10.80
68	1.0328	89.01	3.26	2.87	4.99	.72	10.99
69	1.0314	86.32	3.02	2.73	4.67	.69	13.68
70	1.0320	87.22	4.05	2.39	5.27	.69	12.78
71	1.0320	86.89	4.53	2.98	4.97	.76	13.11
72	1.0334	86.55	4.11	2.87	5.15	.55	13.45
73	1.0317	88.35	3.55	2.73	4.57	.55	11.65
74	1.0345	87.12	3.59	2.91	5.10	.64	12.88
75	1.0310	88.01	3.66	2.69	4.49	.56	11.99
76	1.0340	87.62	3.67	2.45	5.40	.70	12.38

TABLE No. 14.—*Analyses of milk from Maythorpe Dairy*—Continued.

Number.	Specific gravity at 15° C.	Water.	Fat arcometric.	Albuminoids.	Sugar.	Ash.	Total solids.
		Per ct.	Per ct.	Per ct.	Per ct.	Per ct.	Per ct.
77	1.0336	86.16	4.75	2.81	5.13	.79	13.84
78	1.0320	86.80	4.36	2.45	5.15	.62	13.20
79	1.0320	84.73	4.25	2.56	4.90	.54	14.27
80	1.0028	86.34	3.50	2.91	4.89	.66	13.66
81	1.0318	88.71	3.71	2.59	4.80	.54	11.29
82	1.0334	86.94	3.97	2.31	5.49	.57	13.06
83	1.0325	86.01	4.58	2.01	5.13	.74	13.99
84	1.0336	86.41	4.23	2.63	5.22	.76	13.59
85	1.0311	87.73	3.61	2.73	4.60	.70	12.27
86	1.0332	87.69	3.79	2.69	4.09	.64	12.91
87	1.0321	86.54	4.11	2.63	4.90	.64	13.46
88	1.0322	86.73	4.41	2.24	5.30	.66	13.27
89	1.0333	85.75	3.85	3.01	5.25	.71	14.25
90	1.0312	88.66	4.64	2.34	5.23	.68	11.34
91	1.0328	87.87	3.61	2.48	5.25	.68	12.13
92	1.0341	86.94	4.66	2.38	5.49	.67	13.06
93	1.0322	87.63	3.75	2.56	5.02	.69	12.37
94	1.0322	86.59	3.78	2.28	5.29	.58	13.41
95	1.0312	88.30	2.73	2.45	4.93	.65	11.70
96	1.0322	87.42	4.30	2.45	5.25	.66	12.58
97	1.0332	87.65	3.68	2.41	5.27	.69	12.35
98	1.0332	87.22	4.35	2.66	5.37	.66	12.78
99	1.0313	88.93	4.79	2.59	4.95	.70	12.07
100	1.0328	87.29	4.07	2.38	5.37	.72	12.71
101	1.0325	88.31	3.05	2.45	5.50	.63	11.69
102	1.0345	87.40	3.65	2.41	5.45	.70	12.60
103	1.0345	87.78	3.60	2.38	5.33	.72	12.22
104	1.0355	88.38	3.97	2.60	5.75	.59	11.62
105	1.0330	88.24	3.14	2.63	5.22	.72	11.76
106	1.0315	88.60	3.73	2.45	5.67	.72	11.40
107	1.0335	88.58	3.06	2.63	5.30	.55	11.42
108	1.0317	88.86	3.57	2.24	5.05	.65	11.14
109	1.0325	87.89	2.61	2.45	5.07	.60	12.11
110	1.0320	88.47	4.02	2.34	5.23	.66	11.43
111	1.0320	88.97	4.68	2.52	5.27	.70	12.03
112	1.0315	87.85	4.67	2.34	5.07	68	13.15
113	1.0315	87.29	4.19	2.45	4.93	.66	12.71
114	1.0367	86.10	4.74	2.84	5.49	.69	13.90
115	1.0356	86.61	4.28	3.08	5.35	.76	13.39
116	1.0354	87.59	3.13	2.63	5.52	.73	12.41
117	1.0036	86.37	4.41	2.52	5.23	.73	13.63
118	1.0340	86.17	4.45	2.73	5.25	.74	13.83
119	1.0326	86.09	5.12	2.80	5.29	.69	13.91
120	1.0338	85.88	5.09	2.69	5.43	.72	14.12
121	1.0352	86.91	4.16	2.94	5.30	.74	13.09
122	1.0342	87.17	3.80	2.69	5.33	.70	12.83
123	1.0352	85.99	4.57	2.80	5.42	.71	14.01
124	1.0338	86.64	4.47	2.31	5.24	.72	13.36
125	1.0348	87.55	3.78	2.76	5.50	.79	12.45
126	1.0343	85.41	4.91	3.01	5.47	.71	14.59
127	1.0352	86.47	3.99	2.91	5.32	.72	13.43
128	1.0357	87.81	3.15	2.76	5.62	.77	12.19
129	1.0336	87.66	4.74	2.91	5.20	.72	12.34
130	1.0336	86.32	4.50	2.66	5.27	.71	13.68
131	1.0341	85.88	5.02	2.69	5.49	.69	14.12
132	1.0351	86.57	4.65	2.69	5.55	.75	13.43
133	1.0354	85.81	4.51	2.98	5.58	.76	14.19
134	1.0353	87.33	3.66	2.45	5.67	.89	12.67
135	1.0346	86.34	4.68	2.63	5.39	.75	13.06
137	1.0338	85.48	6.05	2.80	5.39	.79	14.52
138	1.0345	86.60	3.74	2.87	......	.77	13.40
139	1.0345	85.60	5.63	2.48	......	.71	14.40
140	1.0320	86.85	4.09	2.63	......	.73	13.15
141	1.0330	87.18	3.49	2.94	......	.73	12.82
142	1.0340	86.18	4.30	2.98	......	.74	13.82
143	1.0330	87.54	3.51	3.04	......	.60	12.46
144	1.0341	86.98	3.82	2.45	......	.67	13.02
145	1.0320	87.66	6.03	2.34	......	.74	12.34
146	1.0333	86.65	3.33	2.87	......	.66	13.35
147	1.0335	86.24	3.57	2.91	......	.58	13.76
148	1.0350	88.02	2.65	3.08	......	.73	11.98
149	1.0332	89.38	3.21	2.87	......	.59	......
150	1.0344	86.72	3.54	3.15	......	.78	13.28
151	1.0333	85.34	5.35	2.45	......	.70	14.66
152	1.0333	86.41	4.18	2.80	......	.60	13.59
153	1.0342	87.35	3.50	3.04	......	.75	12.65
154	1.0338	86.66	3.83	2.66	......	.64	13.34
155	1.0345	87.68	2.91	2.76	......	.59	12.32

TABLE No. 14.—*Analyses of milk from Maythorpe Dairy*—Continued.

Number.	Specific gravity at 15° C.	Water.	Fat areometric.	Albuminoids.	Sugar.	Ash.	Total solids.
		Per ct.	Per ct.	Per ct.	Per ct.	Per ct.	Per ct.
156	1.0353	86.43	3.87	2.37	....	.70	13.57
157	1.0320	86.46	5.29	2.52	....	.54	13.54
158	1.0335	86.99	3.91	2.63	....	.53	13.01
159	1.0340	86.89	3.73	3.19	....	.58	13.11
160	1.0339	86.73	3.97	2.91	....	.70	13.27
161	1.0333	87.59	3.30	2.66	....	.71	12.41
162	....	87.03	3.61	3.15	....	.60	12.97
163	....	87.73	3.43	2.66	....	.60	12.27
164	....	87.09	3.76	2.91	....	.64	12.91
165	....	....	4.04	2.73	....	....	....
166	....	....	5.41	2.27	....	....	....
167	....	....	3.76	3.11	....	....	....
168	....	....	....	3.85	....	....	....
169	....	....	3.91	3.92	....	....	....
Means ...	1.0334	86.95	4.08	2.78	5.05	.70	13.09

TABLE 15.—*Analyses of milk from various sources.*

Number.	Specific gravity at 15° C.	Water.	Fat areometric.	Albuminoids.	Sugar.	Ash.	Total solids.
1*	1.0315	88.14	4.73	2.88	4.67	.69	11.86
2*	1.0320	....	5.86	2.84	5.00	.71	....
3*	1.0316	87.48	5.05	2.84	4.75	.73	12.52
4†	1.0265	90.91	2.35	2.10	3.77	.62	9.09
5†	1.0254	91.59	2.01	1.96	3.63	.52	8.41
6†	1.0245	88.76	4.51	2.06	2.02	.56	11.24
7†	1.0285	89.84	2.68	2.17	4.23	.69	10.16
8‡	1.0335	86.97	4.07	2.91	4.92	.68	13.03
Means ...	1.0292	89.09	3.91	2.47	4.12	.65	9.54

* From C. J. Loomis, 1413 Stoughton Hill. † Department lunch room.
‡ Thompson's Dairy.

KOUMISS.

The use of koumiss, both as a beverage and in the sick-room, is rapidly increasing in this country, and for this reason I have thought it would be of interest to add here the results of the investigations on some home-made koumiss.[1]

Fermented mare's milk has long been a favorite beverage in the East, where it is known as "koumiss." Although the Tartars and other Asiatic tribes use mare's milk for the manufacture of koumiss, yet it is not the only kind that can be employed. Since the consumption of milk-wine has extended westward cow's milk is chiefly employed for making it both in Europe and America. Mare's milk is considered most suitable for fermentation because of the large percentage of milk-sugar which it contains.

König[2] gives as the average percentage of milk-sugar in mare's milk 5.31. The same author[3] gives as a mean of 377 analyses of cow's milk 4.81 per cent. of lactose. Dr. Stahlberg,[4] who brought forty mares from the steppes of Russia to Vienna for the purpose of using their milk for

[1] Am. Chem. Jour., vol. 8, p. 200.   [3] *Op. cit.*, p. 40.
[2] Nahrungsmittel, p. 46.   [4] Tymowskis' Bedeutung des kumys, p. 12.

koumiss, found its percentage of lactose to be 7.26. On the other hand, ordinary mares that were kept at work gave a milk containing only 5.95 per cent. sugar. The quantity of milk-sugar in mare's milk is great, but there is a deficiency of fat and other solids. It appears to contain fully 89 per cent. water, while cow's milk does not have more than 87 per cent.

The process of manufacture is not uniform. In the East the mare's milk is placed in leathern vessels; to it is added a portion of a previous brewing, and also a little yeast. In thirty to forty-eight hours the process is complete. During this time the vessels are frequently shaken.

In the samples analyzed by me the milk was treated with a lactic ferment and yeast. After twenty-four to forty-eight h ours' fermentation the koumiss was bottled. The bottles were kept in a cool place, not above 50° F., and in a horizontal position. When shipped to me they were packed in ice. After they were received in the laboratory they were kept on ice until analyzed.

METHOD OF ANALYSIS.

Carbonic dioxide.—The estimation of the carbonic dioxide was a problem of considerable difficulty. It was evidently impracticable to attempt opening the bottle and determining the gas in a portion of the contents. Fortunately I had access to a large balance which would turn with a milligram. On this I weighed the whole bottle, into the cork of which I had inserted a stop-cock such as is sometimes used with a champagne bottle. With the bottle of koumiss were also weighed two drying flasks containing concentrated sulphuric acid with their connections.

Having obtained the weight of the whole, the gas was allowed to escape slowly from the stop-cock and to bubble through the sulphuric acid in the washing flasks.

These flasks, previously to being weighed, were filled with the gas from an ordinary carbonic dioxide generator. After the gas had almost ceased to flow the bottle of koumiss was frequently shaken. It was also placed in a pail of water having a temperature of 30° C. After half an hour the gas ceased to come over.

The whole apparatus was again weighed. The loss of weight gave the quantity of free carbonic dioxide in the sample. After the analysis was completed the volume of the bottle was measured. It is fair to assume that at 30° C. the koumiss still contained an equal volume of dissolved CO_2. In determining the total CO_2 this volume, or its equivalent weight, was added to that obtained by direct determination.

By this method the CO_2 dissolved under pressure in the bottles is estimated separately from that which the koumiss contains in solution under the weight of one atmosphere. Since it is of no importance to separate the gas into these two portions, I have given it altogether in the tables, in volume, by weight; and in percentage by weight.

Acidity.—The samples examined showed under the microscope the acetic ferment, and a portion of the acidity was therefore due to acetic acid. It is the custom in giving the results of analyses of koumiss to represent the whole of the acidity as due to lactic acid. If ordinary yeast is used, and it generally is, it is possible that acetic acid may be formed. This appeared to be the case with the samples in question, since in distilling them a larger percentage of acid was found in the distillate than could have been expected had lactic acid only been present.

I made no attempt to separate these two acids, but estimated the total acidity, and then represented it in terms of both acids.

The direct titration of the lactic acid in the koumiss was attended with such difficulty that the attempt was abandoned. Whatever indicator was employed, the change in color was so obscured that no sharp reaction could be obtained.

To obviate this trouble the koumiss was mixed with an equal volume of saturated solution of magnesium sulphate. After shaking the mixture it was poured through a linen filter. The first portions running through were turbid. After refiltering these the filtrate was quite clear.

Better results were obtained by using with the koumiss equal volumes of alcohol. The filtrate from this mixture was uniformly bright. In this filtrate the acid was estimated by titration with standard sodic-hydrate solution, making the proper corrections for dilution and using phenol-phthalein as an indicator. I would recommend this alcoholic method of clarification to all who may have occasion to determine acid in milk.

Alcohol.—The alcohol was estimated by distilling 500cc. koumiss with 100cc. water until the distillate amounted to 500cc. This, being still turbid, was redistilled with a small quantity of water. The final distillate of 500cc. was used for the estimation of the alcohol in the usual way, viz, by taking its specific gravity and calculating the alcohol from tables.

Milk-sugar.—The milk-sugar was estimated by the method I recommended in a paper read at the Philadelphia meeting of the A. A. A. S.[1]

Fat.—Twenty grams of the koumiss were evaporated to dryness in a schälchen, the whole rubbed to a fine powder, and extracted with ether in a continuous extractor. The process of extraction lasted six hours.

Albuminoids.—The albuminoids were estimated by evaporating 5 grams of the material in a schälchen, rubbing to a fine powder with soda-lime, and burning with the same in the usual way.

---

[1] Am. Chem. Jour., vol. 6, p. 289 *et seq.*

Water.—In a flat platinum dish partly filled with washed and dried sand 2 grams of material were weighed and dried to a constant weight at 100° C. Following are the results of the analyses:

TABLE No. 16.—*Analyses of koumiss.*

No. of analysis.	Weight of koumiss.	Volume of CO_2.	Weight of CO_2.	CO_2 by weight.	Acidity as acetic acid.	Acidity as lactic acid.	Alcohol.	Nitrogen.	Albuminoids.	Fat.	Water.	Milk sugar.
	Grams.	*Litres.*	*Grams.*	*Pr. ct.*	*Pr. ct.*	*Pr. ct.*	*Pr. ct.*	*Pr. ct.*	*Pr. ct.*	*Pr. ct.*	*Pr. ct.*	*Pr. ct.*
1	747.415	2.543	5.009	.07			.87	.431	2.69	2.21	83.81	4.33
2	729.376	3.140	6.186	.85	.31	.47	.66	.412	2.58	2.15	89.53	4.31
3	768.575	3.179	6.269	.92	.34	.51	.69	.483	3.02	2.07	89.15	4.33
4	736.035	3.281	6.463	.88	.30	.45	.81	.482	3.01	1.99	89.31	4.43
5	746.187	3.579	6.850	.91	.32	.48	.86	.423	2.64	1.67	89.97	4.43
6	750.247	2.973	5.757	.77	.27	.43	.70	.450	2.81	1.75	89.87	4.33
7	738.840	3.204	6.313	.85	.33	.49	.73	.462	2.89	2.41	89.01	4.48
8	752.550	3.263	6.428	.85			.77	.450	2.81	2.34	88.87	
Mean				.83	.31	.47	.76	.449	2.56	2.08	89.32	4.38

It will be of interest to compare these results with those obtained by other analysts, both with koumiss from mare's milk and from other sources. As a mean of fourteen analyses of mare's milk koumiss, König[1] gives the following figures, viz:

	Per cent.
Alcohol	1.84
Lactic acid	0.91
Milk sugar	1.97
Albuminoids	1.97
Fat	1.26
Ash	0.30
Carbonic dioxide	0.952

The mean of two samples of koumiss made of cow's milk is given by the same author, as follows:

	Per cent.
Alcohol	2.64
Lactic acid	0.80
Milk sugar	3.10
Albuminoids	2.02
Ash	0.45
Carbonic dioxide	1.03

In nine analyses of koumiss[2] probably made of cow's milk the means are as follows:

	Per cent.
Alcohol	1.38
Lactic acid	0.82
Milk-sugar	3.95
Albuminoids	2.89
Fat	0.88
Ash	0.53
Carbonic dioxide	0.77

[1] König, Nahrungsmittel, vol. 1, p. 68.   [2] *Op. cit.*, vol. 1, p. 68.

Interesting analyses of koumiss prepared from mare's milk have also been made by Dr. P. Vieth.[1]

The mares from which the milk was taken were on exhibition at the London International Exposition for 1884.' These animals were obtained from the steppes of Southeastern Russia. The mares were from five to six years old, and were cared for and milked by natives of the country from which they were taken. When milked five times daily the best of these mares gave from four to five litres of milk. It is to be regretted that the milk-sugar, the most important ingredient of milk in respect of koumiss manufacture, was estimated by difference. Eleven analyses of the mixed milk gave the following numbers:

Table of analyses.

	Specific gravity.	Water.	Fat.	Albuminoids.	Milk sugar.	Ash.
		Per cent.	Per cent.	Per cent.	Per cent.	Per cent.
Minimum	1.0335	89.74	0.87	1.71	6.30	0.26
Maximum	1.0360	90.41	1.25	2.11	6.82	0.36
Mean	1.0349	90.06	1.00	1.89	6.65	0.31

The koumiss from the above milk had the following composition:

Sample No.	Water.	Alcohol.	Fat.	Albuminoids.	Lactic acid.	Milk-sugar.	Ash.
	Per cent.	Per cent.	Per cent.	Per cent.	Per cent.	Per cent.	Per cent.
1	90.99	2.47	1.08	2.25	0.64	2.21	0.36
2	91.95	2.70	1.13	2.00	1.16	0.69	0.37
3	91.79	2.84	1.27	1.97	1.26	0.51	0.36
4	91.87	3.29	1.17	1.90	0.96	0.39	0.33
5	92.38	3.26	1.14	1.76	1.03	0.09	0.34
6	92.42	3.29	1.20	1.87	1.00	0.00	0.35
7	91.42	2.25	1.22	1.75	0.70	2.30	0.36
8	92.04	2.84	1.10	1.89	1.06	0.73	0.34
9	91.99	2.81	1.44	1.69	1.54	0.19	0.34
Mean	91.87	2.86	1.19	1.91	1.04	0.79	0.35

Collecting the above means together, we have the following comparative table:

Sample No.	Alcohol.	Lactic acid.	Sugar.	Albuminoids.	Fat.	CO_2.	Water.
	Per cent.	Per cent.	Per cent.	Per cent.	Per cent.	Per cent.	Per cent.
1	1.84	0.91	1.24	1.97	1.26	0.95	[2]92.47
2	2.64	0.80	3.10	2.02	0.85	1.03	88.72
3	1.38	0.82	3.95	2.89	0.88	0.77	[2]89.55
4	2.86	1.04	0.79	1.91	1.19		91.87
5	0.76	0.47	4.38	2.56	2.08	0.83	89.32

NOTES.—No. 1, mean of 14 analyses of koumiss from mare's milk; No. 2, mean of 2 analyses of koumiss from cow's milk; No. 3, mean of 9 analyses of koumiss, origin unknown, probably from skimmed cow's milk; No. 4, mean of 9 analyses of koumiss made from mare's milk, London Exposition of 1884; No. 5, mean of 8 analyses of koumiss from cow's milk, made by Division of Chemistry, United States Department of Agriculture.

[1] Landw. Versuchs-Stationen, vol. 31, pp. 353 et seq.

[2] By difference.

The comparison of the above results shows that the American koumiss differs from that of other countries in the following points, viz:

(*a*) The percentage of alcohol is quite low and as a consequence the percentage of sugar is high.

(*b*) American koumiss contains more fat; showing that it has been made from milk from which the cream had not been so carefully removed as in those milks from which the European koumiss was made. Mare's milk, as will be seen by the above analyses, contains much less fat and more sugar than that of the cow, thus making it more suitable for the production of koumiss. Good cow's milk, however, is suitable for the manufacture of koumiss after most of the cream has been removed. Should it be desired to make a koumiss richer in alcohol, some milk-sugar could be added.

The samples analyzed were kindly furnished me by Mr. Julius Haag, of Indianapolis. This koumiss makes a delightfully refreshing drink. When drawn from the bottle and poured a few times from glass to glass it becomes thick like whipped cream, and is then most palatable. It is much relished as a beverage, and is highly recommended by physicians in cases of imperfect nutrition. Those desiring to study the therapeutic action of koumiss should consult the monographs of Biel,[1] Stahlberg,[2] Landowski,[3] and Tymowski.[4]

CHEESE.

No studies of cheese have been made in this laboratory.

Caldwell[5] has given a résumé of the subject up to 1882, as follows:

Literature.—The subject of the adulteration of cheese receives only brief mention either in the journals or in monograph works on adulteration of food.

The Analyst[6] quotes from the Chicago Journal of Commerce the statement that soapstone, soda, and potash are added to cheese.

Hassell[7] states that cheese is adulterated with potatoes in Thuringia and in Saxony, and that bean meal is sometimes added in the place of potatoes; that Venetian red has been detected in several cases in the coloring of the rind, and as this color sometimes contains lead, and the rind is sometimes eaten, the fraud may be dangerous. He also says it is stated that blue vitriol and arsenic (green?) are sometimes added, perhaps to give the appearance of age to the cheese, but he has never found them.

Ellsner[8] says that adulterations of cheese are not known. He mentions oleomargarine cheese as an article recently introduced in Germany. Griessmayer[9] also says that cheese is not adulterated; but he mentions in appropriate terms a practice of soaking certain kinds of cheese, such as Limburger, in urine in order to give

[1] Untersuchungen über den Kumys und den Stoffwechsel während der Kumyscur.
[2] Kumys, seine physiologische und therapeutische Wirkung. St. Petersburg.
[3] Du kumys et de son rôle thérapeutique.
[4] Zur physiologischen und therapeutischen Bedeutung des Kumys. München.
[5] Second Ann. Rept. N. Y. S. Bd. of Health, p. 529.
[6] 1881, p. 29.
[7] Food and its adulterations, 1876.
[8] Die Praxis der Nahrungsmittel-Chemiker, 1880.
[9] Die Verfälschung der wichtigsten Nahrungs- und Genussmittel, 1880.

them in a short time the appearance of ripeness; such cheese can be made to show the reaction for muroxide. He mentions the possible occurrence of poisonous metals, as copper, lead, or zinc in cheese, owing to carelessness in keeping it in metallic vessels or wrappings.

Fleischmann[1] quotes the results of Vogel's examination of cheese for lead; beyond 2 inches from the rind no lead was found, even in cases of cheese wrapped in very inferior tinfoil containing much lead; but in such cases lead was detected in the portions of the cheese immediately under the rind; 0.56 per cent. of lead was found in one instance in the rind of a cheese wrapped in tinfoil containing 15 per cent. of lead. Such cheeses are so little used in this country, however, that this matter has no general importance; but the information may serve as a warning to those who do eat them to be careful of eating the rind.

The same author mentions also the use of veratrin, sulphate of zinc, and arsenic to give to green cheese the strong biting flavor of old cheese, and the addition of blue vitriol to the milk in order to prevent huffing of the cheese.

Liebermann[2] mentions the danger in metallic wrappings, and states that verdigris is sometimes sprinkled over the cheese to give it the appearance of age. Blythe[3] states that washes containing arsenic and lead have often been applied to ward off flies, and as some people eat the rind, such practices may be dangerous.

Lard cheese.—About ten years ago dairymen were much concerned less the manufacture of cheese from skimmed milk and oleomargarine should seriously injure the reputation of American cheese abroad, and in that way hurt the dairyman's business here. Whatever chance this mode of making cheese may have had for success, it is now quite supplanted by the lard cheese which is made at over twenty factories in this State, under patents issued to H. O. Freeman in 1873 and to William Cooley in 1881.

In this process an emulsion of lard is made by bringing together in a "disintegrator" lard and skimmed milk, both previously heated to 140° Fahr. in steam-jacketed tanks; the "disintegrator" consists of a cylinder revolving within a cylindrical shell: the surface of the cylinder is covered with fine serrated projections, each one of which is a tooth with a sharp point; as this cylinder revolves rapidly within its shell, the mixture of melted lard and hot skimmed milk is forced up in the narrow interspace; and the lard becomes very finely divided and most intimately mixed or "emulsionized" with the milk. This emulsion consists of from two to three parts of milk to one of lard; it can be made at one factory and taken to another to be used for cheese, but it is usually run at once into the cheese vat.

In making the cheese a quantity of this emulsion containing about 80 pounds of lard is added to 6,000 pounds of skimmed milk and about 600 pounds of buttermilk in the cheese vat, and the lard that does not remain incorporated with the milk or curd, usually about 10 pounds, is carefully skimmed off. These quantities of the materials yield 500 to 600 pounds of cheese, containing about 70 pounds of lard, or about 14 per cent.; about half of the fat removed in the skimming of the milk is replaced by lard (Munsell). It is claimed that no alkali or antiseptic is used, and that only the best kettle-rendered lard can be employed, because of the injurious effect of any inferior article on the quality of the cheese, and that before even this lard is used it is deodorized by blowing steam, under 80 pounds' pressure, through it for an hour.

According to many witnesses the imitation is excellent, for experts have been unable to pick out lard cheeses from a lot of these and full-cream cheeses of good quality together; and it may therefore be safely presumed that the general public would be quite unable to distinguish one from the other.

[1] Das Molkereiwesen, 1879.

[2] Anleitung zur Chemischen Untersuchung auf dem Gebiete der Medicinpolizei, Hygiene und forensischen Praxis, 1877.

[3] Food.

The statistics of the manufacture of this kind of cheese as gathered from various sources, and partly by Inspector Munsell, are about as follows: Thirteen of the " disintegrators" are in operation, all in this State and none elsewhere. The production of cheese at the twenty-three factories engaged in the manufacture in this State during the six months ending November 1, 1881, was stated to amount to 800,000 pounds. None is made in other States, although it was stated before the Assembly Committee on Public Health,[1] in 1881, that it was made at the West. Before the same committee it was stated that some of the cheese was sold in New York City for consumption, but according to the best of my information, most if not all of it is exported. It is claimed that it brings from eight to ten cents a pound when full-cream cheeses sell at twelve cents, and " full-skim" cheeses at four or five cents; but New York dealers tell the inspector that the cheese brings but four cents a pound when its true character is known, and that it is for exportation only. The inspectors have not been able to find any cheese in the city markets which they had any reason to suppose to be lard cheese.

In two respects this kind of cheese can be considered as a fraud under the new food and drug law, unless sold under its distinctive name. It contains less fat, and fat of a cheaper kind, than the ordinary full-cream cheese contains, and, secondly, there are some grounds for the belief that the fat which is substituted for the butter fat is less wholesome than that. Rubner[2] in some investigations on the assimilation of various articles of food by the human subject found that lard was less digestible than butter; and the objection to oleomargarine butter on the ground of its indigestibility as compared with genuine butter may apply perhaps with more force to lard cheese; it only remains to determine by experiment whether the digestibility of the substances is increased by the operation of emulsionizing.

Skim cheese (" anti-huff cheese ") is made, as is well known, from "full-skimmed " milk, without any attempt to replace the fat removed for butter. It is doubtful whether such cheeses are anywhere sold in a way to deceive consumers as to their character. To prove the quality of these cheeses, and especially to prevent them from puffing out, or " huffing," as it is technically called, from the abnormal generation of gases in the interior before they become fully ripe, patented " anti-mottling" and " anti-huffing" extracts are employed, consisting, it is claimed, only of caustic and carbonated alkali, saltpeter, and a little annat to, for coloring, dissolved in water. A qualitative analysis of one of these extracts by both Mr. Munsell and myself confirm this claim in one case; but another extract, said to be used at the West, was found to consist almost entirely of borax, which is a well-known antiseptic. The quantity of alkali and saltpeter said to be added to the cheese in this operation is small, in all less than five ounces to the milk and sour buttermilk for 100 pounds of cheese, and a portion of this must remain in solution in the whey; and there is no satisfactory evidence that such a quantity of borax as could be added to the cheese without affecting its taste would be prejudicial to the health for any ordinary quantity of cheese eaten. Gruber[3] shows that when this substance is taken into the system it seems to leave the organism very quickly and without affecting the system in any injurious manner.

As to the statistics of the manufacture of " anti-huff cheese," it is stated that in the most important section of this State for dairy products 4.500 cheeses of the best quality were made this year of skimmed milk and sour buttermilk with the aid of this extract. Before the assembly committee[4] it was affirmed that this cheese is consumed to

[1] Fenner Committee. Testimony taken before Assembly Committee on Public Health in the matter of investigation into the subject of the manufacture and sale of oleomargarine-butter and lard-cheese. Hon. M. M. Fenner, chairman, 1881.

[2] Zeits. für Biologie, vol. 15, p. 115. Bied. Centralblatt, 1881, p. 391.

[3] Ber. Chem. Gesel., vol. 14, p. 2290. Zeits. für Biologie, vol. 16, p. 195.

[4] Loc. cit.

some extent in this country, but most of it is exported. It is claimed that nearly the same prices are obtained for the cheese as for full cream cheese, and that it is a good and wholesome article of food, containing nothing but what is found in other food. On the other hand, it is asserted that the excessive quantity of alkali supposed to be in the cheese makes it unwholesome, and that, like the lard cheese, it is a fraud on the public unless sold under a distinctive name; bringing nearly the prices of a full cream cheese, it is taken by consumers to be such. As to the first point there is no evidence *pro* or *con*, and the presumption is, as above stated, that there is no excessive quantity of alkali in the cheese. As to the latter point, it can be left to the interpretation of the law. Without question, a valuable constituent of the cheese has been removed and nothing of the same character has been substituted for it.

Water and fat determined were in small samples, each one of skim cheese made without anti-huffing extract, and with it. Both samples were taken with an ordinary cheese-tryer by Mr. Freeman, the patentee of the process, and sent through Mr. Munsell to me. The results of this partial analysis are given below:

	Water.	Fat.
	Pr. ct.	Pr. ct.
Anti-huff cheese	47.56	14.48
Ordinary skim cheese	47.00	16.77

There is nothing unusual in the composition of these samples as compared with skim cheese in general.

Poisonous cheese.—A sample of cheese, said to have produced sickness on the part of those who ate it, was sent to me by the Secretary of the Board, who received it from Inspector Smith. Cases of so-called "poisonous cheese" occasionally appear in different parts of this country and in other countries. Husemann,[1] quoted by Fleischmann,[2] mentions a number of instances from all parts of Germany, and also in England and Russia, resulting from eating old and especially sour milk and soft rennet cheeses. Scarcely ever is the result fatal, and recovery is rapid, because the vomiting, which is among the first symptoms, relieves the system of the dangerous matter. Voelcker[3] after noticing cases of sickness produced by cheese containing copper or zinc sulphate that had been added often surreptitiously by the dairymaid to prevent "heaving" of the cheese, gives an account of a case where all the cheese of a certain "make" sold in different places produced sickness. The cheese presented nothing abnormal in appearance, but his assistants, on eating less than a quarter of an ounce of it, were taken with violent vomiting and pain in the bowels, and a disagreeable mercurial after-taste was left in the mouth. No metallic poisons could be found in it, however, nor anything else abnormal except an apparently larger quantity than usual of fatty acids, giving a strong acid reaction to the cheese. He suggests that the poison is identical with the so-called sausage poison of German sausages made largely from coagulated blood, and says that a similar poison appears to be generated sometimes in pickled salmon, smoked sprats, pork or tainted meat, and that rancid butter may act as a poison. It disappears from the cheese when quite decayed. I have on previous occasions examined such cheese both chemically and with the microscope, without finding any cause for the physiological effect produced by it, or anything unusual. In one case the cheese was excellent in quality otherwise, but it nevertheless, when eaten to test the truth of the allegation against it, made me quite ill with the usual symptoms for a short time. In the present instance some of the cheese was offered to some kittens which are kept in stock for the use of the anatomical department of the University. At first only one would eat it and that one appeared to be quite sick the

[1] Handb. d. Toxicologie, 1862.
[2] Loc. cit.
[3] Journ. Roy. Agric. Soc., vol. 23, p. 346.

next day. After her recovery the same kitten ate of the cheese again without any noticeable ill effects, and several others also ate of it without harm. It appears, therefore, that the illness of the first animal may as well have been caused by over-eating of rich food as by any supposed poisonous character belonging to the cheese.

I examined the cheese for poisonous metals in the rind, and for matters of the nature of alkaloids in the other part; no metals were found. With respect to the second test, a very small quantity of a substance, precipitated by alkali, soluble in ether, and giving with platinum chloride a yellowish flocculent precipitate, was obtained. These reactions indicate an alkaloid, but I have not been able as yet to carry the examination any further, and, moreover, it is not at all unlikely that a substance of the same character may be found in any ripened cheese as one of the normal products of the putrefaction. Therefore, this result obtained with the poisonous cheese can have no significance till normal cheese has been examined in the same manner without finding any evidence of the presence of alkaloids. For the present, therefore, we can only repeat what others have said who have given this matter their attention, that the cause of this peculiar property of cheese is probably an unknown organic substance, resulting from an abormal process of ripening.

Fickert [1] gives the results of some recent legal investigations on this subject. Cheese is so seldom the object of adulteration that when lately the daily papers stated that it was sometimes treated with urine in order to give it more quickly the desired odor and taste, it was considered as an isolated case. More worthy of note, therefore, was the discovery in a trial at Frankenberg, in Saxony, that mashed boiled potatoes had been used as an adulterant of cheese. This adulteration had already been discussed by Popperheim, and that, too, in cheese made especially for home consumption and not intended for commerce. This adulterant is easily detected by the microscope and by iodine.

Since the intrinsic value of cheese depends largely on its high content of albuminoids, viz, about 30 per cent., and since potatoes contain not much over a per cent. of these bodies, it is easily seen how greatly the value of the cheese is impaired by such an admixture.

TYROTOXICON.

The poisonous substance which sometimes is developed in cheese and milk has been isolated by Vaughn. [2] This substance, the chemical nature of which is not yet fully understood, has been found in cheese, milk, ice-cream, and oysters. For an account of its toxic properties consult Dr. Vaughn's papers.

[1] Chem. Centralblatt, 1886, p. 956; Rep. d. ver. anal. Chem., vol. 6, p. 486.
[2] Paper read at Buffalo meeting A. A. A. S., Aug., 1886, Chem. News, 1886; Medical News, April 2, 1887, p. 369.

ADDENDA.

ESTIMATION OF FAT IN MILK.

Morse and Piggot[1] describe a method of estimating fat in milk by previous desiccation with dehydrated sulphate of copper. About 20 grams of the dried copper sulphate are placed in a porcelain mortar and 10cc of milk added to it, being careful that none of the milk comes in contact with the mortar. The milk is dried in a very few moments, and the mass is then rubbed up with a little clean sand and transferred to an extraction tube. The mortar is then washed two or three times with from 10 to 15cc of benzine, and the fat is extracted by treating in the extraction tube twelve times with the same quantity of benzine. The flask which has received the solution of butter is now placed on a waterbath and the volume of the solution reduced to 10cc or less. The butter fat is now saponified with 20cc of half normal solution of caustic potash. The excess of alkali is determined by a standard solution of hydrochloric acid. The results obtained by this method agree closely with the gravimetric determinations.

ESTIMATION OF WATER IN MILK.

The determination of water in milk is made in the following manner, described by F. G. Short[2]: About 2 grams of milk are placed in a Hofmeister capsule (schälchen) and dried at 110° C. in an oven containing a solution of chloride of calcium, boiling at 110° C.

When the fat is to be subsequently estimated the capsule is wrapped in a piece of prepared cheese-cloth, crushed between the fingers, and placed in an extraction tube.

SUBSTANCES SOMETIMES ADDED TO MILK TO MASK THE REMOVAL OF THE CREAM AND ADDITION OF WATER.

Where much water is added sugar is most frequently used to increase the specific gravity to the normal number.

Chalk, salt, annotto, turmeric, gum, dextrine, and cerebral matter have also been found in milk by Professor Weber.

---

[1] Amer. Chem. Journ., vol. 9, p. 108.   [2] Amer. Chem. Journ., vol. 9, p. 100.

MILK ADULTERANT.

Felix Lengfeld, of San Francisco, has communicated to me the composition of a milk adulterant which has been largely used in San Francisco. The mixture consists of common salt, saltpeter, saleratus, a trace of caustic soda, and a large quantity of sugar. The color is imparted by caramel. These bodies are dissolved in an excess of water and the solution used for adulterating milk in any desired quantity.

OCCURRENCE OF ULTRAMARINE AS AN ADULTERANT IN MILK.

Thoms[1] has analyzed a milk which had a chalky appearance, and on standing showed an accumulation of a bluish liquid at the surface. Ultra-marine was found present in the proportion of 82.3 milligrams per liter.

FILLED CHEESE.

On the authority of the Produce Exchange Bulletin, I give the following account of the manufacture of filled cheese:

The process consists in taking all the cream out of the milk by the separator, and then taking the skim milk up and charging the vat just before it is set with deodorized lard, cotton-seed oil, or other fat. The oil is taken up in the curd and mechanically held there, the cheese curd simply being used as a capsule in which to carry it. There is no assimilation or chemical affinity between the curd and its contents.

Prof. H. A. Weber, of Columbus, Ohio, has made comparative analyses of samples of genuine and artificial cheese, with the following results:

	Genuine cheese.	Artificial cheese.
	Per cent.	Per cent.
Water	35.42	52.73
Ash	2.47	2.69
Fat	31.66	2.63
Caseine, sugar, &c	30.45	41.95
Total	100.00	100.00

[1]Pharm. Zeitung, vol. 32, p. 59.

INDEX.

I